A Note on the Cover

My dad died on April 30, 1982, while watching the *CBS Evening News* anchored by Dan Rather. Two weeks later I received a box with some of his belongings. Among them was the wallet he had in his pocket when he died. I went through it and found this photo of me sandwiched between a couple of credit cards. It is the only picture of me that he ever carried. He kept it in his wallet for twenty-six years.

FULL FRONTAL NUDITY

The Making of an Accidental Actor

Harry Hamlin

SCRIBNER

New York   London   Toronto   Sydney

SCRIBNER

A Division of Simon & Schuster, Inc.
1230 Avenue of the Americas
New York, NY 10020

First Scribner hardcover edition October 2010

SCRIBNER and design are registered trademarks of The Gale Group, Inc., used under license by Simon & Schuster, Inc., the publisher of this work.

For information about special discounts for bulk purchases, please contact Simon & Schuster Special Sales at 1-866-506-1949 or business@simonandschuster.com.

The Simon & Schuster Speakers Bureau can bring authors to your live event. For more information or to book an event, contact the Simon & Schuster Speakers Bureau at 1-866-248-3049 or visit our website at www.simonspeakers.com.

Manufactured in the United States of America

1   3   5   7   9   10   8   6   4   2

Library of Congress Control Number: 2010007846

ISBN 978-1-4391-6999-5
ISBN 978-1-4391-7001-4 (ebook)

Certain names and identifying characteristics have been changed.

All photographs are courtesy of the author, except for photograph on p. 263, by William Grimes.

I dedicate this book to my beautiful wife, Lisa,
who is no stranger to full frontal nudity.

FULL FRONTAL NUDITY

PROLOGUE

August

I don't like to work in August. It's not that I'm lazy, it's just that Huck Finn and Tom Sawyer used to spend August fishin' and catchin' frogs and that's just what I like to do with my two little girls, who are smack-dab in the middle of their "wonder years." Don't get me wrong, I love acting and I've made a good living playing other folks for more than thirty years. At this point in my life, I love my kids more, and August for me and my family is kid time at our cabin on an island, on a lake in Canada. Every August we go there to wash off the past eleven months and start the next eleven fresh.

So I swore I would never take a job in August. Those thirty-one days would be ours, at least until catchin' frogs and the like were no longer of interest to my girls.

I broke that promise when my daughters were eight and ten.

The offer came in unexpectedly the first week of the month. They needed me right away but I'd have to be gone from the cabin for only two weeks. The job was a television pilot being shot in Vancouver and directed by a famous film director whom I admired. The money was good enough and the part was delicious. So, hypocrite that I am, I flew from Toronto to Vancouver, leaving my wife and girls alone on the island. Before I could begin shooting, though, I needed to grab a work permit at the nearest border crossing. Americans can only work in Canada with a bona fide work permit signed by the ministry of labor or some such department. A PA (production assistant), Lyn, had been sent to the airport to pick me up and drive me to the border. Getting a work permit was a no-brainer. I'd picked up at least ten of them over the years as movie and television production "ran away" to Canada, where the greenback went a lot further.

Lyn and I reached the border late Sunday afternoon and ran inside the office to pay the small fee and pick up the permit. There was a cute twentysomething brunette on the other side of the counter and I thanked the stars above that I wouldn't have to face some grumpy old border guard with stale breath. Little did I know that the stars hanging over me that day were not my lucky ones. I sauntered up to the pretty agent in her crisp black uniform, handed her my passport, and announced with a smile that I was Harry Hamlin and that I was there to pick up my work permit for *Harper's Island*. That's when those stars began falling from the sky.

The girl gazed at me through a pair of red-rimmed plastic glasses, cocked her head slightly, and gave me a quizzical look as though she recognized me. But it was not the kind of look an actor gets from a fan who can't quite place the famous face, it was more like she was remembering me from a Ten Most Wanted poster hanging in the back office. She quickly began barking out questions with a snarl.

"Where exactly is Harper's Island?" she asked.

I said that I didn't know, it probably didn't exist in real life, it was a TV show.

"What kind of work are you looking to do?" she barked again.

I told her that I was an actor.

"Do you have your paperwork?" she demanded.

"What paperwork?" I asked.

She looked at me like I was a terrorist. "You need your proof of education and your signed contract," she responded, not looking at me but leafing through my passport in search of stamps from Afghanistan or Pakistan, or some other "-stan."

I told her that the permit was already in the computer and that everything had been prearranged and that all she had to do was type in my name and *Harper's Island* and I should be able to pay the $135 Canadian and be on my way.

"Not so fast!" she barked again. "That's not how it works. You need your paperwork. You need your proof of education and your signed contract."

I explained that I did not have a signed contract because I had just been hired and had not even *seen* a contract. I asked her what exactly she meant by "proof of education."

She said, "Why, your diploma, of course," as though I was the town idiot, which, at that point, I would have settled for.

I told her that I had graduated from Yale in theatre arts some thirty-five years ago and that any diploma I might have had was long since dust but that she should feel free to look me up on IMDb, where my entire pre- and postgraduate history is located.

She looked me in the eye and said with pursed lips, "That's not how it works here. If you cannot produce proof of education, at the very least I'll need a signed contract."

At this point, Lyn and I were going nuts. How could this pretty little thing be such a bitch? What had I done to create this madness?

I once again explained that there was no signed contract and that if she would just type my name into the computer, the permit would probably pop up preapproved. She starred at me as though I was deaf. "I need your signed contract or I can't let you into the country. That's all there is to it."

Then Lyn, who was fit to be tied (I love that expression—fit to be tied! The picture it conjures up is good. There is Lyn, hog-tied and gagged, squirming around and squealing on the floor of the customs house!!), slid a call sheet in front of Miss Lunatic Customs Agent and said, "Look! There's Mr. Hamlin's name on this call sheet. He has to be at work at six. There's the name and phone number of the production company. Please just look for the permit in the system."

Miss Godzilla Face looked at the call sheet, looked up into Lyn's blue eyes, seemed to soften momentarily, and said, "Oh, why didn't you show me this before." And looking straight at Lyn, not at me, she said, "I think I can work with this." That's when it hit me. There was a kind of "I know you'd rather be wearing your keys on your belt" moment between them and I knew why I was in such deep weeds but I could not imagine how deep those weeds would get within a matter of minutes.

It seemed then as though all was well. Ms. "I'll show you who's got more power in this room than you" had found the permit in the computer and was just about to sign off on it when she looked up at me one more time, clearly thinking something very sinister. She grabbed my passport and a couple of forms and asked me to take a seat as she headed through a rear door. As she disappeared she said, "I just have to check on something." I sat down, thoroughly frustrated.

It had now been almost two hours since we started on this work permit saga. I was tired and hungry and fit to be tied. (So now I'm there, too, hog-tied and gagged, squealing and squirming on the customs house floor.) Twenty minutes later she reemerged with a smug little smirk on her face. "Mr. Hamlin, would you step to the counter, please?" came the familiar bark. As she looked down at a fresh printout, she asked in a deliberate and controlled tone, "So, tell me about these narcotics convictions."

Apparently the new piece of paper was the result of a rarely performed "deep background" check. I'll never forget the look on her face as she asked me that question. I laughed incredulously. "Excuse me? Narcotics convictions? I don't have any narcotics convictions."

"Well, it says right here you were arrested for felony possession of narcotics in San Francisco on November 30, 1970, and then again on June 4, 1973, in East Hampton, New York."

Suddenly a time vortex opened up before me. My ears started buzzing and the back of my neck dripped with sweat. I had not thought about those things in almost forty years. I stammered a response, desperately trying to explain what had happened all those decades ago.

"As you may know," Miss Pig Face said, "Canada refuses entry to any criminals who have felonies on their records." She went on to say that if those convictions were for marijuana, it would not be a problem, but since my arrests were for felony drug possession and since they were still unresolved, she had no choice but to assume that I was a convicted felon and should be refused entry into Canada—permanently.

I was speechless. I felt like I had been punched in the gut. "Refused entry permanently!!" But my kids are *in* Canada . . . my wife, all my stuff, the cabin! My father and grandmother are buried there. *Harper's Island!* The director! The job! I was being deported—for good and just because some obscure forty-year-old records were incomplete. I knew I had to do something fast or I was screwed.

I pointed out that if she looked at my passport, she would see that at least four previous work permits had been attached to that document in the last ten years and that all of those were issued to me since the supposed criminal activity nearly four decades ago. I also pointed out that I lived for six weeks of the year in Canada and had come from and gone into the country at least a hundred times over the past forty years and had never been refused entry before. She gave me that smug look again and said that people had not been doing their job before and that she was damn well going to do hers.

Lyn and I were tearing out our hair. All I could think about was my wife and daughters, abandoned on a lonely Canadian island. Lyn was freaking out about the show. Her sole responsibility had been to deliver me to the set, and here we were, trapped in a customs house on the border.

"OK," Little Red Glasses said, "I'll give you the benefit of the doubt this time." And she began typing away on her keyboard and explained that if I ever wanted to reenter Canada, I would have to carry with me sworn affidavits from the courts in San Francisco and

East Hampton that I was not a convicted felon. All of these instructions were being furiously typed into my passport record so that the next uniformed power tripper would be sure to spot me for the felon I was.

But—she was giving me the "benefit of the doubt" this time and letting me work. She told me to take my forms to the cashier, pay the $135 Canadian, and go to work. She said all that with a smile as though nothing unusual had just happened.

That was a year ago. As I said, I really don't like to work in August. I prefer catchin' frogs and fishin' with my kids. Although I hired a lawyer to deal with the narcotics/Canadian border problem, it seems there are no records available from either court to prove one way or the other whether I'm a convicted felon. That means I may never be able to go to Canada again—or anywhere outside the U.S., for that matter. The decision to work that August was probably a mistake, mainly because I am now as good as a twice-convicted felon in the eyes of the vast computer system that tracks travelers worldwide. Harry Hamlin the grizzled felon! How could this happen? What winding road led to my criminal future? Where had my life gone so wrong?

Spot

Three and happy.

When I was three we got a dog from the pound. I was terrified of dogs and spent the first few days of dog ownership climbing around the house on top of the furniture lest I be devoured by the pudgy female Dalmatian now prowling the rooms of our Pasadena Craftsman home. My parents named the dog Spot. If they had had an ironic bone in their bodies, I might have considered such a moniker for a Dalmatian cool; alas, they were Republican—and seriously Republican—and as a result I always considered the choice lame. Thus the whole package, the whole Hamlin thing, was somehow lame in my three-year-old judgmental subconscious. And I included myself in that whole lame Hamlin package.

At the time that we got Spot from the pound, the American military-industrial complex had just finished up with World War II and was working on the tail end of the Korean War. Industry was still punching out shell casings and hadn't gotten around to doggie bowls, so we had to get creative when it came to feeding the dog its half can of horsemeat a day. That was pretty much all that was on the menu for dogs after the war. As I recall it was Kal Kan horsemeat, a tasty treat Spot was kind enough to share with my father from time to time after he had had a particularly long night "out on the town." I would stroll into the kitchen around 9 a.m. on a Saturday morning and there would be Dad, bleary-eyed, a sterling silver fork in hand, rooting around for the perfect morsel of horseflesh in the nearly empty can of Kal Kan. Spot would sit next to him, drooling and wondering why the human was putting her food into his mouth.

My father had peculiar tastes and, like Leopold Bloom, "ate with relish the inner organs of beasts and fowls." Our refrigerator was stocked with everything from pickled pig's feet to calves' brains, which he made us all eat as a ritual Christmas morning breakfast throughout my childhood.

We fed Spot her horsemeat in all manner of containers and bowls from the kitchen until we finally settled on a metal deep-dish bread pan that was just the right size and that had really frustrating right-angled edges so the dog would spend hours trying to get at the bits in the corners. I now know why dog food is served in bowls. We endured hours of scraping and clanging as Spot pushed that bread pan all over the back patio. It must have driven her crazy. All that pushing and scraping meant that the pan had a relatively short shelf life and we got her a new "bowl" about twice a year and retired the old "bowls" to the garden shed for some unknown future use. My parents had been through the Depression and a couple of world wars and you just never threw anything out.

It was one of those discarded bread pans that contributed to my first big life mistake.

It was around the time we got Spot that I discovered I had a very, very small penis. I have a vivid memory of one of the nursery school teachers "teaching" me how to shake the last drop of urine off my tiny penis. She had the audacity to actually take my minuscule member between her enormous red nail-polished thumb and forefinger as I stood before a huge floor-length urinal and shake, shake, shake while she said in a sexy voice, "That's it, shake it, shake it until you get the very last drop." The male member at age three and a half has about the girth of a Ticonderoga No. 2 pencil and is about an inch long in the flaccid form, which is its customary state until around a year later, when it starts to get erect in the mornings for no particular reason. If a man is lucky, it will continue to behave that way forever. That fact notwithstanding, the sight of my little pencil dick being grasped by the gigantic thumb and forefinger of my twentysomething nursery school teacher has forever inoculated me with a sense of inadequacy.

From that moment, sex, urine, red nail polish, and the notion that my penis was way too small have been inexorably connected. Perhaps it was this twisted idea that sent me off on my criminal path. It certainly led me to my first big lie; one that has haunted me for fifty-four years and one that, thank God, removed the "urine" part from the above sexual equation.

Who knows at what point children recognize their sexuality? I've often wondered if boys start getting those twinges before girls and how those "twinges" might manifest themselves. I once had a girlfriend who revealed to me that when she was eight, she slathered her vagina with Bosco and let her basset hound lick it off. Since hearing that, I've never looked at basset hounds quite the same way. Thankfully, the story had no effect on my opinion of vaginas, and I still enjoy looking at them any time I can—with or without chocolate sauce.

I started having vague sexual sensations around the age of four or five, and because the nursery school potty experience had blended pee with sex, I discovered that I would get a boner if I peed somewhere I wasn't supposed to, which was anywhere but the toilet. I had my special spots, which were fortunately all outside the house. When no one was looking, I'd whip it out and let it rip. My favorite of those special places was one of those old, beat-up, forgotten horsemeat "bowls" lying under a bush by the south side of the house.

At four, there's always someone around making sure you're not lighting the house on fire, so it wasn't easy to get those special moments alone with my full bladder and the beat-up bread pan, but I was lucky one week and before long the pan was full of my young yellow pee. It was exciting and forbidden and I would get off like a rocket every time I snuck outside to empty my bladder. All was well and good until one afternoon when I heard my older brother screaming about someone peeing in the dog's bowl. I ran around to the side of the house as a feeling of dread crept up my spine. There, standing over my bowl of forbidden piss, were my brother and my mother.

My mother was not amused and my brother was pointing at me and screaming that I was a pervert. Both looked at me with horror,

My brother Dave and me. Note his devilish grin!
He'd rather me dead.

sure that I had perpetrated this gross transgression. They demanded that I admit to the crime. My brother was especially adamant, and why shouldn't he be? After all, the day I was born he didn't gain a brother; he lost his dominance, his toddler hegemony, his kingdom! He had even tried to poison me with arsenic when I was two by introducing me to a tasty green powder kept on a shelf in the garden shed. I had heard the stories about how I had to be rushed to the hospital to have my stomach pumped, how I had almost died. I'm sure it was my brother's doing and now he was accusing me of this foul deed, which I, of course, had done but would be forever unwilling to admit.

"The dog did it!" I howled, tears streaming down my face.

"Don't be ridiculous!" my mother screamed. "You did this and I want you to confess now, no ifs, ands, or buts—do you hear me, mister?" She had grabbed me by the shoulder and was shaking me. The shame of it all! I wanted to tell them to go fuck themselves but I had not heard that expression yet so I settled for continuing to lie.

"No, seriously," I pleaded. "I saw the dog over here squatting down. It was Spot not me. I promise."

They wouldn't let up. What was wrong with these people? Couldn't they just let this one go? Chalk it up to pre-prepubescent shenanigans and move on? No. Not that bunch.

My mother told me to go to my room and not to come out till I was ready to fess up. I stayed in my room for hours and, until now, have never admitted to the deed. A sacred bond of trust had been broken. I didn't care about that bond with my brother, but my mother and I never looked at each other the same way to her dying day. I was a liar from then on and not to be trusted. I never got a boner when I peed outside again, but I'm sure that was the beginning of my sordid life of crime.

My mother crossed over to the other side on July 6, 1992, at 5:02 p.m. She died peacefully, with my brother holding her hand. I know this because he called me a half hour later to give me the news. I was alone at our cabin in Canada. I had finished dinner and I was in the kitchen washing dishes when the phone rang. My mom had not been well. She had just turned eighty that year and lived in an assisted-living facility in Pasadena. Every time I saw her she would say, "For God's sake, I'm eighty!"

My mother never liked any of the women that I either brought around or married. She had a particularly hard time with my second wife, Nicolette. She always referred to her as "Take A Left," not Nico-lette. As in "So, Harry, how's Take A Left doing?" I would correct her but she just couldn't get it right. I was never sure if it was the dementia or if she just saw right through the girl.

Nicolette was off in London visiting her grandparents when I got the call. My brother told me that Mom had made him executor of the estate and that he would take care of the arrangements while I was away but that we ought to have a little memorial back in LA within a couple of weeks. He described once again how she died and that she really looked at peace. I hung up the phone and went back to the stack of dirty dishes. A few minutes later, as I was finishing up with a glass baking dish, I looked up and caught my reflection in the steamy window above the sink. I was whistling and had a big grin on my face. I was shocked that I was feeling so good having just heard that the seemingly most important person in my life was gone forever. I had that thought—and kept whistling.

That night, as I reflected on the smile in the window moment, I realized what a shitty relationship I had had with my mom. I booked a flight back to LA the next day. The memorial service was indeed small. Just the immediate family, about eight of us. As we left our house for the service, I was mortified to see that my wife, who had returned from her trip to England, had chosen a red outfit with a wide-brim white hat, red lipstick, and huge sunglasses to wear to the funeral. That was Take A Left for you!

As the executor of the estate, my brother spent the next year liquidating anything that was left and presumably finding a final resting place for mom's ashes. We went on with our lives, "Take A Left" ran off with a pop singer, we divorced. I met Lisa Rinna from Medford, Oregon, and we fell in love and built a life together. We did lots of fun things like get married and have kids and travel, and all was as it should be until one fall day in the year 2000 when I went into the basement of our Beverly Hills home to find a suitcase for a quick trip to New York.

Our basement, like most basements, is a repository for all the stuff that we are done with but can't bring ourselves to toss out. Most of the stuff, like old shoes, old clothes, old toys, etc., is stuffed into shopping bags and hauled down into the basement for a while until we get around to putting it in plastic bags and taking it to the garage, where it stays for a few months until it's too hard to open the car doors, and then someone takes the stuff to a storage space where it will sit for decades. This has always struck me as an odd American habit but I guess it's just the way it is. But the day I went looking for my suitcase, I found something unexpected in the midst of all that junk.

That day, the basement contained the usual assortment of shopping bags full of the old shoes and stuff. There was a Barneys New York bag and a Tommy Hilfiger bag and a Ralph Lauren bag and a Saks bag and then there was a smallish bag with a much less familiar logo—at least in our household. There, sandwiched between the Saks bag and the Hilfiger bag, was a little white bag that said J C Penney. Penney? I reached down and grabbed the interloping sack. It was heavy for its size and appeared to be stapled shut. What on earth? I tore open the staples and saw a white plastic box with a label on one side that I couldn't read because it was upside down. I pulled the box out of the bag, turned it over, and to my horror saw that it was . . . Mom! The ignominy! It had come to that! My mother unceremoniously stuffed into a Penney's bag and left to gather dust on the base-ment floor? I immediately dumped out the Hilfiger bag and gently tucked her inside. After all, she had been a Republican and would have loved the red, white, and blue.

I called my brother and said, "What the fuck??!!" He told me that he had come to the house that summer while we were away and con-vinced the housekeeper to let him in. That's when he spirited Mom into the basement. He explained that he had kept her in the trunk of his Cutlass for almost a decade, and as his life had bottomed out, he figured that her ashes being in the trunk must have been a contribut-ing factor. He said he didn't know what else to do with her so he just dropped her off unannounced.

My brother continues to deal with his issues, as do we all, but at that moment I needed to find a suitable resting place for the woman who had carried me to term through a cigarette-smoke-filled, alco-holic haze. How did any of us survive that time when women smoked like chimneys and drank like fish throughout their pregnancies—not to mention the pills? If, as they say, "you are what you eat," then my mom was, and by extension through birth I am, an amalgamation of nicotine, Dexedrine, Emperin No. 2 (with codeine), Seconal, and Bombay gin. There was even a decade when she added a substance she called "hangover juice" to that mix. Created by the good Dr. Max Jacobson, this substance, which was also used by Jack Kennedy when he was president, was later found to be mainly speed with some strong-smelling B vitamin thrown in for effect. My father dutifully injected it into my mother's buttock every morning.

The problem still nagged—what to do with Mom? I decided that she should go home to be with her dad in the town where she was born. She had never really been happy in Southern California and I remembered that she sort of lit up when she talked about her youth in Twin Falls, Idaho. Her father, Clarence Robinson, had been a successful banker in Twin Falls back in the day, and I thought that I could probably find out where he was buried and maybe piggyback Mom onto his grave. Although the idea seemed faintly incestuous, I figured it was the best possible solution. With a little research, I did indeed locate my grandfather's cemetery. I called them up and told them my plan and to my surprise they said, "Come on up."

I told Lisa I was going on a little road trip. I put the Tommy Hilfiger bag in the passenger seat of my 1996 Toyota 4Runner, and installed a voice-activated tape recorder to the visor over where my mother was "sitting." If I was going to spend eighteen hours in the car with her, we were damn well going to have a little chat and I was going to record the "conversation" for posterity.

I still have those tapes but I have never listened to them. Mom and I worked a lot of stuff out on that drive, but not quite everything. When I got to Twin Falls, I gave her to the nice man at the cemetery and watched as a small backhoe dug a hole right where my grandfather Clarence's crotch should be. There was something just a little perverse but at the same time satisfying about the whole thing. It was a gray day and the guy digging the hole turned off the engine of his backhoe and asked if I wanted to say a few words after he laid the box into the ground. I nodded, walked over to the pathetic little hole with the pathetic little box in it, and gazed about the grounds for a dandelion or some other wildflower that I might toss into the hole, but it was the wrong time of year and there were only dead weeds around so I just said, "Bye, Mom," turned around, and left. And that was that.

I have never really grieved for my mother and have never felt guilty about that either. Now that I am closer to the grave than not, I find it odd that I do not and have not missed her. I sometimes wonder if my children will just move on with their lives as I did with mine. Since I have never struck my children either with my hand or a belt and since I have never told them they were good for nothing, I believe that a few tears might be shed and some mourning might take place when I go. I would at least hope that they "tie a good one on"! And if any of them find themselves smiling and whistling shortly after they have heard of my demise, I hope it will be because of some funny thing I said or did to make them laugh. That would be proof of a life well lived!

I'm not sure if my mother ever told my father about the "great pee in the pan" episode or if either of them ever connected the dots between my illicit outdoor urinating and my sexual development. My dad wasn't around much. He'd leave early in the morning and come back late at night. He was working on something secret that required him to have a bunch of badges that were always still clipped to his suits when he got home at night. He would sit for hours at the desk in his study cranking away on an old black adding machine, drinking cup after cup of coffee. He wasn't drinking much then. His work was too important.

I found out later that he was working with an ex-Nazi named Wernher von Braun on a secret project to beat the Russians to the moon. My father called himself an aeronautical engineer. He said that among the other guys working on the project, he was the "thrust man." Actually he was a rocket scientist way before being a rocket scientist was cool. He designed the starting mechanism for what would eventually become the Saturn V, the huge rocket that carried Neil Armstrong and Buzz Aldrin to the moon. (Ironically, years later, I would end up working closely with Buzz Aldrin on a project meant to provide safe, cheap electricity to the world.)

My father was fairly taciturn and didn't think the space program would amount to much other than a big publicity stunt. He remained somewhat of an enigma to me until the day he died, which happened while he was watching the *CBS Evening News* broadcast anchored by Dan Rather, a man my father loathed and who my mother always blamed for his death. Dad was certainly not like the fathers we all know today. There was no playing with the kids or kissing the kids or stories for the kids. The kids were to be seen, not heard, and seen as little as possible.

The letter from North American Aviation to my father about the rocket engine starting method he designed in 1958 (sketch inset). Note the $100.00 check "less standard deductions."

My father was the ultimate pragmatist. A rocket scientist must be pragmatic. There were certain payloads, certain gravitational forces, and certain amounts of thrust that had to be developed to overcome the natural forces Einstein had so feverishly tried to understand. All of that required pragmatism, and such things as emotion were left to the artists and dreamers. Contrary to popular folklore, rocket scientists were not dreamers, they were soldiers of pure pragmatism, armed, in those days, only with slide rules and antiquated crank adding machines. My dad designed the starting mechanism for the rocket that eventually carried the first humans to the moon with only those tools and his totally pragmatic, linear thinking. He was, as they now say, a left-brain man.

I'll never forget the day he called me into his office to have an important "chat." I knew what was coming. I was around twelve and figured it was time for the birds and the bees to be revealed in all their glory. Not so! He looked at me for a long moment as I sat opposite his mahogany office desk and said, with absolute confidence, "Son . . . the most important thing for you to remember in life is that there are no such things as 'feelings.' " According to my father, "feelings" were merely an illusion and not to be taken seriously and that indulging in them would only result in disaster. I remember that moment as though it was yesterday, mainly because that was when I realized that grown men, even grown rocket scientist fathers, could be completely full of shit.

That was Dad. I was conflicted because the man was my father and the archetype, at least, demanded my respect. To this day, whenever I am seriously down in the dumps or depressed, I still cling to the odd sensation that my dad might have been on to something.

The night he died, I was shooting a film in Florida, and as I strolled through the lobby of my hotel on the way back to my room after a long day on the set, the bellman grabbed me and said I had an important call waiting on the house phone. It was my mother informing me of my dad's passing and telling me how relieved she was that he was gone and that, under no circumstances, was I to shed a tear for him. She told me about Dan Rather and how he had killed my father.

I started to cry and she scolded me for my emotional outburst. When I got off the phone, the great character actor Kenneth McMillan, who was also in the movie, overheard my crying and asked me what was up. I told him my daddy had just died and he invited me to his room, where we shared a bottle of Bushmills Irish whiskey. I told him what my mom had said about not crying over Dad's passing and he figured, after that, I needed to get shitfaced. He was right. He stayed up all night with me and we had a proper drunken Irish wake for my dad, the dead rocket scientist. I have always been sorry that I didn't know my dad better.

Two weeks before he died I flew him to LA for his seventy-seventh birthday. He came out from his little house in Lake Havasu City where he lived uncomfortably with my mother. I installed him in a room at the Chateau Marmont hotel, an old Hollywood landmark on the Sunset Strip, and helped him rent a car even though, in his condition, after three heart attacks and a minor stroke, he was in no shape to drive. I knew that he wanted to see someone special and I knew it was a woman with whom he had a very pleasant and sober relationship. My father had given up the bottle when he was sixty-five, which pissed my mother and older brother off to no end. My mother lost a drinking buddy and my brother lost a role model. The distance between my parents had grown palpable and I had become aware of my father's secret relationship after finding a love letter the mystery woman had written stuffed under the seat of Dad's old '78 Audi. Dad had met her in AA and had carried on a clandestine relationship with her for years.

By the time his seventy-seventh birthday came around, I knew that he was pretty close to the end and I wanted him to have at least one last visit with his illicit paramour before he crossed over into the far yonder. As I handed him the keys to his Hertz sedan he looked into my eyes and for the first time in my life said the three words I had longed for him to say since he first bounced me on his knee. He reached out and touched my shoulder and said, "I love you." Then he got into the car and drove straight out into traffic on Hollywood Boulevard, knocking over a trash can on the way out, oblivious to the multitude of blaring horns behind him. I had to leave for Florida the following morning so I never saw my father again. I presume he saw his woman and I know he made his way safely back to Lake Havasu because that's where he died. Like I said, I wish I had known the man better, but there were a few bizarre highlights in our relationship—none more puzzling than Christmas 1962.

Dad and me, Christmas Eve 1962.

In January of 1962 I came home from school one day and my mother announced that I would no longer be going to the Chandler School, a tony private school run by a good friend of the family, Tom Chandler. My parents never explained why I was not permitted to return to school. I was even forbidden to go back and retrieve the personal stuff from my locker. Was it something I said or did? I was certainly unaware of any major infraction, and even though my grades were not stellar, they weren't grounds for dismissal. I had been kicked out of the fourth grade! What on earth could have happened? I always wanted to ask my parents what had gone down when I was older, but I forgot and then they died and so did Tom Chandler so now I'm shit out of luck.

But I have my guesses, and so far, the best one has to do with a book report I wrote in late November 1961. I had a friend at school whose last name was Geisler, obviously German. His dad had a collection of illicit Nazi artifacts from the Third Reich. At ten I had no clue what that meant, I just thought that the Maltese crosses and swastika-covered daggers in his dad's study looked really cool. Whenever I went over to Scott Geisler's house he would pull out all this nifty stuff that appealed to the mentality of a ten-year-old. I was as enchanted as the millions of unsuspecting Germans had been twenty years earlier. He showed me a book he had read by the guy who invented all that stuff and told me I could borrow it; that it was really cool. I took the book home and read it over the next few weeks and, as we had a book report due, I figured, "Why not do the report on this cool book I was reading?" Which is how my fourth-grade book report came to be on *Mein Kampf* by Adolf Hitler.

The weird thing, now that I look back on it, was that my mother helped me with the report and thought that it was really good. I have no recollection of what I wrote but I do remember that my fourth-grade teacher, Mrs. Brewer, was quite possibly Jewish. I never got the report back with a grade. I got kicked out of school instead.

I spent the rest of the year going from one temporary school to another until I ended up at the quintessential school for dummies, where all we did every day was sit on the floor and listen to a man who looked like Captain Kangaroo read *Dr. Doolittle.*

Eventually my folks managed to get me into a fairly good school: the Flintridge Preparatory School for Boys. Aside from being known as a good school, it was also known as the place where the bad boys needing discipline were sent. I figured this was my punishment for whatever I had done to get tossed out of the much more civilized Chandler School. I was depressed and had felt like shit ever since that last day at Chandler, and my parents could sense it. I was also aware

At age eleven, as a student at the Flintridge
Preparatory School for Boys.

that I was evolving into a "pretty boy." I knew that I was cute because
of the reaction I would get from my parents' friends. "Isn't he ador-
able—a real heartbreaker, that one!" "What a handsome young man!"
"Such sex appeal!" Whatever that meant. Little did they know I was a
urinating freak!

I started having some problems with the new friends I made at
Flintridge. They were a tough bunch and I wasn't used to the kind of
rough competition under way at my new school. Plus, all those boys
had Sting-Ray bikes and I was still riding a used racing bike that I had
spray painted red. Basically if you were ten in 1962 and you didn't
ride a Sting-Ray, you were a wuss. This only added to my already
accumulating wussdom. I had to have a Sting-Ray and it had to have
monkey bars and knobby tires and it had to be black! I made up my
list for Santa even though by then I knew the horrible truth about

the fat man in the red suit. At the top of the list was BLACK STING-RAY WITH MONKEY BARS AND NOBBY TIRES. I circled it and underlined it and repeated it at least ten times. I figured Santa would get the message.

I submitted the list early, just after my birthday in October. Of course, I dropped hints around the dinner table and whenever I could so that only an idiot wouldn't run to the Schwinn store to get the bike early. I thought if I showed up with a black Sting-Ray, I would earn the respect that I so desperately needed. Little did I know that I would eventually get that respect, but in a very different way.

Then came the big day. December 25, 1962. I woke up and forced myself to stay in bed until my dad called out that it was time for breakfast. We always ate our traditional braised calves' brains with capers before we were allowed to open presents, but, of course, we always peeked under the tree to see how much Santa had brought. There it was, wrapped in brown construction paper and exactly the shape of a Sting-Ray. Those "calves' brains au beurre noisette" never tasted so good. As soon as we were done with the organs, my brother and I charged into the living room, and I ripped the brown paper off that bike like a madman.

The next ten minutes were quite possibly the worst ten minutes of my life. The situation I found myself in was actually quite complex. I'll never forget the look on my mother and father's faces as I tore into that brown paper. They were standing over me arm in arm with such a look of pride and satisfaction. My folks weren't that well off and bikes were expensive and I guess they felt really good about getting me a brand-new one. But how could they? How the fuck could they? As I tore off the paper I didn't see black, I saw baby blue. I saw a white plastic seat with gold flecks in it and white streamers coming from the white plastic handlebar grips that were on a pair of standard-size handlebars.

They had not gone to the Schwinn store, they had gone to the fucking Huffy store and bought me the most humiliating bicycle imaginable. A powder blue Sting-Ray knockoff. The word *gay* had not yet been coined as a term related to sexuality but I still thought to myself, This is so fucking GAY!!! But what was I to do? They looked so pathetic and proud. I stifled tears and lied, "Thanks, Mom, Dad, this is just what I wanted." I knew I would never, ever ride that bike. Oh, the horror! The horror!

I could barely breathe as my mother pointed to another package under the tree with my name on it. This one was also wrapped in brown paper but it was much smaller, the size of a copy of *National Geographic*. Oh great! I'll have my friends over to look at naked native women from Chad. That'll impress them. My brother handed me the present and I slowly ripped off the paper.

I've often wondered what it feels like to be bipolar, or manic-depressive. The ups, the downs, the highs, the lows—it seems like it would be exhausting. But that Christmas morning I experienced the first of a few bipolar moments that would come in my life. Still reeling from the awful shock of unwrapping a powder blue bike, I went on to unveil not a copy of *National Geographic,* but something much, much better. Suddenly I realized that my friends wouldn't be gazing at the sagging black breasts of the native hordes, but rather at the glossy, toned breasts that were the best that Hugh Hefner had to offer. There, in my eleven-year-old hands, was a copy of the most controversial magazine ever published, with a letter that read: "Congratulations on selecting a five-year subscription to the best men's magazine in the world. Welcome to the *Playboy* family!" Holy Christ!

I never did ride the bike. Pretty soon all I could do was count the days until the next issue hit the mailbox. But what were my parents thinking? Or was it Santa? Whatever was going on, I wasn't about to question it. I decided to just go with the flow. Throughout the

"*Playboy* years" I developed a taste for beautiful women, which has been a good and a bad thing ever since. I saw naked centerfolds and naked film stars and the likes of Woody Allen cavorting with both. I'm proud to say that I never once read an article. I had no use for the print in the magazine, only the pictures. I'll never forget the day I opened up a copy and saw Ursula Andress in total undress standing in a waterfall. I thought the picture of Ursula was amazing but I didn't find her sexy. Her layout was much more art than sex. It's ironic that some sixteen years later I would end up fathering a child with her.

Suffice it to say, I gained the respect of my peers not because I had a cool bike, but because I had the best stash of porn in the neighborhood. Those five years of *Playboy* went by in a flash, and since then I have only looked at a copy of the magazine a couple of times and always because someone I knew—usually my wife, Lisa—was featured in its pages. God knows what would have happened to me if I had gotten both the black bike and the subscription to *Playboy*. I probably would have spent a lot more time behind bars! As it stands, I have spent exactly eleven days in the hoosegow and that's eleven days more than anyone should ever spend incarcerated.

Born Again

My brother Dave, me, and my mom, Christmas 1963.
I'm showing off my Christmas card from Hef at *Playboy*.
Somehow Mom, though suspect, approves.

After tenth grade, which was four years into the *Playboy* subscription, I was sent off to the Hill School in Pottstown, Pennsylvania, a dying Rust Belt village that had once had a profitable steel mill. In 1967 it was a dump—a cold and dreary dump. The Vietnam War was raging and a whole generation of kids was raging as well.

I hated boarding school and everything it stood for. I was from California, the land of the Beach Boys and blond surfer girls and rock and roll. What the fuck was I doing in Pottstown getting up every morning and donning a coat and tie and a little blue beanie? Oh, the humiliation! Didn't these people know I had a subscription to *Playboy*? The whole world was exploding around me and there I was stuck in the Rust Belt eating scrapple and skinned Indian for break-fast every day. Scrapple, for those who have not had the pleasure, is a mystery food made from compressed floor sweepings of the local sausage factory—the stuff doesn't qualify as good enough to get stuffed into the pig intestine for sausage so they grind it up with God knows what and compress the goo into squares that are then deep-fried in leftover bacon fat. Yum . . . Yum! Skinned Indian is cheap chipped beef cooked with heavy cream and served on unbuttered toast—cold. Also yum . . . yum!! Boarding school was a very depressing time for me—so depressing, in fact, that I turned to none other than the big guy himself, the main man, the dude of dudes: Jesus!

It actually happened during spring break in Palm Springs. I went back to California for the Easter break of my junior year. There, a couple of friends and I went to Palm Springs to see a rock concert, which was rumored to have the Grateful Dead as the main attraction. The only problem was that Jerry Garcia or whoever was responsible for such things had failed to get the proper permit, and, at the last minute, the concert was canceled. There we were—thousands of teenagers, hormones raging—in Palm Springs with nothing to do and no music except for some tunes coming from a huge vacant lot with a gigantic neon cross in the middle and a band made up of an eclectic group of hippies and preppies.

My friends and I wandered into the compound and were immediately descended upon by God's foot soldiers. In my case, the soldier was about eighteen, blond with huge boobs, and wearing a see-through peasant shirt and leather cross that kept getting stuck in her cleavage. She had the face of an angel and she wanted to help me meet my maker. She sat me down and told me of the wondrous bounty awaiting anyone who was reborn and swore allegiance to the Lord Jesus. I could only imagine that perhaps she was part of that bounty and I said, "Sign me up!" I gave her a twenty-dollar bill and my address at boarding school and she gave me a copy of a sort of pre–New Age Bible called "The Good News for Modern Man." I asked

her for her address but that turned out to be a dead-end street, so to
speak.

I went back to school and read the Bible, which had been edited
and rewritten to appeal to young, impressionable teens with raging
hormones. I was hooked. I made my own leather cross just like hers.
Her name was Tracy and for years she remained my ideal love object.
Unrequited, of course.

The chaplain at boarding school, which was touted as an "Epis-
copal School for Boys," was so excited at the prospect of one of his
pubescent flock "going Christian," that he arranged for a high "bap-
tismal" service, complete with swinging incense globes and a Eucha-
rist, just for me. That's when I first learned that the Episcopalian
denomination was really "Catholic light." The chaplain agreed to be
my godfather, and I'm sure, if he's still around, he would come to my
aid if called upon. And believe me, I have thought about making that
call many times over the years.

I spent the rest of my junior year wandering around campus with
my hands behind my back, cross swinging from my neck, and mut-
tering oblique Christian epithets from the appendix of the *Good News*
Bible. I stayed in touch with the LA-based organization that had put
on the event in Palm Springs, always hoping that I might get some
word from that blond angel of mercy.

I never heard from Tracy again but I was hooked up with a Mexican guy named Pedro. I had been writing to Pedro about my growing
faith and recent baptism and he determined that I was ready to receive
the "laying on of hands"—whatever that was—upon my return to
Los Angeles. I asked around and discovered that the ceremony was
a really holy thing to do and that if I was lucky I would probably get
the "gift of tongues." Unfortunately the "gift of tongues" had nothing
to do with Tracy. Really it was more like a ritual where the recipient
comes face-to-face with God. He would be infused with the Holy
Spirit and then start speaking automatically in some unintelligible
language. This all sounded pretty cool to me, and anyway, I had long

since stopped masturbating, opening up my monthly *Playboys*, or even thinking about sex or girls as I was focused on God most of the time.

Pedro wrote that I was scheduled for the "laying on of hands" on the last Wednesday in June and that I needed to see the head pastor of the church at least an hour before the ceremony, which was to be held in a warehouse near downtown Los Angeles. Who was this guy, Pedro? I'd never met him. I'd only communicated with him by mail and now I was going to go to some warehouse downtown to have some strangers put their hands on me? But it was all very Christian and I put my faith in God that all would be well.

When I got to LA, I called Pedro for the first time and he answered the phone with a heavy Spanish accent. It was now Tuesday, the day before the big day, and I asked him for directions to the warehouse. He told me where to go and that I should wear all white, including my shoes. He said I should have someone drive me because there was no telling if I would be in any condition to drive myself home after the ritual. I asked him if there was alcohol involved and he laughed and said, "No, my friend. But you might be drunk on God!"

I had one other reborn friend in Pasadena so I called her up to get a lift to the church. Her name was Cathy and I had been her escort when she "came out" at the Pasadena Debutante Ball a couple of years earlier. She had become a strict Christian and would be a perfect escort for me at my "going in" ritual. She asked if she could bring along a friend who was also in the process of rebirth and I said that would be fine. They picked me up just in time on Wednesday and Cathy introduced me to her friend, Whitney Chandler, who just happened to be the daughter of Tom Chandler, the guy who owned the school I was unceremoniously kicked out of in the middle of fourth grade. The plot was getting a little thick and I tried real hard to be as Christian as I could, but I really had grown to dislike that man for dumping me from his school. And even though his daughter was a vision of pubescent perfection, it was hard not to have some negative feelings toward her by extension. She was quite a beauty, though, with straight brown hair parted in the middle and perfectly round, rosy cheeks. I was also enchanted by her name. I'd never met a Whitney before. She looked like Katharine Ross, who had recently starred in *The Graduate* and *Butch Cassidy and the Sundance Kid*. Every high school kid in the country was busy whacking off to thoughts of Katharine Ross, and this Whitney girl wasn't a bad doppelganger. I could feel myself straying from the fold.

We arrived at the warehouse, where Pedro met us in the parking lot and introduced me to Juan, the big cheese. Juan was the head pastor and he explained what was going to happen. I was to untuck my shirt, remove my belt, and take off my white shoes and socks once I was inside the "church." Then he would drape a white cloth over my shoulders and someone would wash my feet while I kept my eyes closed. I was to stand perfectly still while a group of the initiated prayed in tongues as they each put their hands on my body. I was to pray along with them even though I couldn't understand the words, and at some point during the blabber, if I was in tune with the Almighty, I would feel myself in the presence of God and be able to converse easily with him. I would, at that point, be filled with the Holy Spirit and be given the gift of tongues and all the other bounty offered by God the Father Almighty. I thought of Tracy for a split second and wished that I had a whip or something with which to flog myself. Bad boy!

As I imagined this conversation with God, I, of course, pictured myself and an oldish dude with long gray hair and a gray beard on the steps of some Mount Olympus–like temple having a pleasant chat. My idea of God was the usual monotheistic ideal of the old guy in golden robes sitting on a throne passing judgment with an angry scowl on his face. Of course, a bit of fear crept in as I thought about what he might say to me during our imminent chat.

But just before I could panic too much, Juan motioned for us to head into the church, which was really a warehouse. There was a white side table with some flowers and a couple of candlesticks used as an altar. A group of about eight or so Latin men and women all wearing white was waiting for us when we walked inside. Cathy and Whitney and a couple of other "witnesses" were seated around the room. Juan motioned for me to prepare myself. I removed my shoes and untucked my shirt. I wasn't wearing a belt. Juan then draped a white cloth over my shoulders as I closed my eyes and felt someone rubbing my bare feet with a wet washcloth. I began to pray just as I heard a gaggle of unintelligible sounds start to emerge from the men and women in white.

I prayed harder. I shut my eyes tighter and tried to concentrate for dear life. I then felt the warm hands start to pat my body as the sound of the "tongues" grew louder and louder. It was truly freaky and I couldn't wait to see the old guy in the golden robes. The chanting got louder and the hands got hotter and my head felt like it was about to burst! There was a ringing in my ears that I couldn't seem to identify and then, without warning, it happened.

I've tried to describe what I saw and heard at that moment many times, but I know that I will never truly be able to do it justice. I *can* tell you that after that night, I threw away my *Good News* Bible, took off my leather cross, and I have never since set foot in a church with the intention of worship. So what exactly went down?

All I can say is . . . it worked. I didn't start speaking gibberish and I didn't get down with the old dude, but I did get the lowdown. Suddenly the universe, in all its splendor, opened up in my mind. It was truly infinite and utterly chaotic but within the chaos there was perfect order, and it was beautiful and powerful and loud and soft all at the same time and everything was just right. Everything was just right. No old man, no judgment, no problem. Only love, only perfection.

I opened my eyes, looked around at the people thrashing about and babbling. I calmly took off the white cloth, tucked in my shirt, put on my shoes, and grabbed Whitney and Cathy, and beat it back to Pasadena as fast as I could. And that was that. Sex was back on the table and I had a whole year of *Playboys* still in their olive green mail wrappers. Bring it on, baby!

Summer of Love

So, God took on a new meaning for me just in the nick of time because that was the summer of '69 and it would have been a terrible waste of hormones if I had been psychically shackled to some antiquated notion of piety and/or celibacy during the "Summer of Love"!

My friend Charlie and I had heard that there was going to be a big concert that summer at a farm in upstate New York and we were determined to get there. We advertised our skills in the Pasadena *Star News,* calling ourselves handymen who would do almost anything for five bucks an hour. I highly recommend this strategy of creating an income when you're seventeen and know how to do absolutely nothing but sleep and whack off. We were off-the-hook busy working twelve-hour days and by the end of July we had around $700. We still hadn't figured out how we were going to get to Woodstock and we had considered everything from planes and buses to trains and even hitchhiking.

We crunched all the numbers and found that our only choice was to hitchhike, but a few days before we were to set off on our journey across America by thumb, I screwed up my courage and marched into the kitchen—the same kitchen where my dad used to scarf down the dog food—and asked the parental units if I could borrow the Chrysler station wagon for a couple of weeks. I was seventeen, mind you, and New York wasn't Santa Monica. The very last thing I expected to hear was "Sure, just don't forget to get the tires checked before you go." But these were the same parental units who had given me a subscription to *Playboy* six years earlier, so I guess I should have assumed they'd surprise me.

Charlie and I had the tires changed and balanced, bought a Coleman stove, some sleeping bags, a map of the U.S., and off we went. We had decided to take the scenic route up through Nevada, Utah, Yellowstone, and up to Fargo, then on up to Winnipeg in Canada and across Canada's Route 1 to Sault Ste. Marie, Ontario, where we would dip down into upstate New York sliding right into Woodstock (which actually wasn't Woodstock but a little town called Bethel, New York) like a knife through butter.

Charlie and I with his girlfriend, Andy Jorgensen, the day we set off for Woodstock, summer 1969. Andy stayed behind.

Our plan was to camp every night along the way in KOA campgrounds or in the national parks. We had a case of corned beef hash and other canned delectables and we were going to cook our delicious meals each night on the new Coleman stove. In those days Coleman stoves were made a little differently than today's version. The old stoves had a tank attached to the front, where you poured in white gas, pumped a little silver pump for a minute or two till there was some pressure, and then the thing lit up like a rocket. They were pretty cool.

It was halfway through this little road trip when I came very close to being "born again" again. At the very least, I came to think that something I had done or something I was doing had curried God's favor because, all things being equal, I should have been responsible for one of the greatest environmental natural disasters in American history. I should have, but I wasn't, and it could only have been divine intervention that saved me from infamy.

After our second night on the road, we realized that the small bottle of white gas we had brought along was going to run out within a day, so we stopped in a little town in Nevada and purchased a two-gallon jerry can filled with the stuff. We figured that would last us at least until Woodstock. Our other gear was holding up well and everything seemed to be going according to plan as we headed north toward Yellowstone.

I have always been a camper and had always dreamed of camping in Yellowstone. I'd heard about the wildlife and the fishing and couldn't wait to get to the park. Charlie was a bit less of a camper and preferred to gab about girls and sports and the stuff we would do in town. We talked a lot about girls as we drove. There was only AM radio in those days, but we did have an 8-track tape player with only one tape: *Creedence Clearwater Revival.* I know every note of that album. Charlie would mouth all the words to every song and play air guitar as we raced along the interstate. All the while he pined for one girl or another that he wasn't going to be able to see because he was stuck in the car with me.

We peeled off Route 80 at Evanston, Wyoming, and headed north toward Yellowstone, and there, in front of us, just outside of town, was the answer to Charlie's dreams. Standing by the side of the road, backpack at her feet, thumb outstretched, was a vision of beauty. Long auburn hair, patched bell-bottoms, paisley peasant shirt, and a red bandana that framed a face like Julie Christie's, who was, at that time, my and Charlie's ideal sex object. Charlie was driving and without a word he screeched the car to a dead stop right in front of her. Within a split second she was on board and we were rockin' and rollin'!

We cranked up *Creedence,* offered her a smoke, and told her we were headed to Woodstock. She hadn't heard of the concert but thought it sounded cool and would come with us at least until Montana, which was where she was from. We laughed and told stories and laughed some more until we got to our campground that night near West Thumb and Yellowstone Lake. We pitched a tent and set up a little kitchen on the tailgate of the station wagon. Charlie and Megan (her name was Megan and she was from Billings) cooked up the hash while I went fishing in the lake. Turns out Megan wasn't really that much of a hippie. She just had the look.

Megan seemed more like a young housewife on leave from her daily housewifery. She was shy and quite reserved for someone who was taking her life in her hands with her thumb. But I guess it takes all kinds. Anyway, by the end of dinner Charlie and I knew neither of us was going to get lucky that night and we were beginning to hope that Megan would want to get out of the car in Montana. We thought about making a campfire after dinner but we had seen signs that said extreme fire danger so we decided to just hit the hay and get started early in the morning. We left the dishes and other stuff in the back of the car, crammed into the tent, and passed out.

I woke up in the morning to the sweet sound of Megan humming a Joni Mitchell song outside the tent. I rubbed my eyes, poked Charlie in the ribs and swung the tent flap back just in time to see Megan pouring water into a big camp bucket on top of the lit stove. That is cool, she's washing the dishes, I thought as I shook the cobwebs out of my head. But as I crawled out of the tent, the hair on the back of my neck began to stand on end. Something was terribly wrong with that picture of Megan washing the dishes! She had been pouring water into the bucket on top of the stove from a jerry can. We had only *one* jerry can. Too late!!

The sound of the explosion popped my ears and sucked all the oxygen out of the air! Megan jumped back, her eyebrows singed off and her long auburn hair ablaze. She fell back into my arms and I pushed her head into the sleeping bag. She was okay. Her hair was only singed. But I looked up and the tree directly above our car had caught fire! I looked around and could tell immediately that this was going to be a very, very bad day. The trees were close together and there was a slight breeze that would soon spread the fire throughout the entire park—hundreds of thousands of acres. We were in a campground with no other visitors so there was no one to call for help and no way to alert the park rangers. We and the entire Yellowstone National Park were fucked.

But then something happened, something that defies description and can only be explained by accepting the fact that it cannot be explained. It did, however, make me think about giving Pedro a call to apologize for being so hasty in my judgment of all that tongue blather.

I hadn't had time to notice that the sky was gray and dark that morning. But just as the fire in the tree above me jumped to the two trees next to it, the skies opened up and a downpour of biblical proportions extinguished the blaze in a matter of seconds. Then it stopped just as quickly as it started. Five minutes later, the sun was out and the day went from gray to perfect.

In an instant, we had gone from potentially being the most talked-about campers in Yellowstone history to being just another station wagon full of fun-loving visitors enjoying the serene national park. I still was convinced that God didn't have a beard and a crown, but

I figured something must be going on up there, if you know what I mean!

Megan decided to try her luck elsewhere and she never got back into our car. We were clean out of white gas, and when we got to Sault Ste. Marie, we heard on the radio that the big rock concert in Bethel, New York, had been canceled due to inclement weather. We never went south like that knife through butter and we missed the biggest pop culture event in history. Better luck next time.

Charlie and I the moment we arrived back from
our cross-country road trip.

Out of the Frying Pan

W hen we heard Woodstock was canceled, Charlie and I decided to camp out in an abandoned farmhouse in northern Ontario for a few weeks until what little money we had ran out. We made it back to LA and somehow I finished my senior year at boarding school without getting kicked out—as had a bunch of my close friends after someone spiked the dinner punch with LSD. But that's another story for another day. Anyway, not only did I graduate, but I managed to be accepted at Berkeley. I had chosen Berkeley because I wanted to be an architect. The environmental design school at Berkeley, though not a classical architecture school, was renowned for innovation in design perspectives and I was actually really excited about going to work in that field.

I did the graduation thing and my folks gave me three grand to buy a car. That was some serious scratch in those days, and after doing a lot of research, I bought a car that no one had ever heard of: a BMW 2002. At the time, BMW was a little-known company in the U.S. They had only one other model in the country and everyone, including my brother and my parents, thought I was nuts. I drove that car for twenty years. My brother took his three grand and bought a GTO, which disintegrated in four years! Not that I'm gloating.

That summer, my parents decided to spend a month at a ranch in Montana, of which they were part owners. It was an old dude ranch that had been sold to a small consortium of investors from Pasadena. My folks invited the whole family and a handful of houseguests for the month of July. It was going to be great. Horseback riding, fishing, hiking, even the rodeo in Red Lodge on the Fourth of July.

I drove my 2002 from Pottstown out to Berkeley to check it out and then up to Montana for the summer fun. I left Berkeley for the drive to Montana in the late morning and calculated that it would take me eighteen hours to get there. After about ten hours of driving, I started to nod off. It was dead of night and I was somewhere on Highway 15 in Idaho when I started hitting the rabbits.

At first I thought I was bumping into tumbleweeds or branches on the highway, but then, to my horror, I realized that there were jackrabbits everywhere, hopping across the highway. I was hitting the little buggers at a rate of about one per minute. There was little I could do except stop in the middle of nowhere and wait till morning, but I had been driving for hours and had no money to stop for food. By this time, I was exhausted and starving. The growls coming from my stomach were almost as loud as the roar of the BMW overhead cam engine. I had no choice but to press on. Besides, hitting the rabbits was keeping me awake.

I finally made it to the ranch and snuggled into a cozy log bed for a good twenty-hour sleep. I woke up to find that the entire family, including half brothers and their kin, were there. My eldest half brother, Clay, had two young kids who, to my delight, had a babysitter. Barbara was a beautiful girl from Southern California who happened to be eighteen, blond, and very willing. Of course, I was not one to take advantage of a situation like that, but she and I had a connection while we were in Montana.

We were the same age and it was "us against them." "Them" being everyone who was not us. It was quite a good arrangement, in fact. Every night, when my niece and nephew were asleep, she was free to gaze at the Montana sky with me and dream about what was to become of us. I told her of my dream to become an architect and a songwriter. I had decided that rock-and-roll stardom was going to be my backup in case the architecture thing didn't work out.

I had my guitar with me, a Gibson country jumbo special with a cutout and lots of mother of pearl, which only sometimes reminded me of the white metallic plastic seat on that powder blue disaster of a Huffy bike. It was a great guitar and today is the guitar every country singer and even every acoustic rock and roller would love to have. Back then, Martin was the really cool guitar and I was a little embarrassed by the fancy Gibson. I loved to play it, though, and that summer I was determined to write an album full of songs. I'm afraid to say that I failed at that endeavor, but I did fall in love with Barbara the babysitter who was leaving Montana to go off somewhere, never to be seen again.

On the day she left, we were both heartbroken. We hadn't even exchanged bodily fluids but we felt a sense of kinship, a life bond. We decided that it was just not acceptable that we might not ever see each other again, so we made a pact. We swore to meet again, no matter what, in ten years. We picked a location that we knew we would remember and that we knew would still be a landmark after a decade: the box office of the Music Center in LA. We picked a date we would remember (the Fourth of July) and a time (noon). That was it. Our deal was sealed with a kiss and a pathetic song that I wrote for the occasion. Then she was gone. Ten years later, I kept my end of the bargain but, sadly, she did not. It wasn't easy explaining to Ursula Andress, while our three-month-old was screaming in the crib, that I had to go out for a while around noon on the Fourth of July. But I did, and that's another story.

I drove back to LA in early August and put another ad in the local paper for handyman work. My aversion to working in August had not picked up steam yet. I got a pretty good response, and by the time I was ready to drive north for my freshman year, I had about four hundred bucks in my pocket. I was going to Berkeley, the epicenter of the flower child movement, ground zero for the counterculture overthrow of the establishment, where People's Park was famous for its riots and its hippies and its free love. Wow! Out of the bread box into the fire!

But I was not going to let all that bullshit get in the way of my dream. I was going to build houses and buildings and whatever because I was going to become an architect! Or so I thought. They say the road of life is full of twists and turns, and mine was about to get wrapped into a pretzel.

I had scoped out the environmental design department during my short trip to Berkeley earlier in the summer and I had a list of the classes I planned to sign up for. I had read the registration instructions at least ten times and I was as ready as rain. Registration closed up tight at noon on the third Wednesday in September so I put together an itinerary that got me to Berkeley on Tuesday morning with plenty of time to fill out all the forms, pay the $250 for the quarter, and get settled into my dorm room by Tuesday night. My plan was to head up to the Bay Area on Sunday, go to a party at a friend's house in Oakland on Sunday night, hang out there on Monday and Monday night, and drive over to Berkeley on Tuesday. No problem.

The drive up was great, the party was great. One of the girls who had been at the party said that we should all go spend the night at her dad's old summer getaway in La Honda, a tiny forested community west of San Jose. There wasn't much enthusiasm for that idea until she explained what we'd be doing.

There were certain folklore heroes that enchanted the impressionable minds of teenage baby boomers, soon to be hippies in the summer of 1970. None was more talked about than a fellow named Ken Kesey, who apparently had a band of friends and followers aptly named the Merry Pranksters. I had heard of this guy and his infamous gang, but all I really knew was that this smiling Kesey fellow was in the vanguard of the counterculture movement and was always loaded in one way or another.

Word had it that the Merry Pranksters had taken up residence, at least for a time, in a bunch of tree houses in a redwood forest south of San Francisco and that there had been a police raid and a standoff of some kind resulting in a sort of treaty between the cops and the Pranksters. It turned out that this girl's dad's summer getaway was none other than this very same encampment of tree houses. She said the freaks were gone and that her dad never used it anymore because it was all broken down and hadn't been maintained in years, but that it was still a blast to go and spend the night. Now we were listening and within an hour eight of us were headed to La Honda for a camp-out and pasta feast. I told everyone that I was going to have to drive straight up to Berkeley the next morning and wouldn't be able to take anyone in my car so we caravanned over in three cars.

It was everything she had described and much, much more. We drove down a long curved dirt driveway from the little two-lane road above into a glen of some of the biggest trees I had ever seen in my life. The first thing we saw was a one-story lodge with the doors and windows torn out but a roof that still looked good. In front of the lodge was a huge fire pit with logs around it for campers to sit on. It wasn't until we looked up that we saw the main event. Nestled high up in the branches of these majestic redwoods was a village of hob-bitlike tree houses that had ladders and stairs going up to them and catwalks connecting them. It was magical and I could immediately see why a bunch of tripping Pranksters would want to call this place home.

We dropped our stuff and ran squealing up into the trees, each scoping out which tree house we would choose for the night. We could see that, at one time, these places had been totally tricked out. Each tree cabin had a sink and a toilet—long dry. There were switches on the walls for electric lights (also long gone) and bits and pieces of furniture, even some old beds that still had mattresses on them but that were, no doubt, infested with scabies. Since we hadn't been to college yet, we had no clue about such things as scabies and crab lice. This was truly an amazing place and we all imagined what it would be like to be a Merry Prankster with no worries in the world, just hanging out and grooving on free love and flower power. It was intoxicating.

I picked out my crib and hauled up my sleeping bag and clothes, and then we set to work gathering firewood for the fire pit and making dinner. Someone had managed to get hold of a gallon jug of Red Mountain burgundy, which was, as I recall, the drink of choice then among underage baby boomers. We filled a huge pot with water from the little stream that wound through the encampment. We put it on the fire and cooked up enough spaghetti marinara for an army. I was having more fun than I'd had in years.

After dinner, as darkness descended on our merry band, I pulled out my Gibson and began to make up songs as the girls started the "s'more" ritual over the coals. We all felt warm from the wine, and I must say that my guitar never sounded better. It was a pitch black night so the firelight created a little cocoon among the redwoods and we felt totally safe and happy. A true "Kum-ba-yah" experience! Everyone was really into my singing, and just as I thought that maybe my dream of rock stardom wasn't that much of a stretch, the peace in our little glade was shattered by the roar of what could only have been a horde of Sherman tanks.

We looked toward the driveway and could see nothing because of the blackness of the night, but the roar was definitely approaching. Soon the brightest light we had ever seen came through the woods, headed right toward us. There was only one light and by then we knew the sound must be from a huge motorcycle. The light got closer and closer and whoever it was kept revving the unmuffled engine. Suddenly a giant Harley manned by an equally giant hairy dude wearing a jacket emblazoned shamelessly with the words HELLS ANGELS emerged from the woods and came to a halt right next to our fire. We all sat speechless as the rider got off his machine, punched down the kickstand, grabbed his four-inch leather belt, and reorganized his testicles, which I could only assume were the size of bowling balls. He snorted once, and without even saying hello asked in a trumpetlike, gravelly voice, "Anyone here got a wrench?"

None of us moved. It didn't seem like this biker was going to kill us. In the fire's glow, he could clearly see that we were not hippies or Pranksters, but just youngsters without facial hair. An ever-so-slight smile formed under his handlebar mustache as he jumped into an abrupt karate stance. We all tumbled back in unison and he broke into hysterical laughter. He slapped his knee and said, "I ain't gonn' bite 'cha! I just need a crescent wrench to take care of a little plumbing problem up there." And he pointed up to the tree house I had chosen for the night.

I knew that there was an old toilet and a sink in that cabin, but there hadn't been any washing or shitting going on up there for years. I slowly raised my hand and said that I had a tool kit in the trunk of my car and that I was pretty sure I had a crescent wrench. He said something out of place like "Groovy, man," and I went over to my car in the pitch dark and fumbled in the trunk for the tool kit that I, as a closet Boy Scout, always kept close at hand.

The huge man, who we would come to call Hank, marched over to the redwood tree with my cabin on it, which he said was called "Sleepy Hollow." I followed him up the stairs, thankful that he had pulled a flashlight out of his saddlebag so we at least could see our feet.

We got inside and immediately Hank went to work. He got down on his knees, thrust the flashlight at me, and said, "Shine it there," pointing to the S-shaped pipe under the sink. He took a couple of wrenches and, widening them to fit around the rusty pipes, put them in place and started to twist. It took all his strength to get the old pipes to move, but finally there was an enormous crack and the pipe disintegrated, dumping out a pile of small bluish pills. "Aha!" Hank bellowed as he picked up one of the tiny pellets and examined it up close. "Purple microdots!" he exclaimed. "Forty of 'em!!" And he scooped up all forty in his fat hand and headed down the stairs in a hurry. I followed behind him with the light.

It turned out that there had been a big gathering of the Angels at the tree houses and someone had "lost" forty hits of purple micro-dot LSD. Somehow, Hank had figured out that the acid had been dumped in the sink in Sleepy Hollow and he had come back to get it. He was very appreciative of our help so he gave each one of us a pill and insisted that we all wash them down with the Red Mountain, which he had begun to swig in generous slugs.

I don't think many or any of us had yet been down the psychedelic yellow brick road so we didn't know quite what to expect. But Hank stayed with us and sort of held our hands as we rediscovered each other and the world around us.

Tuesday morning dawned and then Tuesday afternoon and still the last thing on what was left of my mind was getting to Berkeley to register. The ferns in the forest and the minnows in the stream were far too beautiful. The redwoods had a strange and enchanting power over us. Our bright-eyed, bushy-tailed "Kum-ba-yah" moment had morphed into a journey down the rabbit hole. Environmental design had been left quite willingly on the surface.

I emerged from the psychedelic haze as the sun was setting on Tuesday and knew that I had to sleep or die, so I slept through the night and woke up when it was just starting to get light. I grabbed my stuff and piled into my trusty 2002, which, by this time, had been anthropomorphized and was called Beulah. I shook off the hang-over and drove as fast as I could to Berkeley, where I would have just enough time to sign up for the fall quarter.

There was a lot of traffic and I didn't get to the campus until around 11:00 a.m. I parked Beulah and raced to the main office of the environmental design school to fill out the forms. I made sure I had my checkbook so I could write the $250 check for the first quarter. Think about it—that's a thousand dollars for a full year of Berkeley! Those were the days, eh?

I bounded into the foyer of the main design building and it was empty. There were some foldout tables and chairs, a couple of trash cans overflowing with scrap paper, and a bunch of scribbled forms on the floor. But no people! Did I have the wrong building? Was it the wrong day? Was I still tripping? Just then, a skinny guy with glasses, a backpack, and a crew cut came through the outside doors. I asked him where everyone was and he said in a matter-of-fact way that registration for the environmental design department was closed, all the classes had been filled up since Tuesday. He checked a bulletin board and left.

I was mortified. Now it was after eleven and I had to get my registration in by noon. I panicked and ran out of the building. I started running toward the main registration office, but I knew that I had to have some class forms in order to register and that if I didn't, I'd have to wait until January to enroll. This was really bad. I kept running.

I stopped when I came to the closest building that had people in it. It happened to be the drama department. There were people sitting at tables and it looked like they were still open for business. I asked if I could take four drama classes—I had only enough time to hastily fill out four forms. The guy behind the desk said that one of the drama classes would satisfy the English requirement and that theoretically I could take four classes from the same department. I grabbed forms for Acting 101, History of Drama 101, Understanding Greek Tragedy, and Dramatic Writing. It was the last one that satisfied the English requirement.

I took the forms and ran to the main administration building, where I got in just under the wire. I gave them my check and the paperwork and I was in. I figured I'd take these drama classes for the first quarter, then migrate back to environmental design in January. What I hadn't banked on was that part of the curriculum for Acting 101 was the requirement that I audition for every play the department was putting up that quarter. I was going to have to audition for plays. Oh, the terror! But first I had to get settled in my dorm.

————

At the main administration building I had been given my dorm room assignment and the names of my two roommates. The room was located in a big multistory building a few blocks from the main campus. I had thought about living off campus in a house or an apartment but my parents had insisted that I give dorm living a try. I was pretty sick of dorms and roommates since I had just been released from the Guantánamo of boarding schools a few months before. I was also feeling a new sense of independence no doubt buttressed by the remains of the lysergic acid still coursing through my body. I walked over to my assigned dormitory and up six floors to my room. The door was closed and I knocked. No answer. I tried the door and it opened. I spent only a few seconds in the room, which had three beds and three closets and three desks all crammed into a room about the size of a shoebox. I took one look and turned around determined to find a room somewhere, anywhere but there. I walked out of the dormitory and never set foot in that building again.

Now I was in a bit of a pickle, though, because it was around 2:00 p.m. and I had no place to stay for the night. The Hotel Durant was close by and I checked to see if I could get a room there. I still had some dough left from planting azaleas in Mrs. Odriazola's garden in August. No vacancy. The guy at the desk told me that I would not find a vacant room for miles because all the parents were in town to drop off their kids. Uh-oh. I figured I'd walk around until I found a FOR RENT sign. After all, there were always places for rent.

Looking back on it now, I wonder how I was ever accepted to this great institution. I've always thought that it must have been a clerical error. What was I thinking? There were forty thousand kids who had descended on Berkeley just days before and they all needed a room or a bed. Forty thousand! Somehow this did not occur to me and I set off on my journey to find the perfect digs.

I walked up and down every street in a grid from Bancroft Street, right next to the campus, to at least a half mile away. No FOR RENT signs anywhere. What was going on? I needed to dump more money in the meter so I walked back to Beulah, which was parked near the corner of Piedmont and Bancroft. I took Piedmont back toward the campus, and when I got to the corner at Bancroft, there it was: the most beautiful thing I had seen since leaving La Honda. Right in front of me, taped to the front door of a beautiful Tudor mansion with a huge willow tree in front was a red and white cardboard sign: FOR RENT!

I forgot all about the meter and marched up to the door. It was a really big oak door, the kind of door suited to a mansion. I looked through the side windows and saw that the floors had beautiful oriental rugs, and I could see a pool table and some leather couches. This was going to be my lucky day. I knocked on the door. Nothing. I knocked again, louder. I could hear footsteps. The door opened just a crack and a guy with really long straight brown hair and who bore a slight resemblance to Neil Young stood there giving me the once-over. "Yeah?" he barked.

Now, I wasn't sure what kind of place this was, and I didn't like this guy's vibe from the get-go, but I needed a room so I swallowed my pride and said, "Hi. My name's Harry Hamlin and I'm a freshman and I'm looking for a room because I just can't stand living in the dorms." He had a funny look on his face, like he knew me from somewhere, and I went on, "I saw the For Rent sign and I wondered if you might . . ."

He cut me off midsentence as he opened the door wide. He reached out his hand and said, "Right, Harry Hamlin! Right! Harry, my name's Mike Stimpson and your room is ready for you. It's over here." He pointed toward the back of the building as he shook my hand a bit too hard. I noticed that even though he had hair almost two feet long, he was wearing a blue oxford cloth shirt, newish blue jeans, and new brown leather boots. He was not quite a hippie but perhaps he was about to become one.

Mike led me toward the back of the house and down a long hallway to a Day-Glo red door. He threw it open, revealing a guy with a goatee sitting on a bed reading a copy of a hand-made book called *Be Here Now!* Mike said, "Harry, meet Gene. He's your roommate and that's your bed." Mike pointed to a single bed on the right side of the room.

Gene just looked at me and said, "Hey, man, have you ever seen this book? It's really wild."

I had two roommates in college at two different universities and both of them were junkies. I didn't stay all four years at Berkeley but I'll get to that later. Gene, my new roommate, was the first person I had ever met who had even seen heroin, let alone shot it into his veins on a regular basis. But he was very forthcoming about his addiction and quite generous too. In our first five minutes together Gene explained that I might come into the room someday to find him lying on the floor all blue and foaming at the mouth, and if that happened I should just drag him into the shower across the hall and turn on the cold water. He also said that I could shoot up some of his junk whenever I wanted. He told me that the book he was reading was by a real enlightened guy named Baba Ram Dass and that it was about living in the moment and that it had changed his life. I wondered what his life had been like *before* the book. I never did try any of his heroin but I have been chasing the "be here now" thing for forty years.

I was still puzzled about Mike Stimpson and the fact that I had a room reserved for me in the back of this beautiful house, until I discovered a few hours later how it all fit together. As I had walked all those streets that afternoon looking for a room to rent, I had noticed a lot of houses with Greek letters on the doors. I knew what fraternities were but I had no intention of ever joining one. It was 1970 and fraternities were way uncool. My oldest half brother had been in a fraternity at Stanford, and a few months before I left for school he mentioned in passing that I should check out his old frat, which had a chapter at Berkeley. Yeah, right! I never gave it another thought, and I scoffed as I passed some of those houses on my search earlier in the day. I considered myself to be far superior to that lame old tradition.

What I hadn't noticed, because of the big FOR RENT sign taped to the door, was that this beautiful house, in which I now had a room and a stoned-out roommate, was actually the Berkeley chapter of the very same fraternity my brother had belonged to at Stanford. Hidden under that red and white cardboard sign was a brass plaque with the bold letters DKE in bas relief. My brother had written to the DKE (Delta Kappa Epsilon) house at Berkeley requesting that I be considered as a pledge. A pledge, as far as I can guess, having never actually been one, is someone who wants to join a certain fraternity and then must endure a long process of scrutiny and hazing that might, or might not, end up with acceptance into the frat. This was not being practiced in Berkeley in 1970. All I had to do was show up at the door on my first day of school and I was *in,* baby!! And in with a room and some junk to boot! I guess the fraternities were having a little trouble in 1970.

My first night in my new home gave me a taste of what was to come for the next two years. Gene didn't show up at all that night and I climbed into bed around 11:00 p.m. I was really bushed from the LSD experience the day before, not to mention the stress of going from becoming a potentially famous architect to a potentially famous actor within the course of a couple of hours. I plummeted straight to sleep.

My slumber didn't last long. By one o'clock there was a terrible brawl going on in the room right across from mine. I hadn't seen that room yet. The door was painted Day-Glo yellow and was always locked because it had a back entrance. I went into the hall, where I could hear male voices screaming something about a VW van and something about rugs. The room was obviously being trashed. I could hear glass breaking and furniture being thrown around. The melee lasted about ten minutes, then calmed to complete silence. There was the pungent smell of marijuana smoke wafting down the hallway and I wondered if it was coming from behind the yellow door. There was no one around and the house was eerily silent. There I was, standing alone in my jockey shorts under a single 40-watt lightbulb, an eighteen-year-old stranger in a very, very strange land.

The next morning, I got up and wandered downstairs to the big frat house kitchen. As I passed through the large common rooms I had seen for the first time the day before, I noticed something different but I couldn't quite put my finger on what it was. A skinny guy in his twenties with shoulder-length black hair wearing a beat-up white T-shirt was pouring a bowl of granola from a huge plastic bag. He said his name was Oliver and I said, "Hi, Oliver. I'm Harry.

He said, "No, not Oliver . . . Oliver."

I said, "Hey, Oliver."

And he said, "No, man, not Oliver . . . all . . . over. Like, you see, man . . . I'm from all over. So you pronounce it 'all over' not Oliver. You want some granola?"

Well, I was glad to get that straight and I said that yes, I would like some granola.

Then Allover said in a kind of stoned-out monotone, "A real drag about the rugs, man." That's when it hit me. The living room! The beautiful oriental rugs that had been there the day before had suddenly, conspicuously vanished!

Allover gave me the lowdown. Some guy named Pete had been living in the house for a few years and he had gotten strung out on opium and had gotten himself into a lot of debt and a load of trouble. Apparently he had reached the breaking point the night before, and he stole the rugs and a VW van that had been collectively owned by the DKE house. He argued with someone else from the house (I never found out who) and then drove off in the middle of the night with $10,000 worth of rugs and the van. He had sort of paid for some of it by leaving behind a half-pound chunk of opium on the floor of the room with the yellow door. That door remained locked for months and I wasn't invited in there until all the opium had been either smoked or stolen.

I saw my roommate only a few times during the quarter. I was never sure if he was a student. And sure enough, one night I came back from a tasty dinner at the Top Dog (a hot dog joint close by) only to find Gene on the floor in a fetal position, blue in the face and foaming at the mouth. I calmly picked him up, dragged him into the shower fully clothed, and turned on the cold water. He didn't die. I saw him a couple of years ago in Fresno. I was on tour with a dance troupe and Gene got the backstage security to let him in. He looked well and it was good to see him some thirty-five years after we had lived together. I wish I could say the same for my other junkie roommate who is no longer with us. But that's another story.

I soon discovered that the DKE house was somewhat unique among fraternities. For one thing there were as many female "brothers" as there were male brothers. I took this in stride and figured that it was just a sign of the times which, of course, it was. Since there were no "pledges," and therefore not enough "brothers" to pay the rent, we filled the ranks with "sisters," which not only covered the rent, but also gave DKE the highest grade point average of any frat on campus. For another thing, the food was all vegetarian and Allover (Oliver) was the cook. Although we didn't pay him, he was allowed to live for free in an attic space under the eaves with his girlfriend, Rose, a fifteen-year-old runaway from Oakland, in exchange for his services as chapter chef. The little wrinkle in that deal was that neither Allover nor Rose could boil water. They were both stoned 24/7 and the food that Allover served was totally inedible.

On the first day of school, I had to audition for Oscar Wilde's *Salome,* which was being produced in the Durant Theatre, a small studio theatre in the middle of the campus. I had only had two previous theatrical experiences: first, when I was ten, I had played the role of a servant boy in a play called *The Egg and I* at the Pasadena Playhouse, and second, my senior year at boarding school I was cast as Mortimer, "the Man who Dies," in the class play *The Fantasticks*—a part I got only because the talented fellow to whom they had rightly given the role got a hefty case of mono during rehearsal.

So, there I was at Berkeley, having to audition for some weird play because a group of bikers had dropped some purple microdots into a sink in a tree house. Life was becoming bizarre but it was about to go from bizarre to bizarre-squared!

I was cast in *Salome* in a minuscule speaking role. I remember my one line: "It is an old cistern." I must have said that line really well because I ended up playing leads in five more plays while at Berkeley. I never did get to the environmental design school and I'll have to wait till the next life to become the architect I could have been, were it not for those damn Hells Angels and that sink.

Franny

That fall, life at the DKE house settled into a routine. I'd go to rehearsals and study at night. I almost never saw my roommate. I got to know some of my other frat brothers and sisters, and I became particularly interested in one girl who lived on the floor above me but who already had a boyfriend. Her name was Franny and she was from a wealthy East Coast family and her boyfriend's name was George, and he was no less affluent. I think George was an officer of the fraternity during the first part of my freshman year.

Franny was interesting and sexy in an East Coast intellectual, bipolar sort of way. George was at least a year ahead of me, and he was tall and very sure of himself. I knew that Franny was forbidden fruit and that any thought of ever getting a piece of that was just nuts. Franny had a little sister, though, and I did get lucky there, but it just wasn't the same thing.

That first Thanksgiving at Berkeley I had planned to fly down to LA to share some turkey with my family in Pasadena. Just as I was packing to go on Wednesday there was a knock at my door, and Franny and George sauntered into my room. This was a big deal. The upperclassmen and particularly *these* upper-class people, would never just wander into a peon freshman's room. They sat down on my bed and George produced a Baggie with some white capsules in it. Franny said that she'd heard I was going to LA and George asked if I would take this bag of pills to a friend of his who lived near USC. George said that the guy would give me a hundred bucks for the bag and that if I brought the dough back I would be doing a huge favor for them both. What could I say? I was secretly in love with Franny and George was an officer of the fraternity. "Okay," I said, and took the pills while George wrote out the guy's address.

Once again, as I look back, I don't know how I ever got into Berkeley. It must have been a mistake. I never thought twice about this request. I had just been recruited as a mule for these two and I never even asked what it was I was carrying, illegally, to LA. Before he left the room, George tossed a little Baggie on the bed and said, "Here— that's for helping." It was a Baggie with about two joints' worth of pot in it. I had smoked pot a few times but it was never my thing. I much preferred Red Mountain if I wanted to get a buzz on, but this was Berkeley in 1970 and you couldn't go five feet without smelling dope in the air.

I took the pills and the pot and wrapped them in a sock and taped the ball of contraband inside my Gibson jumbo with the cutout and the mother of pearl that always reminded me of that blue Huffy bike. I packed a few blue oxford shirts and a pair of dirty blue pinstripe slacks in a little bag and drove Beulah to the airport. The flight down was uneventful.

Over Thanksgiving dinner I told my family that I was kind of enjoying the acting thing and wasn't sure if I was going to try to become an architect after all. My parents were horrified and said that I would be making the biggest mistake of my life if I pursued a career in acting. My mother and I had never really gotten along since the "pee in a bowl" incident and now she became even more distant. Thanksgiving always ended up being rather thankless, and I resigned myself to doing whatever it was I would wind up doing on my own.

That Saturday, I borrowed the white Chrysler station wagon and drove down to USC. I found the house in a very questionable neighborhood and almost thought better of going in, but then I considered how disappointed Franny would be and how I just couldn't live with that. I knocked on the door and a couple of guys out of central casting for gangster movies greeted me.

"Whatta ya want?" one of them said through a crack in the door.

I told them who I was and they took the bag while I waited on the porch for ten minutes with the door closed in my face. Then the door opened and they thrust the bag back into my hand.

"Don't want it," was all the guy said, and once again the door slammed in my face. I thought, Well, I tried. I drove home, packed up my stuff, repacked the sock in the Gibson, and the next day I flew back to San Francisco.

My mother had insisted that I wear the clothes she had washed and pressed while I was at home. I was appropriately preppy in my blue pinstripe slacks, penny loafers, and a yellow oxford cloth shirt. I had left my bell-bottom jeans in Berkeley knowing that if they had seen them my Republican parents would never approve, and Thanksgiving would have been all about the hippies and communists trying to take over the world.

The flight back was also uneventful, but when I went to pick up my Gibson from Special Handling (I always checked the guitar in Special Handling so it wouldn't get banged around in the cargo hold) the guy told me that it had mistakenly gone on to Seattle, but that it would be back the next day and I could pick it up from the same counter. This was a drag because I was playing the guitar a lot and didn't want to miss a day. Plus it meant I had to drive all the way back to the airport again the next day. Bummer!

When I got back to Berkeley, Franny came into my room as though we were old friends. She didn't knock; she just walked right in and asked about the money. I told her that the guy in LA hadn't wanted the pills and that to top it off my guitar had gone on to Seattle. I had not contemplated the criminal aspect of the misdirected luggage but Franny immediately went there. "They must have found the stuff," she said.

"What?" I exclaimed. "No way! The case was locked and the bag was taped inside the guitar under the strings. They'd have to bust the lock open, take off the strings, and look up inside the guitar with a flashlight! They're not going to all that trouble," I said. That seemed to calm her down. Logically speaking, why would anyone go to all that trouble unless they suspected that I was a major smuggler of some kind? It just didn't make sense. After all, I was just a kid with short hair in yellow oxford cloth and penny loafers—hardly the model of a big-time dope smuggler.

I had convinced myself that all was well and I didn't give it another thought as I drove back to the airport the next day. Franny had said she would go with me and, of course, I didn't object because it had been my dream to someday get Franny into my bed, and getting her into my car was a step in the right direction. I never questioned why this girl who was older than I and who had been so aloof just a few days before would suddenly be so interested in my welfare. Franny and I set off for the San Francisco airport at around one in the afternoon, hoping to avoid the return rush-hour traffic on the Bay Bridge.

The conversation in the car on the way over was somewhat stilted, to say the least. "How was your Thanksgiving?" I asked her.

"Good," she replied.

We didn't have a lot to talk about. All I really wanted to say was "How about sleeping with me tonight?" I found out later that probably would have worked, but at that point all I could get out was "Your sister is really great." We talked about her for a while and about her older brother, who was being swallowed up by a new fringe movement in Berkeley called Scientology. Scientology was one of the thousand or so movements being hawked in Sproul Plaza, the main quad for the university. At the time, nobody that I knew thought it would have any legs.

We got to the airport and pulled up to the Pacific Southwest Airlines white zone, where you could park for up to three minutes. There were always tow trucks hovering around to clear away the scofflaws, so I asked Franny to wait in the car while I went in. I told her it would take only a second. I dashed into the baggage claim area, which was crowded with midday travelers picking up their luggage and wandering about. I marched up to the Special Handling window and showed my claim ticket. The pudgy guy behind the counter took the slip and walked into a back room. Two minutes went by and he didn't come back. I didn't wear a watch in those days but I figured that the "three minutes" were almost up.

Where was the guy? Finally, after another couple of minutes, he reemerged with a smile on his face and said the guitar was in storage and that it would be brought up in five minutes and could I please be patient. I told him I had to move my car and walked out to the curb. Franny was sitting in the driver's seat as a cop was about to write Beulah a ticket. I told the cop we were just leaving and I got into the car on the passenger side. Franny drove off and I told her we were going to have to circle around because of the storage thing. Her face dropped and she said she was getting a bad feeling and maybe we should just forget about the guitar and go home. I laughed and told her that the guitar was worth more than a thousand dollars, and that it was my life. I described how the guy was smiling when he told me to wait and that I was not the least bit worried. She drove around the airport and back to the white zone. I got out of the car and once again went through the sliding glass doors into the baggage claim area.

As I got about a quarter of the way into the room, my earlobes started to burn. The room, which had been abuzz with travelers just a few minutes earlier, was now empty. Completely empty—except for the smiling pudgy fellow behind the counter! I could hear the deafening sound of my penny loafers with each step I took toward certain doom. Then, suddenly, all hell broke loose. Men in suits jumped out from all four corners of the room, yelling, "FREEZE, POLICE!!" The pudgy guy ducked down behind the counter as the four men grabbed me and threw me to the floor facedown. Out of the corner of my eye I saw a .45 and lots of gold badges as my arms were twisted behind my back and cuffed together.

Eventually I was dragged down the hallway and put in a window-less room with a desk and two chairs. They sat me down and a small-ish Asian man strolled over and introduced himself as Sergeant Ng of the Airport Police. I looked at his name tag and pondered the name Ng. I'd never seen such a name, let alone such a combination of let-ters. How could someone be called Ng? There must be some letters missing, I thought. But there he was and his name, or lack thereof, was the least of my worries. I knew that life was going to be very dif-ferent from then on. Ng sat down and with a big sigh he said, in per-fect unaccented English, "You are in a heap of trouble, young man."

I wondered what Ng thought of the handcuffed felon in a heap of trouble sitting before him. There I was, with short groomed hair, wearing the preppiest of clothes, and yet I must have somehow been involved in big-time criminal activity. It seemed to me that anyone could see the incongruity or, at the very least, the irony, of the picture. But not Ng. He had his man and he was all business.

"Were you selling the drugs?" he asked. I flashed back to the dog bowl full of pee and my mother ordering me to confess to the improper urination.

I lied to Ng. "What drugs?" I asked, trying to look as innocent as possible.

Ng calmly opened the top drawer of his desk and produced the sock with the drugs in it. "These drugs," he said. Then he unrolled the sock revealing the little white label my mother had so dutifully sewn into all my socks before I left for college. It read in bold red letters: HARRY HAMLIN.

Once again, I wondered how I had ever gotten into Berkeley! I was fucked! Okay, so the pills and the pot were mine, but they really weren't, I tried to explain.

"Okay, so if they're not yours then whose are they?" Ng ques-tioned.

Now I faced a great divide. If I spilled the beans on George and Franny I would not only forever be a snitch, but it would pretty much end any hope I would ever have of winning Franny's respect and then, possibly, her body. I said I couldn't answer that question and Ng didn't press the issue. Without further ado, I was taken down through the bowels of the airport to a waiting squad car, which drove me to the Redwood City jail. There, they fingerprinted me and took my mug shot. I started questioning the processing people, "What is going to happen next? Will I get to make a phone call? Where am I going?" I didn't get a single answer. The processors just grunted and barked orders over and over again. They must have been used to the drill.

Someone took me into a big room with a 20-foot-by-20-foot cage in the middle. There were three or four men huddled in one corner of the cell and one middle-aged guy standing in the other corner crying his eyes out. The guard opened the cage door, took off my handcuffs, and shoved me in. Immediately I knew why the huddle in the far corner. The guy who was crying had shit his pants, which were expensive khakis, and the smell was unbearable. The poor guy was so humiliated that I'm sure, if the tools had been available, he would have killed himself on the spot.

After a couple of hours they took the stinker out of the cage and we breathed a sigh of relief. Sandwiches were brought around and the prisoners traded stories. There was a pimp, a couple of drunks, and some hard-looking guys who were part of a gang that stood accused of robbing a convenience store. It turned out that none of us was guilty of what we were accused of doing. Obviously the system was not working.

I spent the night on the floor of the holding tank. As the night progressed, more and more drunks were shoved into the cage. Just before dawn, a cop banged on the cell with his nightstick and ordered us all to form a line by the door. One by one we were shackled together until there was a line of about fifteen of us. We were then to walk, single file, through the building to a big black and white bus waiting at the curb. The bus was going to take us to the courthouse for our "arraignment," whatever that was. I had never heard the word before and it sounded like something that happened at a wedding.

After a short drive, we were hustled into the courtroom to await our fate. I was by far the best dressed of the bunch, but that didn't seem to impress anyone. After the judge came in, we were told to stand up one by one and answer the charges made against us. I, of course, had no lawyer, and though I had been given a dime to make a call the night before, my one call to the DKE house pay phone had gone unanswered. I was all alone in this and was just trying to take it all in.

Suddenly I heard a girl's voice screaming outside the courtroom, "Can somebody please help me?" The whole courtroom turned toward the commotion. Could it be that Franny had come? The voice had sounded vaguely like hers, but I didn't dare get my hopes up. Then the courtroom door opened and, sure enough, Franny marched in, flanked by a handlebar-mustached guy sporting a gangster-style pinstriped suit and carrying a briefcase in his right hand.

The two of them sat down and Franny pointed to me. I nodded that I saw her as the judge called my name. As I rose, the guy with the mustache and the suit stood up and said in a loud voice, "Michael Stepanian for the defendant, your honor, waive reading and plead not guilty. Request release on his own recognizance." The judge simply said, "Request denied, bail set at one thousand dollars." He pounded his gavel once and that was that.

Franny and the guy in the suit stood up and left the courtroom. Three hours later, I was crammed in between Franny, who was driving, and her little sister, Anne, in Franny's green convertible MG. She had, of course, figured out where I was, gone to the courthouse, and racked with guilt and having no other option, pleaded with any-one and everyone in the courthouse hallway to defend her friend. It just so happened that Mr. Stepanian, who was one of the most successful drug lawyers in San Francisco and was rumored to repre-sent David Crosby of Crosby, Stills & Nash, had heard Franny's plea.

Intrigued by this pretty young girl with the balls to make a scene in the courthouse on behalf of a friend, he decided to take my case "pro bono," whatever that meant. After my arraignment, Franny paid a bail bondsman one hundred dollars in crisp new one-dollar bills—a little "fuck you" to the establishment of which Franny is proud to this very day.

On the way back to Berkeley, Franny and I bonded in a curious sort of way and I began to see a crack in the door, sexwise. We decided it would be best if we stayed mum about the whole jail thing; I would only talk to Franny, George, and Franny's sister, Anne, about it. No one else at the house would know that I had been arrested for felony possession of narcotics. It was going to be our little secret.

George didn't want any part of my predicament and was in serious denial about his role in my new criminal record. At one point, he actually asked me how he was going to get his money back for the drugs that I had "lost"! That was, ironically, the moment that I sealed the deal with Franny. I think she was so disgusted by George's take on the whole thing that she told him to fuck off and with that the door swung wide open. That night, Franny stayed with me. Thankfully Gene didn't come back, which was nothing unusual; I never did find out where he spent most of his time.

Sex with Franny was different. At that point, I really didn't have much experience in the sack. I had flailed around with a couple of girls in high school, but then there was the "Good News" time and I had been celibate for a couple of years. Before the Jesus years, I had really only had what you might call "sex" (that would be penetration) with one girl. Her name was Sarah and she was a babysitter for some little kids who lived near our Canadian cabin. Sarah was fifteen and I was thirteen, and we had been hanging out together in a kind of boy-girl Huck and Tom way for a couple of years. We started kissing and touching the summer of my thirteenth year, and the night before she left to go back to her home in Boston, I found myself in a sleeping bag with her in the room of her two charges while they slept like the babes that they were.

We kissed and touched while the two little girls snored peacefully. Soon our shorts were off and our young, virgin bodies were touching ever so lightly. Within minutes, penetration became inevitable, and I positioned myself above her, thinking, Oh God! What am I about to do? She tried to spread her legs but we were in a sleeping bag and there was only so far she could go. I went in for the score. I poked and prodded with my prepubescent penetrator but couldn't seem to find the opening. Then she said a few words I have remembered verbatim since that moment.

One's first coital experience is never forgotten, much like the moment those of us of a certain age were told that Jack Kennedy had been assassinated. You just don't forget the "first time" and this "first time" was not just memorable for the moment itself but also for those words so gently whispered into my right ear.

In a breathy voice reminiscent of Marilyn Monroe, Sarah whispered, "It would facilitate matters if you were to exert downward pressure."

She was fifteen! Where did that come from? I had never heard the word "facilitate" and I had no clue what it meant, but I somehow got the gist of her advice.

I did what she recommended and I found my way inside, but as I had never reached a climax before, I had no idea whether I had indeed shared bodily fluids with her. I just didn't know what an orgasm felt like. Now, of course, I know that I did *not in fact* experience one that night. At the time, though, I was unsure, and for a few weeks I was terrified that I might become a dad at thirteen. I saw Sarah a year or so later at her parents' summer home in Maine and we tried it again after an evening spent robbing lobster pots in the fog, an endeavor for which we were later told we could have been shot. The lobster raid, not the sex. The sex didn't work anyway and I never dated Sarah again. I was fourteen and had only my subscription to *Playboy* for a romantic companion.

I had a few other false starts throughout my teens, and I had even spent a night or two with Franny's little sister, but Franny was the first "real woman" I had sex with. That meant that she sort of knew what she was doing. I remained clueless.

Franny had a little dog named Mimi that was her constant companion. Mimi was a female Dachshund, a wiener dog, who always and only slept with Franny. Where Franny went so went Mimi. So, that first night it was the three of us. Franny and I made passionate love three or four times while Mimi looked on probably wondering what the hell had happened to George. I wondered if George and Franny put on as good a show as we did.

The next morning I woke up to the sound of a dog scratching and whining at my door. I looked over to see that Mimi was in bed asleep next to Franny, who was also fast asleep. Then I noticed blood on my sheets. I lifted up the sheet and there was blood everywhere. Mimi woke up and jumped off the bed and started barking at the door. Then the dog on the other side started to bark and I realized that it was Buck, a huge German shepherd that belonged to Allover and was forever leaving giant stinking piles of shit on the floor where the oriental rugs used to be. Now Franny was awake and, when she saw the blood she looked over at Mimi and said, "Oh, shit! Mimi's in heat again." I guess we had put on a helluva show because we really got Mimi worked up and now Buck was a wild man.

We spent the rest of the week doing our show for Mimi and trying to keep Buck from fucking the wiener dog—something a lot of people might have paid good money to see!

I'm not exactly sure what happened or who did or didn't do what to whom, but by the end of that week it wasn't looking so good for me and Franny. I knew something was up when I saw George and Franny huddled together on the lawn outside the house. George was a big guy, at least six two, and sitting next to Franny he looked like a giant. I was a little shrimp in comparison, and moments like that always seemed to dredge up those nursery school thoughts of huge fingers, little penises, and total inadequacy. Franny came to my room and said we should take a drive. The only people who say "We should take a drive" are the really bad guys in the gangster movies who you know are going to send you to the fishes if you get in the car. But this was Franny, so we drove to north Berkeley and parked the car in the rain. She said we should stop seeing each other. No surprise. But then she said the reason was because she had decided to become an alcoholic and that she would make a miserable companion because she would be plastered all the time. She said this with a straight face. She was dead serious.

La Lutte Continue

Franny and George got back together but their union was a bit rocky. They shared a third-floor room with Mimi and were forever locked in some knock-down, drag-out codependent ruckus that made Mimi bark like a maniac. One day when my roommate, Gene, was in town, they scored a bag of several hundred "reds" from him. Reds were Seconal sleeping pills—the same substance that my mother was mostly made of. After Gene sold Franny and George the reds, he asked if I wanted to fly to Hawaii with him for the weekend. It seems that he had a pocket full of cash not only from the reds sale, but Gene had also filched some poor sod's Diner's Club card the day before. "Come on," Gene said. "No one will ever know and we'll come back Monday in time for your classes." I had always dreamed of going to Hawaii and he almost had me but I thought about my growing criminal record and felt I was in enough trouble as it stood.

I politely declined, said good-bye to Gene, who tore off for the airport, and went up to the third-floor roof to watch the sunset, a ritual that Franny and I had started a couple of weeks before. It was also an excuse to walk past George's room and to possibly run into Franny. A couple of hundred reds? I thought. They must be going into business! I wondered who the poor soul was who would be their drug mule this time.

I got to the top of the stairs and saw that George's door had a fresh coat of paint. It was now Day-Glo blue with a hand-painted slogan in French written in an orange Day-Glo arc across the front that read

LA LUTTE CONTINUE! Just then, the door opened and Franny emerged with a stack of stamped envelopes in her hand and a scowl on her face. She brushed past me and went down the stairs without a word. Oh well, I thought, and went out onto the roof. The sunset over the bay was glorious and it felt good to be alive.

I woke the next morning to hysterical pounding on my door. It was Franny, who was furious. She was screaming at the top of her lungs, "You fucker! You motherfucker!! You motherfucking bastard!!" She was pounding and screaming and crying all at the same time. I pulled on my bell-bottoms and opened the door. Franny collapsed into the room and looked around. "Where the fuck is he?" she demanded. "Where did that fucker go?" It turned out she wasn't pissed at me. No. The object of her fury was my roommate, Gene, who was probably sipping mai tais on the beach in Honolulu by now. "He burned us!" she gasped. "The motherfucker burned us!"

The expression "burned" was used when one purchased some form of illegal dope that turned out not to be dope at all but some other benign substance. What neither Gene nor I had known was that the two lovers had not bought the dope to sell. They had no intention of making a profit. Instead, their plan had been to use it, all of it, the same night they bought it.

The letters that Franny had had in her hand when she passed me in the hall were suicide notes she was planning to mail to her close family and friends. (She told me later that she never did.) Later in the evening, she and George split up the sleeping pills and each took enough to kill a bear, while forcing a handful of dissolved capsules down Mimi's throat as well. Then they waited for the peaceful end to what must have been a tormented existence. No luck. It turned out that Gene had indeed "burned" them, selling them pills filled with baby laxative and then hightailing it off to Hawaii to escape their certain wrath. The only thing that happened to Franny and George also

happened to the dog, and there was dachshund shit all over the house for days.

George, when he woke up, had wanted to finish the job some other way but Franny had second thoughts and decided to live on— without George. She moved out of the house and I saw her only a few times after that. I looked up the words *la lutte continue* in a French dictionary. They translate to . . . "the struggle continues." And so it does.

Evie and the Monkey House

Michael Stepanian, my hotshot drug lawyer, had my court date set for March of the next year, thinking that delaying it would work in my favor. It was now late December and exams were over and it was time to drive down to LA for Christmas with the parental units and brother Dave.

I was very low on cash and had heard that there was a bulletin board in some dorm where people put up requests for travel companions to share expenses over the holidays. I posted a notice: WANTED: PASSENGER TO RIDE TO LA AND SHARE GAS $. I left the DKE house phone number and waited. A couple of days later I got a bite and a girl came to the house to find out if I was on the level. She called herself Evie. She had the face of an angel, brown hair that fell down below her waist, jeans, a T-shirt, and no shoes. She was a vision to behold. The quintessential goddess of flower power and free love, she smelled of patchouli incense and Herbal Essences shampoo. She was way out of my league but she needed a ride and I was glad to oblige.

We set off for LA on a Thursday morning and Evie seemed totally comfortable with herself. Free and easy, without a care in the world. She went on and on about her great life and her love of dance. I, on the other hand, was totally off balance with this beautiful free spirit sitting next to me. I wanted to find out if she had a boyfriend but the conversation just never went there. It sounded like her life was so full that she wouldn't have time for a boyfriend anyway. I was envious of her freedom and her passion. We talked about everything under the

sun, and as we pulled out of Fresno, where we had stopped for a bite to eat, I was really sad that at nine that night I would be saying good-bye to her, possibly forever. She didn't need a ride back from LA to Berkeley, so this drive was it. I purposely slowed down a little bit to squeeze out a few more minutes with her when it started to rain.

Normally a little rain on the highway is no big deal, but soon the traffic stopped dead. We waited in the downpour for a few minutes until we saw a cop in a yellow rain slicker walking toward us and stopping to talk with each driver. Cars in front of us started peeling out of the formation and driving back the way we came. The cop got to us and told us that the highway was closed for the night and that we would have to find someplace to stay. It was cold and rainy and we had twenty bucks between us. We turned around and went back to Bakersfield.

Things were getting interesting! I had never rented a motel room with a girl before and in those days it just wasn't done unless you were married. But we had only enough money for one room and I wasn't about to drive all the way back to Berkeley. We found a Holiday Inn and I went in and did my best Dustin Hoffman impersonation from *The Graduate*.

Evie stayed in the car while I got the key to the room, and after I went up, she snuck up and slipped inside without attracting any attention. I was really nervous but she seemed to take everything in stride. She said she was tired and wanted to go to sleep right away. That was fine with me. She went into the bathroom and I sat down on the bed wondering what I should do or say so that I wouldn't seem like a total geek. Then the door to the bathroom opened and a four-year-long obsession began.

Evie stood in the doorway absolutely naked as though it was the most natural thing in the world. She had a dancer's body, long slender legs, a perfect waist, and beautiful breasts. The kind of breasts that would-be movie starlets will pay big bucks for today. Her hair was so thick and long that it covered one of her breasts and even part of her crotch. She yawned and repeated that she was tired and climbed into bed next to me. I was speechless, sitting frozen next to her like a statue.

I was confused. Did she get naked because she wanted to roll in the hay? Or did she get naked just because that's what people like her did with strangers and it meant nothing at all? I figured that I should also get undressed and get into bed. So I did and, of course, one thing led to another, and like I said, I remained obsessed with Evie for four years.

The next day we got back on the road and I dropped her off at her folks' house and didn't talk to her again until almost a year later.

That winter was filled with a lot of meetings with my lawyer. He figured I had gotten a bad break and that I didn't really deserve the felony rap the state was trying to pin on me. Stepanian was apparently well connected, and he told me he was in the process of making a deal with the DA regarding my case and that he wanted me to meet with him and the DA at a restaurant in the city. I have to admit that I didn't know what a DA was, nor did I know what a deal with him meant. But Stepanian was my only hope so I went to the lunch meeting. We ordered enormous cheeseburgers and the DA asked me about my life up to then. I told him about the DKE house but I left out the part about the girls, the opium, and my roommate, Gene the junkie. I had made the honor roll for the first quarter in spite of all the hijinks, and I told him that I had gone to boarding school on the East Coast. He seemed impressed and wondered how I had become mixed up with these narcotics. I told him that I didn't really know what the drugs were and that they weren't really mine.

Once again he asked me where the drugs came from and I said that I couldn't tell him. Why was I protecting that Neanderthal, George? Have I mentioned that I often wonder how I was accepted to Berkeley?

The DA said that he would work out a deal in which I would plead guilty to misdemeanor possession of prescription drugs without a prescription and that I would get summary probation for a couple of years—basically a slap on the wrist. He said the judge, who was a woman and a good friend, would understand that I really wasn't felon material and that I had just made an idiotic mistake. He promised it would all be prearranged and that he would even be there to make sure everything went smoothly. Stepanian assured me that everything would be fine. I was relieved to say the least. It was mid-February and my court date was more than a month away. No sweat.

The month went by like lightning. I was in a production of "The Scottish Play" in the small Durant Theatre. (As an actor, I am not permitted to say the actual name of this play by Shakespeare because any utterance of the name *Macbeth* will cause mountains of bad luck to be heaped upon me. Oops!) I played Malcolm—or rather I massacred Malcolm. It was my first attempt at Shakespeare, and even though I sucked I found that I liked the challenge of doing the classics. Twelve years later I played Hamlet professionally to packed houses, rave reviews, and standing ovations at Princeton's McCarter Theatre and, as it happened, it was the Danish prince that started me on my crusade to save the world. But that's another story.

The last performance of the Scottish play was a couple of days before my court date and I was looking forward to putting the whole "felon" chapter of my life behind me. When the day came, I polished my shoes, put on some clean blue slacks, a yellow oxford cloth shirt, and dusted off my old boarding school blazer, which was the only sport coat I owned. My hair had grown out some but I could still make it look pretty geeky with some Brylcreem and water.

I drove Beulah over to the courthouse and went in expecting to see Mr. Stepanian in the foyer. I waited for a few minutes but I was on the docket for 9:00 a.m. and it was 8:50, so I went inside and sat down while keeping an eye on the door. I looked around for the DA, but he was also nowhere to be seen. I then noticed that the little silver nameplate in front of where the judge sat said DELARIOUS, not MILLER, as Stepanian had assured me. I thought I must be in the wrong court-room. I was about to get up when the bailiff grunted, "All rise!" and in swept the judge, a balding middle-aged man without a smile any-where in his DNA.

Just then, a kid a couple of years older than I and completely out of breath swept in beside me and asked under his panting breath, "You Harry Hamlin?" I whispered, "Yes." I noticed that his suit was too big for his slight build and that his tie was one of those fake jobs with metal clips. He told me in a whisper that Stepanian had been called to Alaska because one of his rock-and-roll clients had been busted the day before in Anchorage (must have been David Crosby) and that he, the kid, was going to represent me at the hearing. Then the kid looked up and said, "Oh, shit! Delarious!" I said, "What?" and the kid explained that Delarious was the "hanging judge" and that Judge Miller must have been sick. I didn't know there was still hang-ing going on.

The kid was starting to look panicked. I asked him where the DA was and he whispered that the DA had gone to Hawaii for a vacation. I asked the kid if he knew the deal and he told me to be quiet. Just then, the judge called my name. The kid kicked me and I stood up. Stepanian had told me that if I pleaded guilty to the charges, I would just get probation, but that was a deal he had made with a different judge. Delarious looked down at my rap sheet and without looking up asked me how I would plead. I didn't know what to do. I just stood there. The judge asked me again and the kid whispered through the side of his mouth, "Guilty!" "Guilty, Your Honor," I said. What hap-pened next was truly surreal.

Judge Delarious looked over his bifocals to see me sitting there with my boarding school blazer and oxford cloth shirt, and I must have reminded him of the childhood he would like to have had but didn't because his father was probably a no-good alcoholic garbage-man and his mother whipped him with a butcher strap. He stared at me for an eternity and then said with a grunt that I looked like I had had all the opportunities in the world and that I had wasted them on a life of drugs and crime. He told me I should be ashamed of myself and that I was a disgrace to my family and to my peers, who would give their eyeteeth to have had the chances I must have had. He said that he was, quite frankly, disgusted with people like me and that he had had enough of it. Then he sentenced me to three years in the state prison at San Quentin.

I looked at the kid sent by Stepanian and he looked like he had just had the wind knocked out of him. I looked at the judge and then around the courtroom for someone, anyone, who might intervene and straighten this mess out. My heart was pounding like a jackhammer as I tried to make sense of what I had just heard.

I looked back at the kid and something was happening to him. He was growing up really, really fast. Right after Popeye downs a can of spinach, his body starts to build in strength until he is ready for anything Bluto might throw at him. The same thing was happening to the kid. I swear, I have to find that guy, the kid (I never caught his name), who must be in his sixties today, for what he did next was nothing short of genius.

The kid shouted that the judge couldn't do that, not just because of a prior plea bargain reached with Judge Miller but, more important, because I was an honor student who was not only president of his fraternity but who also taught underprivileged children math and English three days a week in Oakland. Only the first of those things was accurate and when Delarious looked down at me and asked me if what the young attorney had said was true, I hesitated for only a second, instantly revisiting that moment with my mother standing over the old bread tin filled with pee. The kid kicked me with his left foot and I cried, "Yes, Your Honor."

There was a long moment of silence while the judge must have relived the butcher strap one more time before saying, "All right, then, I'll give you a break this time, but if I ever see you again in my courtroom, you will rue the day!" Then he said, with much less relish than the first time, "One year in the county jail, all but nine days suspended." The kid went into action again and somehow got the judge to let me serve my time on weekends so that I wouldn't miss teaching any of those inner-city kids, and he got the judge to let me start doing my time after Easter, which was coming up in one week. I often wonder what my life would have been like if that young fresh-faced lawyer had not been so quick on his feet. I would probably have at least one tattoo.

Perro

Because of that genius young lawyer, I got an Easter vacation before I had to report to the county jail. I was especially happy about this because an old childhood friend of mine had invited me to join his family for an Easter feast at a remote hacienda somewhere in the desert of Baja. So, the Friday after my court appearance, I drove down to LA, this time, lamentably, without Evie. A few friends and I piled into Carter's old 1949 Ford woodie and, along with a couple of carloads of parents, we caravanned across the border and out into the desert wilderness of Baja. After a couple of hours on a well-groomed dirt road, we came to the hacienda, which looked like an oasis in the middle of the Sahara. We drove down a long cactus-lined driveway and came to a beautiful adobe home.

Although the house was maintained, it had not been occupied in some time and all the provisions for the Easter feast had to be hauled in from the cars. It was Saturday and we had brought enough food for that night and Easter Sunday. The Easter menu was pretty exotic: spit-roasted pig with all the trimmings. I wasn't sure how a pig on a spit was "trimmed" but I knew it would be a great feast, a fitting final weekend before my incarceration.

We had a pretty lean meal on Saturday night as the adults kept repeating that we should all "make room" for the big Easter feast the next day. That night we sat around a big fire pit outside the house and I played the guitar and sang a few lame improvisational songs about Mexico and roast pig. Everyone was really excited about the porcine feast to come. There was an outdoor brick barbecue that one of the dads had converted into a spit roaster with some rebar, a small electric motor, and a car battery. The idea was to take a whole pig, dress it, and skewer the thing on a rod attached to the motor and a car fan belt. The hacienda had no electricity so everything was lit by candles and oil lamps at night and all the food was in Coleman camp coolers packed with ice. The pig would slowly turn over the coals until it was golden brown, we would then unskewer the beast and carve it up into the most delicious and unique Easter dinner ever. Yum! Yum!

As the night wore on, one of the dads produced a jug of Red Mountain burgundy and I had my first "flashback." I excused myself and walked alone out into the desert night to reflect on some of the things that had transpired since that fateful night in La Honda. I told no one I was going to jail the next week. I still was spending a lot of time trying to figure out how to cover the whole thing up since I was probably going to make a run at the White House someday.

I slept in the next morning and when I woke up the grown-ups were furiously preparing the Easter feast. There were great bowls of corn and salad and a giant plate of sliced vegetables to be roasted along with the pig, which was already turning slowly on the spit over a bed of mesquite coals. It would take several hours to cook the animal. We had coffee and barbecued toast for breakfast. The dads kept saying, "Don't eat too much, save room for the feast!!" We had no choice but to oblige as our stomachs groaned, pleading for eggs and sausage to accompany the toast.

By one o'clock, the sun was high in the sky, the long outdoor table was set, the veggies and salads were packed on ice and tucked under the table out of the sun. The pig had started to turn that golden brown. The adults kept poking and prodding the pig to see how much longer it needed to turn on the spit. It seemed that there had been a slight miscalculation. The pig needed to cook for at least two more hours. The feast would be delayed.

Someone suggested that we take a hike through the desert chaparral to see the wildflowers that were just starting to bloom. There was nothing else to do except sit and watch the endless rotation of the pork carcass, so we all agreed and set out to look at flowers. During the walk it occurred to me that there was some irony to the fact that this convicted criminal who was about to check into a county jail to be strip-searched and shoved in a cage was peacefully walking through the Baja desert being lectured about larkspur and the California poppy. If these people only knew about the hardened criminal in their midst.

We walked forever until the chorus of stomach growls had become so loud that we could no longer hear the wildflower lecture. We turned around and headed back at a good clip. This was going to be a dinner to remember. As we got closer to the house, we could smell the mesquite smoke and our mouths began to water. A little black and white dog came bounding down the path toward us and I knelt down to say hi but the dog just ran by, paying no attention to the humans. One of the dads yelled, "Perro, Perro!" which even I knew meant "dog" in Spanish. The dog didn't stop. Someone said how cute the puppy looked. I wondered who his master was since it seemed there were no humans around for miles.

Before long another dog ran down the path. Then we saw more dogs running across the desert. There were big dogs, and small dogs, black dogs, white dogs, and black and white dogs—about twenty dogs in all were running all around the hacienda. We had not seen one dog until that moment and by the time we reached the patio, we found ourselves looking at what could only be described as Armageddon.

The pig, no longer a golden brown orb rotating on the spit, lay in pieces on the dirt floor of the patio. It was unrecognizable as a pig, having been reduced to ribs and bloody flesh. All the coolers with the vegetables and desserts had been torn open and most everything had been eaten by the wild dogs. There was nothing left. In the middle of the patio, lying motionless, was a smallish dog, maybe a puppy, whose belly was almost bigger than the dog itself. It was dead as a doornail. Too much pig! Then we noticed another dog with a huge belly limping and looking guilty as sin as it slowly hobbled, tail between its legs, out of the patio and into the desert. The most distinctive thing about the mongrel was how full its belly looked while the rest of it was just thin skin over bones. The dog limped off. It was obviously the lead *perro* who had been the one to walk on the hot coals to get the pig off the spit. He was the hero of the group and I could only feel an odd kind of admiration for him. His feet were probably burned to the bone! There was a lesson in this somewhere.

Our starving band of Easter revelers shooed off the dogs, packed up what was left, and moved the feast to the first Denny's we came to once we got over the border. I felt that Easter dinner at Denny's was actually much more appropriate for a convicted criminal on his way to prison than "pig on a spit."

Welcome to the Monkey House

When I got back to Berkeley, I had a message from Mike Stepanian, my famous drug lawyer who had not been there to save my skin. I called him up and he said that he was really sorry that things had gotten so screwed up. He promised to do everything he could to make it better. When he returned from his tropical vacation, the DA had been horrified to find out that I had been sentenced to jail time. He told Stepanian that he would do everything in his power to make my time in the Redwood City jail as comfortable as possible. I thought, How the fuck can jail ever be comfortable?

The DA had explained that, coincidentally, the warden of the Redwood City correctional facility had a brother who was a student studying acting at Berkeley and that, in fact, the brother was currently playing the title role in *Cyrano de Bergerac* on the main stage of the Zellerbach Playhouse. Stepanian said that he would arrange a meeting between me and the two brothers, which was how I came to meet the warden of the Redwood City correctional facility, my home away from home for the next three weekends.

Jeff, the warden, told me that I would be well taken care of in jail and that I had nothing to worry about. He said he would be there the following Friday night when I was checked in and that he would see to it that everything went smoothly. He even paid for my hamburger at the greasy spoon where we met. I wished his brother good luck with *Cyrano,* told him that I was in rehearsals for the next play at the Zellerbach, and said I'd come to see his show when I got out of the hoosegow.

Breathing a bit easier, and feeling like I had an in with the manager of an impossible-to-get-into high-class resort, I arrived at the jail parking lot at around four thirty on Friday afternoon. I was scheduled to check in at 5:00 p.m., and the one thing Jeff had emphasized was not to be late. I put a pen, a pack of cigarettes, a toothbrush, and my journal into a brown paper sack per the warden's instructions and headed into my weekend penance.

At the check-in window they took my wallet and the stuff from my pockets as the warden walked into the room. He gave me a wink but didn't say anything to me, and I heard him tell the guard on duty that I could keep the contents of the paper sack and that he was to take good care of me. What a relief. The guard shoved a towel and a roll of clothes, prison-issue blue jeans and a denim shirt with the words REDWOOD CITY stenciled in black on the back into my arms and took me into a small holding room. He told me to change into the jeans and blue work shirt, put my clothes into a canvas bag, which was hanging on the wall, and to keep the towel. The guard then said something like "You must have some friends 'cause usually this is when we do a strip search, and you know what that means." I actually didn't know what that meant but found out later that it involved the guard, a flashlight, and a pair of rubber gloves. I was just glad I was being "taken care of."

I was led down a long corridor past two or three cell blocks until we came to cell block F. The guard barked some code, there was a loud buzzing noise and the cell door opened as if by magic. I walked into the cell, which was about 16 feet by 20 feet with bunks lining the walls and a cement table with cement benches in the middle of the room. A plastic shower with no curtain was attached to the left wall next to the stainless steel toilet bowl that stuck out into the room. As we made our way into the cell I noticed that four or five large African-American men were sitting in a circle on the floor passing around what looked exactly like a joint! How could this be? I'm in jail for less than a minute and people are already breaking the law!?

I couldn't smell any pot so I figured that they must be low on tobacco and were sharing a hand-rolled smoke. I discovered later that the smoke of choice in jail was Bull Durham tobacco hand rolled into ZIG-ZAG rolling papers—probably because it was cheap.

I settled into my new bunk and lay down on it to test it out. "Hey, man! Off the bunk!" shouted another prisoner. There were nine African Americans and one short Mexican guy with gold teeth in the cell with me. Needless to say, I didn't quite blend in.

"I said off the fucking bunk!" the guy screamed again. I didn't know the drill. No lying down on the bunk until lights out. The guards wanted everyone to be really tired come bedtime so the monkey house inhabitants wouldn't make any trouble at night. This guy was obviously some kind of inside enforcer and he stared at me like I had just raped his daughter. I got off the bunk.

The big black dudes were still passing around hand-rolled cigarettes like they were joints and it seemed like they were getting louder and laughing a lot. I thought, Nah. It must have been my imagination. Four other big black dudes were playing hearts or something at the cement table. The Mexican guy was sitting alone on the only other cement bench, staring at the bars. There was a whole lot of squawking going on. Prisoners are a loud bunch and there never seemed to be a lull. The cement walls and floors created a huge reverberation chamber and the sound was deafening. There was also loud sixties rock-and-roll music being pumped into the cell block nonstop.

After what seemed like an eternity, I heard a loud voice shout, "Lights out!" And thus began one of the longest nights of my life.

The lights dimmed, the music went off, and everyone except the guys passing around the smokes headed for their bunks. The smoking dudes groaned in unison when the music went off but kept sitting there in a circle passing around their smokes and laughing and howling while the prisoners in other cells were shouting for them to shut up. It was obvious to me by then that our guys were lit up by something. They started rolling around on the floor and laughing so hard that I thought they might split open. These were very big men very out of control and I began to get scared.

I was the only white guy in the cell and I was a fresh-faced kid with no experience with these sorts of folks. I wasn't just a fish out of water; I was flopping around on the deck! I pulled my one brown blanket over my head and asked that Scotty please beam me up. The BBDs (Big Black Dudes) were now taunting the rest of us and even taunting the guards who were nowhere to be seen. Where were the authorities? We were in prison, for Christ's sake. This was precisely the place where this was not supposed to happen. What the fuck was going on??

The BBDs had begun taking off their shirts, dancing on the tables, and howling like wild animals. I had visions that at any moment they would turn on us, specifically my little white ass, ripping me limb from limb to eat my still-beating heart with relish. The whole jail joined in the chorus and there was screaming and singing and howling and just general insanity. The BBDs then turned their attention to the shower and yanked and pulled until it pulled away from the wall with a huge creak. There was more shouting and dancing and howling for about an hour until the BBDs began to fall asleep. Some of the other guys were talking in low voices now about what a bad situation we were in. I just wanted the whole thing to end. I drifted off to sleep sometime after three and woke at around five thirty when I saw the Mexican get up and take a suit out of a hanging bag next to our bunk. He dressed and stood in front of the door. The door opened and he walked outside without making a sound.

Most of the other guys were still snoring away. At six, the lights

came on abruptly and the music blasted from hidden speakers somewhere above the cell. The place was a mess and still there was no sign
of any guards, or anyone who was not a prisoner, for that matter. Had
they not heard the noise? Did the guards go home at night and leave
the prison to the inmates to do as they pleased? What was this place?
And why did the Mexican guy put on a suit and walk out of the cell
unattended? Why? Why? Why? There were more than a few dots that
I was having some trouble connecting.

I got the answer to the Mexican question from one of the hearts
players while we brushed our teeth in the sink, which, thankfully, the
BBDs had left alone. The toilet was still intact as well. The Mexican
guy was going to court, hence the suit. Apparently, he had killed his
wife some years before, chopped her up into pieces, and strewn her
dismembered corpse along I-80. He had managed to get away with
the horrible crime until he saw a TV show about how an old case was
solved because a skull was found by police and the dental records had
revealed the identity of the victim. He had panicked when he saw the
show and, shovel in hand, had gone back to the spot to dig up the
skull and destroy the possible incriminating dental evidence. I guess
he had some trouble locating the bones because he was soon arrested
for digging holes along the highway.

The police, who had found human remains there some years
before, put two and two together, and now the Mexican was on trial
for the heinous crime. I now had another vision to contemplate
because the Mexican wife chopper-upper had been sleeping not two
feet from me. This brought new meaning to being "between a rock
and a hard place."

I sat at the table to write about all of this in my journal. One of
the hearts players asked me, "How come you got to bring that book
in here?" I didn't think I would get many brownie points if I told
him that the warden was looking out for me and that he had even
bought me a burger the week before, so I told him that nobody had
said anything about it and I didn't know it wasn't permitted. They all

grumbled and I heard the word *white* a couple of times. Then one of the BBDs came over, sat next to me, and handed me a lit rolled cigarette like the ones they had been smoking the night before. "Here, man. Have some of this. It'll cure what ails ya!"

"No thanks," I said in as nonchalant a manner as possible.

"Come on, man. Don't be a pansy. Here, this stuff is jazz." He poked the joint into my face.

I never liked being called a pansy, especially in those days. It always got a rise out of me—probably because of my history with that baby blue Huffy bike.

"All right," I said, and took a big drag on the smoke. There was hardly any taste to it but within seconds the whole cell was rolling around.

"Angel dust!" he said proudly. "Makes you fly like an angel!" he sang as he walked away taking a huge toke from the joint. It was 7:00 a.m. I was in a jail cell with eight lunatic felons and I was stoned out of my gourd.

I kept writing in my journal, which I still have and refer to now to get some of this stuff right. Suddenly and without warning, six uniformed guards armed with pump action shotguns marched in front of F tank and pointed their weapons at us. "Shakedown!" one of the officers bellowed. "Everybody out now! Up against the wall!" The door opened, the armed guards retreated, and we filed out and formed a line against the wall while other guards went into the cell and started tearing it apart, obviously looking for whatever had made the BBDs crazy the night before.

We were told to spread our legs as wide apart as we could and stretch our hands up to the ceiling against the wall. Then one of the guards started a pat-down of each prisoner. Just before they got to me, Jeff, the warden, came into the picture. When he saw me up against the wall, he told the other guards to bring me out of the group and take me to another cell block. As I passed him he stopped the guard and said, "What the fuck is he doing here? This is the felony side. He's supposed to be on the misdemeanor side!" The original booking officer had sent me into the wrong cell. So, before I knew what was happening, I was pulled from F tank and ushered into P, which was for convicted misdemeanor offenders and was another world altogether.

There were no BBDs smoking angel dust, no murderers or violent offenders; just guys who had veered off the tracks in one way or another and now found themselves shitting in front of each other and eating stale bologna sandwiches for dinner behind steel bars. I was allowed to keep my journal for the remainder of the first weekend but for the following two incarcerations I was allowed nothing but my birthday suit, and only after it had been thoroughly searched by a guard wearing rubber gloves and holding a flashlight.

As I discovered during my time in P tank, there were a few guys who actually looked forward to the rubber glove/flashlight thing. One such fellow was a gay, twentysomething, skinny, black offender who called himself Brother Robinson. He wore bright red Speedo underwear and always referred to himself in the third person. Brother Robinson said that he was innocent of the charge of destruction of public property, specifically jamming parking meters in his neighborhood. I tried, in my mind, to draw some *Cool Hand Luke* comparisons but came up empty. He was actually a pretty sweet fellow and I don't think I would have made it through the next two weekends without him. He was my savior behind bars and had no fear about telling the other inmates to fuck off and leave me alone when they got going on the "new kid."

Each cell had a hierarchy, and the oldest guys who had been in the longest had seniority. When someone new, especially someone white and under twenty and naive, was introduced to the population, the senior guys had a field day. I was no exception and the older folks, most of whom were black or Hispanic, immediately let me know the drill. First, they wanted to know my "beef," which is prison speak for whatever offense the "man" thought I had done to get me convicted. I told them it was for possession of narcotics and they asked me if I was

guilty and I said, "Not exactly." They all laughed and said that not one
of them was guilty either. Wow, I thought, all these innocent people
getting arrested and sent to jail! The mind boggled!

It was my job to clean the toilet and the shower and to pick up
any trash in the cell. The toilet and shower cleaning happened once
a day around 11:00 a.m. and the trash pickup was an all-day affair.
The word *gay* had not entered the mainstream lexicon as of 1971
and, in fact, I did not know anyone who was openly gay. But Brother
Robinson was a flamer! He was totally miscast among this bunch
and was even more of a sore thumb when he cavorted around in his
red Speedo. The guards would come by periodically and scream at
Brother Robinson to stop his perversions and get dressed.

Every time one of my cell mates dropped a match or cigarette
butt on the floor someone would yell, "Hamlin! What the fuck! You
asleep, motherfucker? Get your ass over there and clean that shit up!"
That's when Brother Robinson would shout at the screamer, "Shut
your yap, asshole, leave Brother Robinson's boy alone!" Thankfully I
never was his "boy," but I was glad that he treated me as such around
the thugs. I finished out my first weekend as a convict quietly and
under the protection of Brother Robinson. Had I known what the
next two weekends would bring, I would have requested to be transferred to San Quentin.

During the weeks between jail time I dutifully went to classes and
rehearsals, and, of course, told no one where I was headed on the
weekends. The first week between "correctional obligations" went by
like lightning and I showed up, once again, at the Redwood City
jail at 5:00 p.m. sharp. This time there was no Warden Jeff and no
special treatment. I was pushed and shoved and searched like a slab
of beef and then thrown back into P tank, where Brother Robinson
squealed when he saw me. There were a couple of new guys and I
thought, for a second, that I would be upgraded to another chore,
but no, I was forever to be the new guy and was back on janitorial
duty. Somehow this didn't seem fair to me, and after I had been del-

egated my job by the head goon I said, "Excuse me, but I had that job last week and . . ."

He cut me off. "Shut the fuck up, pissant, and I don't want to see or hear you till you leave on Sunday! You hear me, motherfucker??!!" I was terrified. No one had ever addressed me in such a fashion during my short lifetime and I was taken aback. I looked around the cell where all the guys were just staring at me to see what I was going to do. My first visceral response was extreme nausea, but I realized that I would puke all over the boss man if I let go so I swallowed hard and just made the sign of the zipper across my lips. That seemed to break the ice and a couple of the guys laughed nervously.

Something was up and I could sense that a chill was not only coming from the inmates but from the guards as well. Apparently, since there's not a lot of new stuff to talk about in jail, the little incident that had taken place on the previous Saturday had caused quite a stir and had been the "talk of the jail" for the past week. The rumor was that the warden, Jeff, had been suspended because he had allowed special treatment for a young white inmate who had not only *not* been strip-searched upon entering the facility, but had also been allowed to bring in a brown paper bag with personal effects. Since I was the only person who had entered the jail without being searched and since the stoned-out riot had happened the day I arrived, it was assumed by the guards that I must have brought in the drugs. But that's not all! Since the warden pulled me out of the line-up by F tank during the shakedown, the inmates thought that I was the snitch, planted there by the warden. And why wouldn't all these different people think these different things? From each perspective, it made perfect sense.

From then on, I was reviled by both the inmates, and the guards. There was nothing the guards could do to prove that I was the smuggler because I had been released and I had no drugs on me when I came back. All they could do was make my life as miserable as possible for the next six days. When they gave me coffee, it would spill on the floor— "Oops!" If I asked for a deck of cards to play solitaire, the deck had forty-nine cards. If I asked for a book to read, they tore out the last chapter. Incidentally, the book that I was given minus the final chapter was *The Collector* by John Fowles. Those who know the story will be tickled by the irony.

Inside P tank, I also got the cold shoulder from "the guys" who would somehow "miss" the toilet bowl when relieving themselves— "Oops!" Or they'd kick over the trash can by "accident"— "Sorry!" Or spill their beans and rice on the floor— "Silly me!" The only person in the Redwood City correctional facility who treated me civilly over the next two weekends was Brother Robinson, and I'm sure he had an agenda of his own.

I served out my time in silence and made no friends. I never told Brother Robinson that I lived in Berkeley, but I did tell him that I was going to be an actor. He looked at me funny and said, "Man, we are all actors in here, but if you gonna be a actor, you better be a star, 'cause then they can't touch ya!" Brother Robinson was filled with wise advice. He also taught me a little barroom trick that has come in handy on many occasions. To wit: how to tie a cigarette into a knot, stomp on it with the heel of your left foot, and throw it against the wall as hard as you can and still smoke it! This trick has never failed me and has paid for itself many times over. Thank you, Brother Robinson.

The Scorpio Master

It was spring in Berkeley when I got out of jail, and spring in Berkeley in those days meant social unrest, particularly riots in the street. I was not aware of this annual phenomenon until one late April day when Allover arrived in the DKE kitchen with a dozen gallon bottles of white vinegar. He asked me to help bring them in from the two shopping carts that he and fifteen-year-old Rose had pushed all the way from the co-op to the house. Allover and Rose said they didn't believe in cars and refused to ride in them. They did a lot of walking and cart pushing, especially since they were responsible for getting all the supplies for our inedible meals from the store to the kitchen. On this day, however, it was vinegar and lots of it that had been pushed up from Telegraph Avenue. Allover was quick to explain that riot season was coming and that the Blue Meanies would be using pepper gas to disperse the crowds and that white vinegar was the best antidote for tear gas.

Blue Meanie was the name affectionately given to members of the Alameda County Sheriff's Office after their excessive use of force in 1969 against the protesters who "took" People's Park away from the university and turned it into a community gathering place. They wore blue jumpsuits, visored helmets, and carried shotguns loaded with buckshot. Their MO was to first fire tear gas into a crowd and, if that didn't work, fire buckshot into the crowd. That usually worked.

Allover cautioned that the riots could start any day and usually happened in the first week of May. I had, of course, heard about the first People's Park riot when one person was killed and another blinded by buckshot from the Blue Meanies, but I had thought that all that stuff was behind us now. People's Park was, at that point, part parking lot and part park. It was not really being used. It was surrounded by a chain-link fence and no one seemed to care much about it anymore. I didn't really think that it might once again be the focus of counterculture rage. As it turned out, it wasn't, not that year anyway. It seemed that 1971 had chosen Bank of America as its focus, and on the Sunday following the Big Vinegar Buy it happened.

There had been some talk about the possibility of a mob forming on that first Sunday in May, but places like the DKE house, even though we were a "hybrid fraternity," were out of the riot loop. I had spent the morning reading Thomas Mann's "The Magic Mountain" for my German Lit class and was surprised when someone dashed into my room and announced that the riots were coming up Bancroft Way. We ran out of the house and, sure enough, there was a crowd of at least a thousand young people way down by Sproul Plaza, maybe a quarter of a mile away, heading up the street pursued by armed men in blue jumpsuits.

I could see billowing tear gas canisters landing in the crowd and then being tossed back at the Meanies. The crowd was getting closer and we could see people being trampled and could hear screaming as they pushed toward us. I ran in the direction of the oncoming riot as if drawn by a mysterious force. The injustice of it all coupled with the injustice I had endured from all sides in jail just made me snap. I raged at The Man who was still far enough away so as not to be any real threat. I screamed and raised my fist as I ran toward the gas. I was suddenly surrounded by panicked rioters and I could smell the fear mixed with the gas on their clothes.

Everyone was out of breath and sweating, and soon I changed direction and started to go with the flow back up the street. I could hear the sound of gunfire behind us, and with every shot the crowd screamed in unison and ducked down. Now, when I look back on it,

I don't think that we were actually being fired upon, but there was no way of knowing that at the time. Suddenly a girl fell to the ground in front of me. She was coughing wildly and tears streamed down her face. She curled up into a fetal position as people tried to avoid her in their panic. I reached down and grabbed her but she was limp as a rag doll. I hoisted her up with all my strength and got her in a "sack of potatoes" hold over my shoulder. I picked her up mainly to get her out of the way because at any moment she could have been trampled to death. I tried to put her down by the curb but she held on for dear life. Even though she was thin and not too tall, she was too heavy for me to carry all the way back to the house, which was now only a hundred or so yards away.

She was a mess. Her clothes were torn; she had bruises and scrapes on her arms that were accentuated by the fact that she was a sandy redhead with easily bruised fair skin. I asked her if she could walk and she grunted through nonstop coughing. This girl had gotten a very healthy dose of pepper gas and I had just the thing for her back in our kitchen—thanks to Allover. I put her arm over my shoulder and dragged her toward the house. I knew that if we got inside, the mob would pass us by and we would be safe.

I got my first whiff of gas just as we reached the back door of the DKE house, and luckily Allover was there to unlock the door and let us in. We staggered inside and bolted the door behind us. The girl collapsed to the floor, coughing and oozing from her eyes and mouth. Allover rushed into action for the first time since I had met him. Normally Allover moved very slowly and deliberately, like those folks you see from time to time practicing tai chi in the park, but now he was on fire. He grabbed a gallon bottle of vinegar as Rose unbuttoned the girl's shirt, which had started off the day as a crisp white button-down cotton affair with epaulets and rolled-up sleeves but which was now a torn, greasy mess. She was wearing a bra, which was somewhat unusual for the time but was a good thing on this particular day.

I figured she was around eighteen judging from the maturity of her body. I was waiting for them to douse a rag with vinegar to wipe her off when Allover just poured the vinegar on top of her, dumping out the entire bottle. She didn't know what hit her and she started to flail at Allover, coughing and spitting vinegar all over everything. Rose started screaming at Allover to quit and back off but he yelled that he knew what he was doing. Then the girl stood up, stuck her hands straight out, and, clear as a bell, shouted, "Cool it!!" Her long red hair was stuck to her face and she just screamed, "What the fuck was that?! What the fuck was that?!"

Allover shouted that it was vinegar to counteract the tear gas and she seemed to calm down. She wasn't coughing anymore, and after a few seconds she cried, "It's working!" And indeed it was. It was an unforgettable sight, a bit like that iconic photograph of the young Vietnamese girl running naked down a country road, arms out-stretched, after being doused with napalm. She started to cry, and Rose got her a towel and took her upstairs to wash in the same shower across from my room where I had saved my erstwhile roommate's life. I told Rose to put her in Gene's empty bed in my room since he hadn't been back since the *la lutte continue* incident.

After she was cleaned up and in bed resting, I knocked on my own door and went in. She was lying in bed with the white sheets pulled up to her chin. Her red hair flowed over the pillow and she was a vision of nubile cultural discontent. She said her name was Jay Ann. I told her she was welcome to spend the night. The pepper gas had really knocked the wind out of her; she was clearly exhausted and barely able to keep her swollen eyes open. I slipped back out of the room as she drifted off to sleep.

I wondered what this pretty girl's story was. She had spoken only a handful of words and she was now asleep, mostly naked, in my room. I checked on her a few times throughout the evening and she didn't move a muscle as she slept. Finally, around midnight, I crept into the room and, as quietly as possible, slipped into my own bed against the opposite wall. She still had not moved and was snoring ever so gently. Sleep came easily to me but it didn't last long.

I woke with a start, my mouth full of red hair, as Jay Ann mounted me and began a primitive bump and grind on my groin. What the fuck?? She was kissing my face all over and was, at that moment, the single horniest human being I have ever encountered. My first thought was that she was drugged and I pushed her off me with one thrust. She landed with a thud on the floor and immediately started to cry. I wasn't sure if I was lucky or cursed to have this naked beauty crying in a puddle at the foot of my bed. I made the decision to go with lucky and reached out to calm her. "I'm sorry," I said, "I was asleep and you scared the shit out of me." She then said she was sorry but that she was just so thankful because I had saved her life and she wanted to show her appreciation.

"Lucky" was the right choice and I hoisted her back onto the bed and we started over, with a little less passionate appreciation and a little more romance. Things got very hot and once again she "mounted" me and she did more of her primitive thing, but this time, we were connected. I had never "done it" that way before and was thrilled to death, in the biblical sense. Years later I discovered that the post-sexual-revolution cinema had come to refer to this act as a "cowgirl"!

Whatever it was, Jay Ann and I did it over and over until she collapsed and started calling me a "Scorpio Master"! For some reason, she thought that I was, in some way, not just a passive participant in the "cowgirl." In fact, all I had to do was lie there and think about garbage so we could keep on doing it. I had discovered that images of putrid garbage being poured into scum-covered trucks were able to keep me from reaching a climax, which always meant the temporary end of playtime. She kept on about my sexual prowess, which I had not known about before but which I was perfectly willing to accept. I had not been able to shake the "shake" episode in nursery school and had always felt that just about any other guy was going to be better in bed than I. To this day, three wives and *People* magazine notwith-standing, I still think I was right about that.

Our magical cowgirl extravaganza came to an end as daylight began to seep through the one small window on the east side of my room. The south side had two high windows covered with a black sheet, but the window on the east side wasn't really a window at all; it was more like a porthole on a ship—only about 12 inches by 14 inches. My roommate, Gene, had, for about a week during the fall quarter, adopted a cat that used to use that porthole to do its business and thus the window remained constantly open. This never concerned me because I figured that no human would be able to get through it.

I told Jay Ann that I had to get to German Lit early and that she was welcome to eat breakfast downstairs but that I was going to have to lock up. She said that was cool and we both got ready and left: I to school and Jay Ann to her own devices.

I had had a thing about locking my room ever since the first day at DKE when the former brother stole so much stuff from the house. I didn't really own much of value but there were still some boxes belonging to my ex-roommate, Gene the junkie, and I sort of felt responsible for that stuff.

If anyone had gone into my room to steal something they would have been foiled simply by the mess. I guess I was a pretty typical college student. I would straighten up my crib about once a quarter. Otherwise it was only marginally organized chaos. I knew where stuff was under piles of clothes, books, and trash, but anyone else would need a map.

On that postcoital, post-cowgirl morning, I closed the door on my disgusting world and locked the dead bolt. I bade good-bye to Jay Ann and was sure that I would never see her again, and I was okay with that for some unknown reason. There was a part of me, in fact, that was exhausted by her and wished that sex would forever, from then on, be on my terms and never again at the whim of some street urchin pulled from the rubble of the counterculture wars. I was off to learn and I had seen quite enough of riots, Blue Meanies, and red-headed sex goddesses.

The streets were still littered with the detritus of social unrest—discarded clothing laced with pepper gas, bandages, broken glass, and stones that had been thrown in vain at riot police. There were police everywhere and students darted from class to class without stopping to discuss the events of the previous day. The word was that the police would fire on any group of more than two people. Apparently that had been the case in 1969 and no one was willing to test this new batch of "pigs."

I got back to the DKE house around four and checked in with Allover about the evening menu, which was to be brown rice and cucumber-mushroom casserole, a favorite of Allover but one of the single most unappetizing meals I have ever been unlucky enough to eat more than once. We had brown rice and cucumber-mushroom casserole at least twice a week. I decided that I would skip the DKE meal and grab a kielbasa at Top Dog, the local hot dog joint. I ran up to my room to get some cash, but when I unlocked the door, I felt as though I had entered the land of Oz.

My room was immaculate! The beds were made, my clothes were all clean and folded, my desk was organized, and the floor had been vacuumed. My junkie roommate and I had the only keys to the room. I had the locks changed myself and was the official keeper of the keys so I knew that unless Gene had returned to face the wrath of George and Franny, it was impossible for anyone to get in.

Then I saw a note on my pillow addressed to "The Scorpio Master." It said, "Hope you like it! I'll be back someday. . . . Love, J.A."

It dawned on me that she had somehow squeezed through the tiny window on the east wall of the room. Impossible! She was not only a cowgirl but a contortionist as well! The possibilities seemed endless. I waited for her that day but she never showed. She did end up coming around several more times, but nothing would ever compare to that rodeo the first night. Each time she returned she cleaned my room and, from then on I started cleaning my digs myself, and have continued to live my life in orderly surroundings ever since. Thank you, Jay Ann.

Night of the Living Dead

The spring quarter was coming to an end and the drama department strongly recommended that we audition for summer jobs with the two or three local summer stock companies. Summer stock is basically inexpensive amateur theatre; some companies are far superior to others. The most respected summer theatre in the Bay Area was the Marin Shakespeare Festival, which had a reputation for mounting productions that were at the very least watchable, and that sometimes rose above the mediocre to receive critical acclaim. The down side for the Marin Festival was that it was considered "establishment"—and that was a nasty word during the counterculture movement.

The Berkeley theatre community was struggling with the choice between a mainstream, classical approach to theatre, such as Shakespeare, Molière, and Tennessee Williams, and plowing new ground with more avante garde, guttural, and raw material. *Guttural* and *raw* were adjectives we threw around a lot, but really they just masked the true nature of this new theatre, which was excruciatingly poor and inaccessible to the rational mind. It was often performed in dirty basements, garages, and back alleys, and presented under circumstances better suited to violent crime than art.

The debate continued as we finished the year and I was torn between pursuing a life in "back alley" theatre or the bright lights of Broadway. But I guess we all secretly wanted to be movie stars because at the last minute we decided to "sell out." One bright Saturday, three of my friends from the department and I crammed into Beulah and drove up to Marin County for what I believed, at least in my case, would be an exercise in futility.

My confidence level was at a low point on pretty much every front, though I was still occasionally dining out on the "Scorpio Master" thing. It was the end of my freshman year and I had already become a convicted criminal, done time in jail, been dumped by the woman of my nightmares, and been vilified for my portrayal of Malcolm in "The Scottish Play" (*Macbeth*). The *Berkeley Daily Gazette* had some strong words for our production and didn't get what we were trying to do. It had been my first review, and though I was not mentioned by name, it was clear about whom they were talking when they said that some of us should find another major.

As we drove north over the Golden Gate Bridge, I couldn't help but wonder what to expect from my first professional audition. It was considered "professional" because there was money involved; not a lot—$250 for the summer if you got cast. But in those days that was a living wage for a couple of months and, since I had made a deal to stay on at the DKE house for the summer as the "caretaker," I had a free place to stay. We arrived at the festival site and signed up for our audition along with close to a hundred other would-be thespians. We waited for hours in the baking sun until our group was called. When it was my turn, I did a little piece from the Scottish play along with a bit from Stanley's tirade against Blanche in *A Streetcar Named Desire*. I was terrified throughout the whole audition and felt like puking when it was over.

Of the four of us, I was the one with the least experience. Of the four of us, I was the one with the least confidence. Of the four of us, I was the only one cast in three of the productions to be mounted by the Marin Shakespeare Festival for the 1971 season. My friends were heartbroken and not too happy with me, but they had found another outlet for their creative juices. They had decided that if the establishment wouldn't accept them, they would create a new paradigm. So, with some other fringe theatre folk from Berkeley, they formed the People's of Berkeley Workshops and Improvisational Group, or POB-WIG. They asked me to join them and blow off the Marin establishment.

I recently went through some of my father's old papers and I found a letter he wrote to me that summer imploring me to take the job with the Marin company and admonishing me for even considering the gig with POBWIG. My father lost that battle. I blew off the establishment and the two hundred fifty bucks and chose instead to do guerrilla theatre for $10 a week. I became a founding member of POBWIG. I learned a few years later that, had I chosen door number one in Marin, I would have been working with Robin Williams who was also cast that year. Instead, POBWIG mounted a production of Ibsen's *Peer Gynt* in a church only a few doors away from the DKE house. I played numerous roles in the play, which ran four hours and had been staged with several "total nude" scenes, which almost always scared the four or five audience members out of the "space" by the intermission. We mainly played to empty houses.

However, our crowning achievement that summer was not *Peer Gynt* but a single act of outdoor terror theatre that caused a miniriot of its own.

Our director gave us a mandatory assignment: to go see a horror flick that was playing at one of the local movie theatres. It was called *Night of the Living Dead* by a new filmmaker named George Romero. He gave us all a couple of days to see the film and told us we would regroup on the following Saturday morning for our next "production." I didn't sleep for two nights after seeing the movie. It is about a twenty-four-hour period when, for some unknown reason, the dead come to life to feed on the living. The dead people of all ages and persuasions march across Pennsylvania, stopping at nothing to get at warm, living human flesh. *Night of the Living Dead* remains, to this day, the most frightening film I have ever seen.

Cast members of POBWIG just before our
Night of the Living Dead experience.

When we came together on Saturday, we were told that we would be working that night until 2:00 a.m. We were instructed to choose zombie roles from the movie and to re-create the dead using makeup, torn clothing, blood, organs, and bones that we would buy from local butcher shops. We were to get into costume and makeup and gather our body parts and proceed to the theatre, where *Night of the Living Dead* had a midnight showing, just in time to "greet" the traumatized moviegoers as they exited the theatre. This "greeting" was to be in character, complete with the same grunts and gurgling noises coming from the bloodthirsty dead folk that had entertained the audience only moments before.

I and two other POBWIG thespians went to the local co-op and were able to get a few raw calves' livers and some large leg bones as well as some bits that looked like intestines. Around midnight, once we had donned our costumes, we traveled in a convoy of three station wagons to the street opposite the theatre, where we waited until the show finished. While we were getting ready, someone produced a gallon of Red Mountain and some capsules purported to be mescaline, and by the time we left for the theatre we were pretty lit up. As the theatre let out, our little band of fifteen zombies emerged from the station wagons, crossed the street, and began to infiltrate the crowd coming out of the movie. What happened next confirmed that our artistic director had a nose for shock theatre.

The first people to notice us seemed nonplussed, but within seconds chaos prevailed. The first screams came from women, but soon the men were screaming too. One of the girls in our troop had become a little dead girl with a sharp garden trowel that mimicked one of the most chilling moments in the movie. When the primed moviegoers saw her, there was pandemonium. The poor people went to some primitive defensive place as they were gripped with terror.

I was the fifth zombie into the crowd, which was quickly becoming a mob, flailing and striking out at the "living dead." I walked with a limp, dragging my left foot, and held a raw liver up to my mouth. I was socked in the face and knocked down by a twentysomething man whose eyes were filled with rage and terror. We were beaten and kicked and pummeled by the crowd, but the director kept yelling for us to "stay in character." Some of the people started to threaten us with more violence, and I got up and started to run. I ran for a few blocks until I was safe, wiped the makeup off my face, and walked alone back to the DKE house.

We were paid thirty dollars each for participating in the *Night of the Living Dead* thing, so that event qualified as my first "professional" gig. I quit POBWIG after that and have no idea if they went on to more glory.

Mac

As "caretaker" of the DKE house, it was my responsibility to see that the house remained reasonably clean and free of "street people," who were in the majority in Berkeley that summer. I closed off the first and second floors and took up residence in the huge room on the third floor, which was intended to house at least five freshman pledges. Allover and Rose, who never paid rent, stayed on, living under the eaves of the top floor. One or two other members drifted in and out, but for all intents and purposes, the house was shut down.

Sometime in late July, as I was kicking back in my "penthouse suite," enjoying the silence of an empty fraternity house, I was interrupted by the sound of what could only have been a sick elephant making its way up the stairs to my third-floor sanctuary. There was wheezing and huffing and puffing and coughing and the floor creaked as though Paul Bunyan was shaking the house. I looked up from my paperback copy of *Siddhartha* and there, standing at my door, was the fattest human being I had ever seen. Drenched in sweat and unable to speak because of a severe oxygen shortage, a man who must have been the inspiration for the "Nowhere Man" in the Beatles film *Yellow Submarine,* and who later admitted to weighing in at just under four hundred pounds, greeted me. "Hi!" he said, between huge draws of breath. "I'm Mac and you're supposed to have a room for me."

Apparently this very fat man had driven in from Chicago, having made a deal with someone that he could stay at DKE if he paid some rent. He was not a student and didn't seem to have any connection to

Berkeley other than to this supposed person whose name he couldn't remember who had promised him a place to stay. What was I to do? He gave me $50 and I gave him an empty single room on the first floor. I figured that he had better live on the first floor since his climbing stairs could have been fatal.

Mac seemed to be around thirty years old and had a wide, engaging smile and an infectious laugh that got the attention of anyone within earshot. He turned out to be just as charming as he was fat, which was a good thing for him since he was really, really fat.

A couple of weeks after he moved in, he invited me to have a burger with him across the street at the International House, a university-sponsored housing project where students from foreign countries could stay and mingle with other foreign kids. I ate at the "I House" commissary when Allover's food was impossible, which was actually a lot of the time. Mac met me at the "I House," and over a cheap burger and fries, asked me how it was that I decided to be an actor. I told him the story about La Honda and the tree houses and the acid and he went wild. He had read about La Honda and thought that it was just urban legend, and he couldn't believe that it was actually there. He wanted me to take him there immediately. The fat man was beside himself.

The next day three of us—Mac; Michael, a student staying at the house temporarily; and I set off for La Honda in Beulah. I was driving with Michael in the back and Mac in the front. Beulah let out a groan when Mac forced his way into the seat. The car leaned down on the passenger side as its tiny German suspension system tried to cope with four hundred pounds of ambulatory protoplasm. Mac was all smiles. He never seemed to even notice that he was the size of a grand piano.

We arrived in La Honda a couple of hours later and Mac was transformed into a little boy when he saw the tree houses. He pried himself out of the car and ran to the nearest set of stairs that wound up to a tree house. Michael and I yelled for him to STOP! as loud as we could. Mac turned around with a quizzical expression, looked back at the tree, then back at us as he realized that we had just saved his life. There was no way he was going up into a tree house. That day had passed back at two hundred pounds. I told him about a trail into the forest that led to the little creek next to the camp. I promised that a short walk into the giant redwood grove would make the day just as magical.

We set off along the fern-lined trail as it climbed upward next to the creek bed. It was a perfect late summer day. The ferns were emerald green and every forest creature seemed to be on display as we marched along. Mac squealed when he saw a cluster of Monarch butterflies, and again when a hummingbird darted across the path. We were happy that this overweight city boy from Chicago was having such a blast amid the huge California conifers. Then came a third squeal, and as we looked back to see what magical creature had crossed his path, we saw him, arms akimbo, disappear as the ground beneath him gave out under his four hundred pounds. The squeal morphed into a scream as he tumbled straight down the fifty-foot cliff into the creek bed below, landing with a crash and a cracking sound like a big tree branch breaking in a storm.

The screaming never stopped as Michael and I found our way down the steep incline to the creek below. Mac's four-hundred-pound body was half submerged in the river. The only thing moving was his left leg, which was swaying in the water, perpendicular to his body. Every time the current caused his lower leg to drift, he screamed bloody murder. His left femur was shattered in a compound fracture that caused the bone to stick right out of his tight pants.

I couldn't stand the screaming and the sight of his leg drifting with the current so I took off my belt and found a piece of bark and fashioned a crude splint to sort of keep the leg straight. I gave Michael the keys to my car and he ran off to find help. Mac screamed with pain until the fire department showed up, but when they saw how big he was they called in another company. The first paramedic on the scene gasped when he saw my makeshift splint, demanding, "Who the hell made that mess?" I refused to cop to it and pointed to the woods hoping that he wouldn't notice how loose my jeans were.

It took thirteen men and two stretchers tied together to hoist the Nowhere Man out of the forest. The next week, Mac was back at the house with a cast all the way up to his hip. He was in amazingly good spirits, though—probably because of the morphine tablets he was swallowing like candy. The only real complaint he had was that his huge gold ring that said MAC in 1-carat diamonds across the top must have come off during the fall. This devastated him, as though his whole identity was somehow contained in that lump of gold and diamonds. Gradually he became despondent and pretty much stayed in his room for eight weeks, busy discovering the wonders of opiates, hashish, and lysergic acid diethylamide.

El Presidente

The fall quarter started and I was determined to tread the straight and narrow. I guess I had done a bang-up job "caretaking" over the summer because I was being considered for president of the DKE house that fall. The term "president" was loose, to say the least. Mike Stimpson was president by the time a transition was necessary, and there were only two of us living in the house that September who had any managerial experience with the place. The other fellow was a kid named Brad who was very ambitious and seemed hell bent on becoming president. He lobbied hard with Mike and the other officers, who were responsible for appointing the next president. I, on the other hand, showed little interest in the job and just made sure that all the lightbulbs worked and that the kitchen and the public rooms were reasonably clean.

Mike sat us both down one Saturday and asked us point-blank if we wanted the job. Brad said that he not only wanted the job but that he needed the credit on his résumé so that his chances for getting into a good graduate school would improve. Brad pleaded with Mike, essentially saying his life would be ruined if he didn't become DKE president. I said that though I enjoyed taking care of the place, it was quite a distraction from my studies. I had no need for the credit because I was going to pursue an acting career and having the presidency of a fraternity on my résumé could actually hurt my chances of getting into a good postgraduate acting program. I said that I would take the job if asked, but I remained ambivalent about it. I was being truthful and was sure that I would walk out of the room as a member of the DKE rank and file. No such luck!

Mike turned to Brad and with a handful of words sentenced him to a life of mediocrity. "I'm appointing Harry the next president of DKE!" And that was it. I could not have known how drastically those words would alter the course of my life.

As president, I had the responsibility of vetting the various people who wanted to live at DKE. There was no rush period and there were no pledges. Typically, within the Greek system, a large number of freshmen would "rush" a fraternity and "pledge" that if accepted they would join the club. Only a few of the candidates would make the cut and that was after a period of hazing and ridicule that no one in 1971 was willing to endure. In 1971, nobody wanted to join a fraternity and we were lucky to be able to rent out the rooms so that I, in turn, could cut a monthly check to the local chapter chairman, who, of course, had no idea that DKE looked more like a co-ed vegetarian hippie commune than a frat house.

We had a certain number of beds that had to be filled in order to make our monthly nut and there were always a lot of students and nonstudents looking for a place to stay. I had to sift through them and pick those I thought would make the best contribution to the group and be the most amenable to our communal lifestyle. Since there were never enough men to fill the rooms, I had no choice but to rent to girls. What a darn shame!

My main duties were administrative. I collected the rent and made sure there were enough lightbulbs and toilet paper and that the food was edible and there was as little dog shit as possible on the living room floor.

Ever since the exquisite oriental rugs had been stolen, the dogs living in the house, inspired by Buck, Allover's German shepherd, had taken to defecating on the hardwood floors. We called it "Buck shit,"

Members of the Delta Kappa Epsilon fraternity, fall 1971. I was the
president and standing next to me is the secretary, James, and next to
him is Brad, the vice president. I am in the top hat and vest.

and as president it was my responsibility to see that it was cleaned up
regularly. Since no one else seemed to care about the Buck shit, the
job fell to me, the chief executive shit-cleaner-upper. No matter how
much I mopped and scrubbed the floors, the dogs kept pissing and
shitting huge piles of digested kibble in exactly the same three spots.
Life at the DKE house wasn't all bad, though, and as long as we stayed
out of the living room, things could be very pleasant.

Another "perk" of the job was that I got to live in the "president's
suite," which was a beautiful corner room with French windows all

around. Though I had no girlfriend in the fall of 1971, I decided that the position of president of DKE required that I sleep on a water bed. Water beds were the latest thing in '71 and my new digs had just enough room for a queen-size version. I bought some two-by-twelves from the local lumberyard and built and painted a frame, and, with the help of some of the freshmen, I installed the DKE house's first water bed. Now all I needed was a warm body to share it with. After all, I was the Scorpio Master. But since Jay Ann had disappeared that June, I had only daydreamed about girls—and mainly about Evie, who had crystallized my notion of the ideal love object on that snowy December night at the Bakersfield Holiday Inn.

Evie Redux

To my delight, I bumped into Evie on campus in mid-October and she mentioned she was looking for a new place. She had broken up with her boyfriend and was staying with friends until she could find an apartment. I told her that I just might be able to help her. God was obviously smiling on me as I had been dreaming of such an opportunity for almost a year.

As president, I had complete authority over who stayed in which room and with whom, and since we still had a considerable number of female students peppered throughout the house, what difference would it make if we had one more? I just had to find a room for her. A young blond freshman had moved into my old room on the first floor and I broke the news to him that he would have to share a room with two other guys on the third floor. He didn't object as much as I had thought, and he moved his stuff two floors up that afternoon. That cleared the way for the woman of my dreams to move in exactly one floor beneath me. And move in she did.

Much to my chagrin, it immediately became obvious that Evie did not share my enthusiasm for our future together. She paid little or no attention to me and seemed completely absorbed in her studies and her friends. She never ate with us and never spent any time in the communal rooms. The house had a kitchen, dining room, poolroom with a beautiful antique pool table, TV room and living room, which, of course, was never used because of the horrific smell of Buck shit. Evie only went to her room and never socialized with any of the other inhabitants. The only time we ever saw her out of her room was when she bathed, buck naked, in the second-story communal shower.

There was something about that time in Berkeley that lent itself to the mass acceptance of full frontal nudity on the part of just about everyone. The DKE house had a shower on the second floor that had six showerheads and was built for a kind of locker room bathing experience among the brothers of the house. The addition of ten women to the list of inhabitants created a new and interesting bathing dynamic for everyone. Boys washing naked in the shower with naked girls was commonplace and seemed just like the natural thing to do during the counterculture years. There were no complaints and, amazingly, no rapes or reports of any hanky-panky in the shower at all.

I would step into the shower in the morning and there would be Evie, naked as a jaybird, and then I would be soaping up next to her, naked as a jaybird, while she whistled and washed her long auburn hair. She would have been mortified, I'm sure, had she been privy to the thoughts swimming around in my postadolescent head. I was determined to make this girl notice me. There I was, everything hanging out, standing right next to her as she went on about her business as though the naked twenty-year-old buck preening in front of her didn't exist. It was no use. I was invisible. She would just turn off the water, grab her towel, and march out of the shower. Not even a good-bye. I had my work cut out for me.

The world works in mysterious ways, sometimes bitter, sometimes sweet, sometimes . . . who knows? One fall night as I was laboring over a paper on *The Tin Drum* by Günter Grass, I heard a faint wailing sound coming from the floor below. I left my desk and crept downstairs, seeking the source of the phantom cries. At first it sounded like a cat was stuck between the floorboards, but as I investigated, I discovered that the noise was coming from behind Evie's locked door. I had been very respectful of her privacy till then and was hesitant to knock. What on earth could be wrong? This girl was really, really upset!

I waited to hear the cries die down but they only got stronger. I couldn't hear her talking to anyone so I assumed she was in there alone. I knocked. The crying stopped for a second then started again with a vengeance. I knocked again. The crying stopped again and didn't start up. Then the door opened a crack. The pain on Evie's face was evidence of some terrible disaster. Seeing that it was I, she opened the door and grabbed me as though I was the last person on earth. Through her sobs she told me that her mother had gone to the hospital that afternoon for a routine knee operation and had died on the table from a reaction to the anesthetic. I held her and felt the greatest sensation of love I had ever experienced.

I had never been that close to death or in the presence of that kind of loss, and Evie's vulnerability in that moment was stunning. She was inconsolable and I offered my whole being to her as if to raise her mother from the dead. Of course, I remained mortal, her mother remained dead, and Evie slept in my bed that night and almost every night thereafter for almost a year. Evie had found in me a kind of soul mate and confidant, and after she came back from her mother's funeral, she kept coming to my room to sleep. Evie was my first true love and I ate from that apple with relish. We talked for hours and hours about life and art, theatre and the dance world. At the beginning, we would just spoon, and I would hold her while she wept, which she continued to do for months. But eventually the old "one thing leads to another" effect crept into our nights together and we started doing the nasty like rabbits.

Albino Rhino

The fall of 1971 marched on. As president, I had made the executive decision to let Mac stay in the house, even though he wasn't a Berkeley student. By October, his cast had been removed and he had begun hobbling around the house on crutches with remarkable ease for a man his size. He had gained some weight during his drug-filled convalescence and clocked in at close to 425 pounds on the day of the big game between Cal and Stanford. In celebration of the big event, someone had provided this quarter-ton behemoth enough LSD to incapacitate a rhinoceros. In fact, by the time Mac started to hallucinate, he was calling himself the "Albino Rhino," insisting that he only be addressed as such. If anyone tried to call him Mac, he would fly into a rage, and the last thing anyone needed was a stoned four-hundred-pound wild man on a rampage.

We did everything we could to calm him down, but at some point he became convinced that it was the sole duty of the Albino Rhino to join the Cal–Stanford game in progress across the street at the stadium. Mac threw off his crutches, undressed to his red and white striped boxers (size 60), grabbed a pool cue, and made a beeline to the stadium, which was packed with fans watching the third quarter of play. Mac, or I should say, the Albino Rhino, ran onto the field in the middle of a play waving the pool cue and screaming that he was going to "put the quarterback into the corner pocket."

Of course, pandemonium ensued, and fans and campus police tried unsuccessfully to subdue him. Mac ran, mostly naked—when you weigh more than four hundred pounds it's hard to tell where one thing starts or another thing ends—for half an hour before being corralled into a police van. He must have become coherent enough to tell the police where he lived because it wasn't long before they called the house pay phone begging me to pick him up from the station, where he was making a lot of noise and threatening to make trouble. The police said that under normal circumstances they would arrest someone who was threatening police, but Mac was obviously stoned out of his mind, and he was so large that they didn't think they would be able to contain him without killing him. They wondered if I might come and take him off their hands until he sobered up.

Mac no longer fit into Beluah so we found someone with a camper van and relieved the Berkeley Police Department. We got him back to the house but he was now clearly insane, having been awake and tripping on acid for more that twenty-four hours. He babbled about being the Albino Rhino and that he was going to rule the world and kill anyone who didn't agree with his divine plan for global salvation. I remembered that I had a bottle of a substance called Librium, which I think was the tranquilizer of choice in those days. I had never taken any of the pills myself, and I think I had ripped them from my mother's medicine cabinet. I took the whole bottle and emptied the contents of the capsules into a glass of orange juice. We told him that the juice was the nectar of the gods, which would give him powers beyond his wildest dreams. He laughed, looked at us like we were all insane children, and poured the whole glass down his throat in one gulp. Mac slept for two days, and when he woke up, he packed up his things and drove back to Chicago, fearing that the Berkeley police were not finished with him. I never saw him again.

Ten years later I went back to the spot where Mac had fallen off the cliff and, as I recounted the story of his fall to some new friends from Hollywood, I saw a glint of reflected light coming from the stream below. I climbed down to the very place where Mac had landed a decade before, and there, lying in a few inches of water, was an immense gold ring with MAC across the top in glittering diamonds. As luck would have it, one of my agents in Hollywood knew Mac and I was able to get the ring back to him. A few years later, I got a call from Mac. My old agent had given him my number. He was in jail on a cocaine charge and wanted me to send him $20,000 to bail him out. I told him to call his mother and hung up the phone. I've always felt bad about that, but 1987 was a big year for me and the last thing I needed was to have big Mac back in my life.

By mid-January 1972 life was looking pretty good. Evie had moved into my room, my probation officer told me I didn't need to see him anymore, the DKE house was fully rented out, and we even had money for a few parties and a cleaning crew to come in once a month. Because we now had ten female students living in the house, our overall grade point average was higher than it had ever been, and every quarter we got congratulatory letters from the dean, who was just "so happy with our academic performance." As long as we registered Allison Parker as A. Parker, nobody was the wiser and the Dekes could do no wrong! I was also becoming something of a star at the drama department and had been asked if I would be in the spring Durant Theatre production of *A Streetcar Named Desire,* playing the part made immortal by Marlon Brando, Stanley Kowalski. Life was good! I had somehow made this college thing work in spite of my felonious behavior.

Then one day Evie burst into our room more excited than I had ever seen her. She was waving a letter in the air, exclaiming that she had been accepted to Bennington College in Vermont. What?? Apparently she had forgotten that she had applied in the fall to the prestigious Eastern girls' college, or at least she had forgotten to tell me. She said she had applied on a whim with another friend and that she never thought she would get in. She said she had promised her mother that she would go if she got in, so that was that.

Front Royal Mohel

So now our connubial bliss was finite? Come September we would be separated by thousands of miles. That just wouldn't do, so I sent for an application to Yale, which was roughly in the same neck of the woods. At least we could see each other once in a while if I was in New Haven. It looked like Vermont was only a couple of hours away by car. There was just one hitch: I had to get into Yale as a transfer student with my application getting in just at, or just after, the deadline. I did a little research and discovered that Yale accepted transfer students, but historically the average was five per year. I was going to have to pull off some kind of Hail Mary if I was to have a prayer of being accepted.

I decided to write a satirical, tongue-in-cheek essay about my experiences at Berkeley that I figured, at the very least, would be fun to read, but which displayed no academic acumen whatsoever. I sent off the application "special delivery," hoping that it would make the deadline. I called the admissions department to set up an interview but I was told that I had missed the deadline and in-person interviews were no longer being conducted in California. They would set something up on campus if I could make it to New Haven. Someone there could see me during the second week of March, which happened to be spring break at Berkeley. Evie said that she wanted to see Bennington as well and suggested that we fly to New York and drive up to Bennington and New Haven and then drive down to her ancestral home in Virginia to visit her grandmother. This sounded like a good plan.

I had a TWA "Getaway Card," which was a credit card just for airline tickets, and we had some dough saved up, so as the quarter ended, Evie and I set off to chart the new course of our lives, a course that would hopefully take us from the riots of People's Park to the halls of Ivy League academia. We flew to Newark and there picked up a tiny Datsun 1600 that belonged to someone in Evie's family. We were given the little car to drive for the two weeks of our journey. The trip up to Bennington was uneventful and we saw a bit of the campus before drifting south to New Haven.

At Yale I met for a few minutes with a dour bespectacled assistant professor wearing a tweed jacket and bow tie. He told me not to get my hopes up as my chances of being accepted were slim to none. And that was that. The meeting was over before it started. Not a lot of face time for having flown all the way across the country. Oh well.

Evie was getting more and more excited about the visit with her grandmother. She had spent her childhood summers at her grandmother's home in Front Royal, Virginia. She described it as a classic antebellum plantation house with acres and acres of grounds, lakes, ponds, and carriage houses. It sounded positively grand and surprisingly opulent for this little girl from West LA whose dad was a middle-class executive for Occidental Petroleum. She swore that it was all true and that we would be there soon and she would show me herself.

We drove south through Pennsylvania and Maryland and then down into Virginia. Since I had already driven across the country a couple of times, I felt more comfortable behind the wheel and did most of the driving. After driving a BMW across the country, driving a Datsun 1600 was like driving a toy car. It had no pickup and had a maximum speed of around 65. It was a joke but it could do the job.

I heard story after story about the grandparents and what a wonder-filled childhood Evie had. She told me that her grandfather had died years before and that her grandma now shared the old mansion with her sister. Who were these magical people I was about to meet? I was getting excited too! We stopped at a Howard Johnson's for lunch near Winchester, Virginia. I had been driving for almost six hours straight and could barely keep my eyes open, so after lunch I handed the keys to Evie, put on my coziest wool sweater, and plopped into the passenger seat for a good snooze. Then I did something completely out of character for me: I pulled the seat belt across my lap. Though automobiles were required by law to have seat belts, people rarely used them in those days and I was no exception. I clearly remember thinking, "What the hell?" as I snapped the buckle.

Thankfully Evie could see that I was bushed and she stopped with the stories. I fell asleep immediately to the drone of the little Datsun's four cylinders whining to keep pace on the highway. Before I drifted off, Evie said she was going to take the scenic route to Front Royal. I had thought about trying to stay awake for that but I was just too dang tired, and right before I drifted off, Evie turned our little bucket of bolts onto Highway 340. The next thing I heard was her shrill, piercing voice as she shouted, "I don't think I'm going to make this!"

I opened my eyes to see her crouched over the steering column of our little toy car futilely attempting to make the thing go faster by pounding on the wheel. I looked to my right and saw that we were traveling uphill, going around a curve, and passing two huge eighteen-wheel trucks. I looked to the left and saw that we were flanked on the driver's side by a cement abutment perched on a cliff that overlooked a steep valley hundreds of feet below. The tiny Datsun was straining at the top of its capacity to get up enough speed to pass the trucks. As we rounded the bend, I looked ahead of us and saw, coming straight for us, a huge Country Squire station wagon going at least 60 and unable, as we were, to avoid a head-on collision.

Then came the screech of brakes and an eerie kind of silent acceptance washed over me. I knew we were going to crash, and most probably die, and yet it all seemed okay for that split second. No problem! I just relaxed and let it come.

I regained consciousness outside the car on the cold grassy shoulder. I couldn't move. I saw Evie in a heap a few feet away from me and I heard some kids screaming. I looked around and saw a bunch of people running toward us. Then there was a circle of faces looking down at me.

One man, probably one of the truckers who had witnessed the horrible crash, asked if I was okay, which was actually a really dumb question considering the circumstances. But, having just crawled out of the wreck, I was in acute shock and completely unaware of the absurdity of both his question and my response, which was to say I was fine. And as I reached out to shake the strange man's hand, I invited him to dinner. (I was clearly out of my mind.) At that moment someone else approached, saw my wounds, and said, "Oh my God, don't look, it's horrible!"

It took a moment for me to realize that they were referring to me. By then I could feel the ooze of blood on my face and neck, and I looked down to see that my new, cozy rope cashmere sweater was drenched with blood. I loved that sweater and it was ruined! Shit!

Apparently the Datsun had been absorbed by the Country Squire and now occupied the station wagon's engine compartment. The toy car was no match for the tank we hit with a combined speed of at least 100 miles an hour. By the laws of physics we should not have survived.

I heard Evie mumbling and saw that she was cradling an arm with a bone sticking straight out near the shoulder. Now there were more people milling about and I saw an African-American woman in her forties. She was clutching her throat as other African-American onlookers tried to comfort her. I heard people saying how horrible the whole thing was and how it was amazing that anyone lived through it.

As I have come across theories of alternate universes and multidimensional realities in my life, it has occurred to me that I may indeed have died on that country road just outside Front Royal, Virginia. There may be a universe in which there was a funeral for me and grieving parents and friends. I may have just casually slipped into this universe, where I survived to go on to have more whacky things happen to me. Just a thought.

Eventually I could hear the wail of an ambulance, and I saw uniforms and badges and knew that the cops were there. The ambulance pulled up and paramedics were swarming around us. As I was being hoisted onto a gurney, I heard men screaming at each other and saw that a black gentleman was yelling at a cop while waving his arms and pointing toward the ambulance into which Evie and I were being wheeled. There was one ambulance with plenty of room for three victims, but this was Virginia in 1972, and if there was one ambulance, the white folks were going to take it alone. I later learned that the black woman was driving her two kids home from school. The kids had not been wearing seat belts and had tumbled around in the crash but ultimately they were fine. Their mom, on the other hand, had not been so lucky. Her neck had been penetrated by the steering column and her vocal chords were damaged. She and her kids were driven to the hospital by a Good Samaritan passing by.

Years later there was a court case and I had to sign an affidavit that Evie had been completely at fault, which she had been. What the fuck was she thinking? *Let's see, I'll just try to pass these two huge trucks going around a curve, uphill, with a five-hundred-foot drop on my left in a Datsun 1600 being powered by rubber bands. Sounds good!* I'm pretty sure the woman lost her voice, but she got a huge settlement from Evie's insurance company, which she deserved—and then some.

We arrived at the hospital and were transferred to an OR. A doctor looked down at my face and frowned. I still couldn't move my legs. I told him that I was going to be a movie star when I grew up and that if there was anything he could do to fix my face it would be greatly appreciated. He looked at me like I was off my rocker, which I was, and said, "You've got a badly broken nose and a star puncture in the middle of your forehead. It'll give you character." He put some stitches in my face and sent me to X-ray to find out why I couldn't move the gams.

If, in fact, I did not enter a separate universe and if I did survive the unsurvivable crash, my living through it must have been because of that uncharacteristic click of the seat belt outside of the Winchester Howard Johnson's. I would surely have been ejected from the Datsun like a cannonball had I not had that belt around my lap. Shoulder belts had just been invented and the vast majority of cars on the road had lap belts. Undoubtedly a lifesaver, those belts did have a drawback, as discovered when the doctor looked at the X-rays of my spine. The impact had been so forceful that the buckle on the belt had rammed into my spine, pushing the kidneys and intestines and stuff to the sides. The buckle fractured three vertebrae in my lower spine and the inflammation pinched the nerves, making me temporarily paralyzed. They said I'd be up and about in a few days but that it would be about a year before my spine was fully healed. I contemplated how it would look if I had to play Stanley Kowalski in a wheelchair.

I was transferred to a room with two beds, the other one being occupied by a fifty-year-old African-American fellow named Clarence. They put Evie on a different floor as she was recovering from surgery on her compound fracture. Clarence and I exchanged hellos and he asked me what happened. I told him and he winced as though experiencing sympathy pains. In fact, I was not in much pain. I had been put on a morphine drip and was feeling quite pleasant. Clarence seemed fine to me and indeed he was. I asked him why he was there and he told me a story that made me feel like the lucky guy in the room.

Clarence was a very outgoing and happy-go-lucky kind of guy who had an infectious laugh and who seemed to be the kind of fellow who got the very last drop out of life. Clarence announced that he was getting married. Here he was, fifty years old, and getting married for the first time! "First" was pronounced "Foist." He was, on the one hand, like a little boy on Christmas morning and, on the other hand, like a condemned prisoner on death row.

Clarence explained that he had met the woman of his dreams and that he had asked her to marry him. He was very open about why she was perfect. She was young, she was pretty, and she let him eat fur burger! He asked me if I had ever had "fur burger." Pronounced "foy boyga." It took me a while to figure out just what delicacy he was referring to, but when I did finally get it, an immediate sort of male bonding took place in that hospital room in Front Royal, Virginia. Yes, I had tried foy boyga and I liked foy boyga! I congratulated him on his good fortune and told him that my "foy boyga" was in bed on the fifth floor nursing a compound fracture. Then came the "dead man walking" part.

His beloved wife-to-be, who was young, pretty, and a fan of cunnilingus, was not a fan of uncircumcised men. Unfortunately Clarence's parents had spared baby Clarence the indignity of the mohel's knife only so that fifty-year-old Clarence would have to endure the painful ritual as an adult. The young, pretty, furry fiancée insisted that Clarence get the cut before she would walk down the aisle. Such was the fate of the man lying opposite me in that hospital room in Front Royal who had the double misfortune of having not been circumcised at birth and having been named Clarence.

The next morning, Clarence was prepped for surgery and finally wheeled out at around 9:00 a.m. By noon he was back and sleeping like a baby. I drifted in and out of morphine-induced sleep and wondered how much I would have to love a woman to accept those terms for marriage. Then it started.

Clarence screamed as though he were being dragged down to hell by the devil himself. He was awake and looking with horror at his crotch. I could see a massive bloody, bandaged "hard-on" poking from under the sheets. The doctor rushed in and gave him some painkillers and explained that he could expect the hard-on thing to go on for a couple of days every few minutes. He said something about the nerves being exposed and that there would be automatic stimulation of the penis, causing it to get hard, stretching the sutures every time. The doctor apologized and said there was nothing he could do and that in a few days it would all be over. Let me just say that when my son was born, there was no question about what to do in that department.

Clarence was still screaming every few minutes when I was released a couple of days later. As I left, I wished him luck and pictured him and his new bride locked in the 69 position, he blissfully eating out his cute new wife, thick black fur all around his mouth, and she taking in all of his newly cauterized member with a smile.

When I was released, I was given a back brace and a cane and met up with Evie in the lobby. A limo was waiting for us outside to take us to the plantation. We were bruised, broken, and battered but still alive, and soon to be transported to the antebellum South.

We had been in the hospital for three days and had no visitors. I had called my parents to tell them of the crash but I made it sound as though it wasn't a very big deal so they wouldn't feel the need to fly across the country. Evie's grandmother was old and couldn't be bothered, but she did send a car to take us from the hospital to the plantation. And plantation it was!

Evie had not exaggerated when she described the place. Giant white columns adorned the front porch in classic antebellum style. Inside the house were huge dark rooms with twelve-foot ceilings. A black maid in a black and white uniform whom Evie did not recognize greeted us and said in a high voice, "Let me escort you to the drawing room." What the heck is a drawing room? Back in the day, any mansion worth its salt had a "drawing room." Robert Mitchum was always smoking and drinking brandy in the "drawing room" along with Clark Gable and occasionally Cary Grant, but I never saw anyone drawing anything but Scotch from a decanter in the drawing room. Maybe that's what they meant.

In the middle of said room sat two ancient women poring over what looked like travel brochures. The thought occurred to me that they must be planning that one last great cruise. They stood up when they saw us, introduced themselves as Evie's grandmother and great-aunt, and asked how we were. It was all very formal. Either that or they were suffering from dementia and weren't quite sure who we were. They motioned for Evie to come forward for a hug but there was no such move indicated for me. I did not get the feeling that we were very welcome in the house, and I definitely didn't sense the warm-and-fuzzy stuff that I'd heard so much about before the crash. More than likely, they were unaware that Evie had been behind the wheel at the time of the crash and they thought that I had brought this horror into their family.

I glanced down at the brochures spread across the coffee table only to realize that they were not travel pamphlets at all, but rather catalogs of coffins and coffin hardware. There were also swatches of silk and other fine textiles obviously meant to cradle these two crazy women for eternity. The old dowagers were picking out their final resting places as though they were picking fixtures for a new bathroom!

I immediately got the creeps and asked if I might use a phone to call the house in Berkeley. I had not communicated with anyone from the DKE house and, of course, they had no knowledge of our mishap. When I got through to the downstairs pay phone, my sad story was immediately eclipsed by the news from there, which was not good.

It turned out that a fire had broken out in the basement the night before and the kitchen and the pantry had burned to a crisp. The house was full of smoke and some officials from the university were poking around the place asking questions about our boarders. No one had been hurt but the fire had gutted part of the ground floor. The house was still habitable, though the smoke smell was really bad. I got off the phone and informed Evie that we were going to have to cut our stay at Tara short. I was still the president and the responsible party in situations like this.

Burned Again

We arrived back in Berkeley the next day to find yellow tape around the door on the ground floor. There was a pile of charred wet wood in the driveway, and a chubby fire inspector with a clipboard stood next to his red and white sedan making some notes. I introduced myself and he asked me why I was using a cane. Had I been injured in the fire? I explained that it was unrelated and he had me sign a couple of forms. He gave me a very strange look as he squeezed back into his car. At first he looked very stern, but that look morphed into a slight knowing smile as though we shared some dirty little secret. I thought it was odd but continued my inspection of the damage. The kitchen was a wreck but it was still usable. The pantry and storage room next to the kitchen were lost and would have to be rebuilt over the summer. Until then we would just close that area off with plastic. All in all, it could have been worse. Little did I know what was brewing within the university and the Board of Regents of the entire UC system because of that little fire.

I had been told that the fire had started around two o'clock in the morning. The theory was that some street person had found his way into the house on the cold March night and had hooked up a space heater to stay warm. The heater was kicked over, which started the fire. What I had *not* been told was that the fire department had used a cherry picker to take people off the roof because the house had filled with smoke. That was not remarkable in and of itself. What was remarkable to the firemen and the local newspaper, the *Berkeley Daily*

Gazette, was that they cherry-picked nine women in various stages of undress from the roof of the DKE house at 3:00 a.m. The following day, it was reported that a fire had broken out in the venerable frat house and that the university was investigating not only the cause of the blaze but also the curious discovery that nine females were living in the house. That story was picked up by the Associated Press and I got my first national press as the fellow running a brothel out of the Delta Kappa Epsilon house in Berkeley. It was a story that was popular in the South. A relative in Florida sent me a clipping.

Spring quarter got under way. My broken back was recovering bit by bit. I wore the brace, which was more like a corset with vertical metal ribs. I could only walk slowly and couldn't bend over or lift anything. My face wasn't swollen anymore and Evie was on the mend too. She had a huge cast on her arm, which was very cumbersome in the water bed when we got down to the nasty. I started rehearsing for *Streetcar* and it was all I could do to stay vertical up on the stage. I waited patiently for the letter from Yale.

The story about me and the "Frat House Brothel" had reached someone on the Board of Regents and I was called into the dean's office for a chat. He told me that the board was dismayed by the reports of sexual misconduct at DKE and that they insisted that all females be evicted from the house. In 1969 Ronald Reagan, then governor of California and as such president of the Board of Regents of the UC system, had been quoted as calling Berkeley a "haven for communist sympathizers, protesters, and sex deviants." I fell into the last category but would find myself falling under one more category before too long.

By the spring of 1972, I had morphed from nubile preppie into a full-blown hippie. My hair was down to my shoulders and I sported muttonchop sideburns. I only wore bell-bottom jeans and poorboy shirts, which Evie sewed for me. I fit right in on Telegraph Avenue but was a fish out of water in the well-appointed dean's office. I sat across from the buttoned-down dean of men as he told me what I needed to do to comply with university regulations. First, I had to evict all the women immediately. Then I had to write a letter of apology to Governor Reagan and the Board of Regents and to the headquarters of the Delta Kappa Epsilon organization, which was located somewhere in the South. Then I had to open the house to an inspection by the university.

The dean laid all these requirements out and then sat back and waited for me to say "Yes sir!" But I simply said, "No." His jaw dropped and he asked me what I meant by that, and I told him that I would not kick anyone out of the house, that I would not apologize to Ronald Reagan, and that the house was off limits to "inspectors" from the university. I told him that my responsibility was to the people who had paid rent for their rooms and that I didn't feel I had done anything that required me to apologize to anyone.

I got up and walked out of the office as he shouted that I had not heard the end of this. I was wearing a brown leather vest over my poorboy shirt that day and it gave me a sense of power that I have since tried to rekindle on several occasions but to no avail. The power must have been in the vest because I have been that forthright with figures of authority only a very few times in my life and I was always wearing a vest. I went back to the house and told everyone that there might be a skirmish with the university and that they might try to forcibly remove the girls. I didn't know what was going to happen but I knew that it was certainly not over.

The following week, I got a letter summoning me once again to the office of the dean of men. I once again put on the brown leather vest and walked over to the administration building. This time the dean asked me to close the door behind me when I went in. He sat down as did I, and in a very deliberate tone he said that after careful consideration, the university and the Board of Regents had decided not to take any action against me or the DKE house. They had concluded that they could not legally force the tenants to leave the house. I breathed a sigh of relief. I had won! Then the dean took a deep breath and said that though the university could not legally dismiss me for my actions and could not dismiss me for academic reasons because I was on the dean's list with honors (an irony that was not lost on me), the Board had requested that I move on voluntarily. I asked him what that meant and he said, "You need to transfer—to another school." He said that everyone was willing to let the incident go for the remainder of the school year if I agreed to "move along." The inference was that the University of California would help in that effort as long as I "disappeared."

So they couldn't kick me out but they could strongly encourage me to "relocate." Good thing they didn't have computers in those days, as I'm sure my felonious behavior as a freshman would have given them the grounds they so desperately wanted. I told him that coincidentally I had made an application to transfer to Yale and was waiting for a response. He said, "Yale! That's good. That's very good." And he shook my hand as he showed me to the door.

I never saw the dean of men again and I never had to write that letter of apology for being a pimp to Ronald Reagan, and that's good, because sixteen years later, while he was president of the United States, he was a big fan of *L.A. Law,* an NBC-TV drama in which I starred. At the time, he invited me to the White House on a regular basis. But that's another story.

Three weeks after my last visit to the dean's office, I got the letter from Yale. I was in! Bye Bye Berkeley! Evie and I were heading East. But first I had to finish out my obligations to the drama department. I had one big paper to write and Stanley Kowalski to play and an understudy role in the big spring main-stage production to learn.

Power to the People

Spring was in the air. The rehearsals for *Streetcar* were going fine and I thought that I was going to be far better than Brando in the role. I was putting in hours a day on a paper about Greek tragedy, which, for some peculiar reason, I had come to love. And I was starting to learn an understudy role in the chorus of a curious adaptation of one such Greek tragedy called *Antigone* by Sophocles, which had been renamed *What the Blind Man Saw* for the purposes of the adaptation. The title referred to the character Tiresias who appears in many Greek tragedies. Tiresias was an old blind guy who could "see" clearer than anyone else. Tiresias and Cassandra were my two favorite characters from that period. Cassandra was this chick who was always right about what was going to happen but whom no one ever believed. I think I related to Cassandra because, after the "pee in the dog bowl" incident when I was four, my parents never believed me about much of anything, even when I was spot-on about something. Because of some pre-prepubescent perversion involving unregulated urination I have forever had a "Cassandra complex."

What the Blind Man Saw was to be a spectacular anti–Vietnam War statement and it was going to be the crowning achievement of the head of the drama department at Berkeley. The play was set in a Vietnam-like country and all the characters wore fatigues and carried M-16s. I was understudying a member of the chorus (all Greek tragedies have a chorus that sings at intervals to give emphasis to the story) so I didn't have to go to every rehearsal, but the dress rehearsal was mandatory. The play was getting a lot of buzz around Berkeley because in 1972 Vietnam was getting a lot of buzz around Berkeley.

On the first Saturday in May, I showed up at the rehearsal around 11:00 a.m. and settled into one of the auditorium seats to watch. On stage there were soldiers in fatigues brandishing fake M-16 rifles and speaking in mangled mid-Atlantic tones as they attempted to say lines that had not only been conceived thousands of years ago but were also originally written in Greek. Under the best of circumstances, with the greatest actors in the world, Greek tragedy is a tough thing to watch. The last thing anyone should be subjected to is a four-hour production of a Greek tragedy being played by untrained college students. It would be easier to take four consecutive hours of fingernails being dragged across a blackboard.

The rehearsal went on and Bill Oliver, the head of the drama department, bellowed out instructions over the PA system from an unseen booth in the back of the theatre. A short time into the second act of the play, during a particularly lugubrious speech by Antigone, the daughter of Agamemnon, there was a commotion outside that we could hear from inside the theatre. I heard what sounded like women screaming and men yelling. It was odd that we should hear anything inside the theatre as it was known for having one of the most sophisticated acoustical systems ever made. Some of the actors on stage became distracted and looked toward the wall of doors that led out to Sproul Plaza, the main courtyard of the university.

The doors were all shut but the noise outside was getting louder and louder. Bill Oliver shouted into the PA that everyone should remain in their places and pick up the dialogue where they left off. Just then, the doors started rattling and there was a deafening pounding sound as one door after another burst open and a huge crowd of screaming students flooded into the theatre.

Now Mr. Oliver was beside himself. "Actors! Stay where you are! Do not leave the stage!!" But it was too late.

It was now apparent that we were in the midst of a full-blown anti–Vietnam War riot! There, filling the theatre, was a crowd of coughing and wheezing rioters who had just been pummeled with tear gas by the Blue Meanies. And there, up on the stage, were faux soldiers in army fatigues with plastic M-16s at their sides. The clash of the two realities was one of the single most ironic moments of my life, highlighted by the pleading screams of Bill Oliver over the PA system as he tried to keep control of his antiwar play in the midst of a real antiwar riot. By then, a lot of the actors, including myself had said, "Fuck it!" and joined in with the mob. We made our way through the bowels of the theatre and out again onto the street where the rioters regrouped and headed toward People's Park.

We never really knew for sure when or if a riot would take place. There had been talk about a rally if Nixon went ahead with his proposed plan to mine the main harbor in North Vietnam, but it was only a rumor. But now it was rumor no more and at least a thousand frenzied kids were marching up Durant Avenue toward the legendary park. People's Park was ground zero for the counterculture movement of the sixties but it had been cordoned off by an eight-foot chain-link fence. The fencing was ordered by Governor Ronald Reagan and his chief of staff, Edwin Meese III, after a riot in 1969, and there was always talk that someday People's Park would be retaken by the people after whom it was named. That day had arrived, and when the mob reached the park, the fence didn't stand a chance. We pushed it over in a second and began to rip up the asphalt parking lot with our bare hands. The police, seeing how large the crowd had become, intelligently backed off and let the inevitable happen.

It took only a few minutes to return the park to bare earth. We made a huge pile of asphalt chunks in the middle of the street. Our hands were scraped and bloody but, by God, the park was ours again. Time to party! The hippies had won the day and the symbolism of a People's Park retaken energized the whole community. By evening there were fires and guitar music and conga drums as the flower children who had so longed to re-create the Dylanesque innocence of the sixties partied into the night.

The police were nowhere to be seen. The first hog rolled in at around two thirty, then another and another and another until the sound of the conga drums and flute music had been drowned out by the guttural roar of unmuffled Harley-Davidsons. The Angels had arrived to claim their moment! The appearance of Hells Angels freaked out a lot of the flower children and soon the peaceful party had devolved into drunken, raucous anarchy with the big smelly dudes on motorcycles threatening the long-haired, incense-burning commie draft dodgers. By the next day, there was no more flower power in People's Park. The hippies left, the Angels stayed, and we all knew that Berkeley, once the epicenter of the movement that changed the world, had jumped the shark.

Good Luck with Yale!

The following week we opened *A Streetcar Named Desire* at the Durant Theatre. I was very satisfied with my work in the play and felt that the weak link was the girl playing Blanche. I felt like my performance was going to save the play, in spite of my broken back and whatever medication I was taking for the pain. Brando Schmando . . . I was the new Stanley Kowalski! When the curtain came down and it was time for our bows, I was sure the place would go nuts when I came out on the stage.

I wiped the sweat off my brow and had run out to take a bow when the applause, which had been quite healthy, dimmed to about half its volume. I felt a kind of hot centipede-like sensation travel up my spine. Then the girl who played Blanche came out for the final bow and the place went nuts. I was still wearing the back brace and was taking some pretty strong medication for the pain. I think it must have been the drugs that had led me to believe I was anything but horrible in the part. There wasn't a soul who wanted to talk to me after the play and I snuck out through a side door. Luckily we only did a handful of performances and by the final night I had improved a little bit. But I had been, and I remain to this day, humbled.

I finished my final paper on Greek tragedy and breathed a huge sigh of relief. It was my last assignment at Berkeley, and a week later, Evie and I packed up all our stuff, I handed the keys to the DKE house over to the ambitious, young president-to-be, and I marched down to the drama department to pick up my paper and collect my final marks.

That paper on Greek tragedy was the most comprehensive essay I had ever completed. I had burned the midnight oil to finish it and I was extremely proud of it. I had been accepted to Yale provisionally, contingent, of course, on finishing Berkeley in good standing. I never gave that a second thought because I was and had been on the dean's list for the entire two years I was there.

Not so fast!

The work on the essay was good, all right. So good that the professor accused me of buying it from one of those services rumored to be around. The following is a verbatim transcription of her fond note to me scribbled on the last page of the essay: "There is absolutely no similarity, either in writing style or ideas between this paper and your other work. I will assume, to be charitable, that it is simply a mass of unattributed quotes, though it does seem a bit unlikely that you should suddenly burst forth with an 11 page research paper. If I'm misjudging you, my apologies—bring me your notes, etc. that you used in writing it and I will get the grade changed. My assessment is purely my own, considering the fact that you're planning to leave and need the grade. I didn't relay my impression elsewhere. Grade: F. Good luck with Yale."

As I recall, throughout the quarter we had been assigned to write a three- or four-page paper each week on some subject having to do with the classical theatre. I had been a bit preoccupied with the car crash and my broken back and the fire and the dean of men and *A Streetcar Named Desire* and the riots, not to mention the sweet spot between Evie's legs, and I had dashed off those little papers in minutes, usually on Monday morning before class. Admittedly they sucked, but I had put my heart and soul into the final essay, which was much longer and more in-depth. Now, my whole future hung in the balance. If I couldn't go to Yale, Evie would run off to Bennington while I stayed behind with the more-than-likely fate of having to transfer somewhere else.

I had burned my bridges at Berkeley and no school worth its salt

11

regeneration. He is a man who, through his passion for truth and self-awareness, was able to transcend his tragedy and become the man among men.

Tragedy, as a literary vehicle for expressing man's interpretation of life, may very well outlast any other literary form. Here I have discussed three ancient authors and I have presented ideas as to the purposes of their work and tragedy itself. All three authors have much to offer as they seem to deal with ideas basic to the nature of man.

There is absolutely no similarity, either in writing style or ideas, between this paper + your other work. I will assume (to be charitable) that it is simply a mass of unattributed quotes, though it does seem a bit unlikely that you should suddenly burst forth with an 11-page research paper. If I'm misjudging you, my apologies — bring me your notes etc. that you used in writing it + I'll get the grade changed. My assessment is purely my own — considering the fact that you're planning to leave + need the grade, I didn't verify my impression elsewhere.

GRADE Changed

F.

A

The last page of my last essay at Berkeley, with the professor's note and the grade changed to an A.

would accept a cheater jailbird who ran a brothel on the side. I was screwed! Unless, of course, I could produce my "notes, etc." The problem there was that I had pretty much moved out of the DKE house. The mounds of academic flotsam and jetsam that populated the floor around my desk had been scooped up and tossed out days before as

Evie and I prepared to leave Berkeley forever. The "notes, etc." were history.

I am proud to say that I have only once been inside a Dumpster. My sole chance at redemption lay buried in the DKE house trash bin along with hundreds of pounds of end-of-the-year fraternity house waste. I climbed into the mostly full container and tore through the reams of crumpled paper covered with some kind of smelly slime, old brown rice, and empty bottles of Herbal Essences shampoo until I thought I had turned over every single sheet of paper in the bin. Covered in goo and at the end of my wits, I reached down one final time to turn over the last bit of cardboard at my feet and realized, in that moment, that the God I had so recklessly turned my back on three years before apparently didn't hold a grudge. There, on the foul floor of the Dumpster, untouched by slime or coffee grounds, lay my "notes, etc." I was saved!

I took a long hot shower and later carried the notes down to the drama department for my redemption. I couldn't wait to see the look on the professor's face. She would have no choice but to apologize and eat a mouthful of crow. Why do we get such pleasure from witnessing the eating of crow? And what exactly does it mean to eat crow?

Anyway, I never got the chance to see that bird go down the hatch because the professor had left town for the year. I gave the notes to her superior and explained the situation. The grade was changed to an A. I never saw the professor again but am sure she still thinks I bought that paper and that I didn't deserve to go to the Ivy League. The truth is that I did not cheat on the paper, but neither did I deserve the Ivy League, which is just something I have to live with.

The next day, Evie and I crammed all our stuff into Beulah and left Berkeley for the last time, heading to Southern California and Italy for the summer and to our new academic lives in New England in the fall.

Because It's There

Evie's father had rented a farmhouse in Tuscany for the month of June and had invited the whole family, including me, to come to Italy for a mini-reunion to celebrate Evie's mother's life. It would be the first time the family had all been together since her death, and what better place to attempt closure than a rustic Italian farmhouse?

By that time, I had become obsessed with backpacking, and my passion and enthusiasm for the sport had infected Evie. The two of us spent hours dreaming about where and when we would take our first hike together. We bought backpacks and equipment and had planned to take a lengthy hike into the high Sierras in the late spring but all of those best-laid plans changed on that two-lane highway outside Front Royal, Virginia; the backpacks and camping stuff lay unused in the closet as we recovered from our broken bones. We found out about the Italian trip in early May and thought that by mid-June we would have recovered enough to take a hike into the mountains. We even spent a month building our own high-tech, two-person tent based on a pattern we copied from a company based in Berkeley called Sierra Designs. To buy a tent like that would have cost $200—a huge sum in 1972, and definitely not the kind of dough a couple of hippies had burning a hole in their pockets. So we built the tent and decided that since we were going to Europe, and they had these great mountains in the north of Italy called the Alps, we might as well do our big hike there. Why not?

My father, when he wasn't playing with his slide rule or eating the dog's food, was also a big camper. A couple of times a year we'd pack up the old bubble-top Lincoln with sleeping bags, an ice chest, and a metal grill, and head out to some remote spot in the desert or the local mountains. It was pretty basic camping and I learned how to get by in the great outdoors. Just before I turned eleven, I joined Troop 5, the local chapter of the Boy Scouts, mainly because they frequently went on two-night camping trips. Precocious little kid that I was, I figured I was such an experienced camper at the age of ten, I could probably show all the other scouts a thing or two.

Dad, me, and my brother Dave as we left for our fateful camping trip.
I was not yet officially a Boy Scout so I didn't have a uniform.

You were supposed to be eleven to join the Boy Scouts but I was allowed to join two weeks before my eleventh birthday so that I could go on a camping trip that my father had helped to organize. It would be the first and last camping trip I would ever take as a Boy Scout.

The plan was to caravan fifty boys and a truck filled with tents and equipment to a remote spot near Mount Palomar in Southern California. We arrived late Friday afternoon and began to pitch our five-man tents in a clearing at the foot of a gently sloping hill. The ground was flat and grassy—a seemingly perfect place for tents and Boy Scouts.

However, we hadn't been paying much attention to the sky, and as this trip preceded by many years the advent of "Live Doppler Radar," there were no accurate five-day forecasts. Had there been "Live Doppler Radar," we all, most assuredly, would have stayed home in our cozy living rooms watching *Leave It to Beaver* on our black-and-white Zenith TVs. As my five-boy group set up our tent, I noticed that the sky had turned black and that the wind was starting to get angry. I turned to the oldest, highest-ranking boy in our group and recommended that we reconsider where to put the tent. I suggested that it might rain and that if it did, we would want to be on higher ground in case runoff from the hill flooded our flat clearing. He told me to button it up, that we'd be fine, and that he was feeling really sick anyway and was going to get one of the fathers to take him home. He walked away and I didn't see him again all weekend. After he left, there were four of us and we all had the same rank. I saw an opening and took charge. I told the other boys to gather up the tent and the other stuff and follow me up the hill.

I had noticed a relatively flat spot about two hundred feet up the hill surrounded by some pine trees that we could use to tether the tent. The wind was really starting to whip up by then and I looked down at the other nine tents already up on the plain below. I could see the canvas flapping every which way and kids running around sticking extra tent pegs in the ground. My little group of four got to our new campsite on the hill where the clearing was just big enough for the tent. We went to work right away and in no time we had our home away from home up and tethered and pegged. It was starting to get dark and the first raindrops had begun to ping on the roof of our tent.

Within minutes the rain was coming down in buckets and the wind was howling through the trees. We opened our tent flap and peered into the storm, which was strangely lit by a full moon high above the angry clouds. All hell had broken loose below. My prediction about flooding had materialized and the other tents were inundated with water. We could see the little glow of flashlights running in every direction and then, as a monster gust of wind raced through the valley, one tent after another lifted up in the air and blew away. All nine tents were either uprooted or collapsed as the screams of the Boy Scouts and their fathers grew louder and louder. Just then, our door flap was drawn open and my father, soaked from head to toe, burst in. He asked if we were okay and we all said we were fine. He never asked whose idea it was to put *our* tent in such a safe place, but I'm sure he never dreamed it was his own flesh and blood. He said that everyone else was going to load their wet tents and gear into the truck and head down to the coast to a campground by the beach but that we could stay if we wanted to since our tent was in no danger. Some of the dads were staying in a cabin down below so we felt reasonably safe and decided to stay.

It rained all night and every couple of hours I would wander out into the bushes just outside the tent to relieve myself. By morning we were all soaked. World War II–issue canvas tents couldn't withstand the fury of the night's storm and the seams had all leaked. At daybreak, the rain stopped and we broke camp as fast as we could. By noon we were down by the beach repitching our soaked tent and drying out in the poststorm afternoon sun.

One of the guys who had come to the beach the day before welcomed us by reporting that "Bumper is open for business." We all knew what that meant and dropped what we were doing to go be a part of the spectacle. "Bumper" was one Jason Bumper, a sixteen-year-old Eagle Scout candidate who hailed from England. It was legend in Troop 5 that from time to time on the overnight trips, for a mere fifty cents per boy, Bumper would display his enormous British penis for a few seconds. There was a line outside Bumper's tent and the look on the boys' faces when they emerged from the viewing was one of disgust, shock, awe, and envy. Bumper was the only Brit any of us knew so of course we thought that all Englishmen were hung like horses. I never saw the pudendum myself—probably didn't have the fifty cents—but if the stories were true, Bumper put Dillinger and Holmes to shame.

But he wasn't the only show in town on that trip; that night there was a grunion run on the beach. A grunion is a small, sardinelike fish that lays its eggs on dry sand on certain full moon cycles each year. When the grunion "run" they seemingly run up the beach on their tails, lay their eggs, and then flop back down to the water to ride a wave out to sea. Humans tend to go crazy when witnessing this phenomenon, and they dive and grab and try to catch as many of the hapless fish as possible. Being human, that is precisely what I and fifty other Boy Scouts did that night. The grunion is and was a protected fish, and catching them by hand as they lay their eggs is not only cruel and stupid but also illegal. Scofflaws that we were, we caught hundreds of the little suckers and built a fire to try to eat them. The fire and grunion for dinner was my father's idea.

Despite my father's chosen profession of rocket scientist, he had a certain recessive caveman gene triggered by the sight of any wild thing that could possibly be eaten. He shot and killed jackrabbits for breakfast in the desert (if it was a male jackrabbit, he would fry up the testicles and make us eat them with garlic salt and butter); he clubbed a partridge on a camping trip in Idaho, making me pluck the feathers and cook it for dinner; and he bashed in the head of a porcupine at our place in Canada and cooked it for lunch. As the story goes, he shot and killed a cow moose on a canoe trip in northern Ontario so that he could have some fresh meat for dinner. He was with three other guys. Two thousand pounds of moose for dinner. Yum. Yum.

But the grunion meal didn't work out, so it was hot dogs and hamburgers without the buns, which had disintegrated during the storm.

That night, in my sandy, salty sleeping bag, I started to itch. At first I thought it was the combination of sand and salt from my romp in the ocean with the grunion, but soon I came to realize the worst. The bushes outside our well-tethered tent, into which I had regularly ventured to pee during the previous night's storm, had been poison oak. By morning it was evident that I was covered from head to toe with poison oak, and within a day I'm sure the size of my swollen penis came at least close to that of Mr. Bumper.

Two weeks later, after my birthday, I was summoned to the troop headquarters for a special meeting with just me and the troop leader, an imposing man in his fifties who must have dreamed of being a marine drill sergeant. My hunch was that word had gotten around that I moved our tent to higher ground and saved our guys and I was sure that I was going to be promoted from tenderfoot to at least second class, if not first class. After all, what I had done was practically heroic.

I walked into the troop leader's office and he asked me to explain the whole grunion catching and grunion dinner thing. I was not getting a promotion, I was getting a reprimand. He told me that catching grunion by hand was illegal and that he was having the same conversation with all the boys. I asked him if he had heard about my tent and the rain and he said that we had done a great job and that he was recommending that I be promoted to tenderfoot. I explained that I already was tenderfoot and then he reminded me that, since I was still ten at the time of the camping trip, I was technically not anything and that I should be proud to become a tenderfoot. That was the moment I quit the Boy Scouts. I didn't know it at the time, but in a few weeks Santa was going to bring me a very special treat along with a really shitty bike. Who needed the Boy Scouts?

That camping trip and a couple of others along the way had inspired me to try backpacking in the Sierras, and in the summer of 1971, shortly after the *Night of the Living Dead* incident, I set off on a weekend hike into Desolation Valley with a bunch of friends from high school. I had the time of my life. I fell in love with the wilderness. It was absolutely peaceful and so fresh and clean. When I got thirsty I'd just dip my canteen into a stream and guzzle the sweet mountain spring water. When I was hungry, I'd cast a lure out into a stream or a lake and there would be dinner. The trout were enormous and far too easy to catch. We built huge campfires and sang and told ghost stories after dinner. It was heaven. The weather had been perfect and the scenery glorious. I was hooked.

So, it was only natural that with my extensive Boy Scout experience and that three-day trip under my belt, I should plan to take my girlfriend, who had never been backpacking, high into the Swiss Alps for a weeklong hike from the Italian border to the Matterhorn. I was even more qualified to do this because I spoke no Italian, German, or Swiss German, and I had broken my back just three months before. No sweat!

We arrived in Italy in mid-June, backpacks and newly minted tent in hand. Evie's father had rented a rustic four-bedroom farmhouse that had few amenities. He was fairly progressive and Evie and I were given our own bedroom—an unusual setup for a couple of unwed twenty-year-olds and something that would most certainly not have been tolerated under my parents' roof. As I got to know Evie's father, I began to see where Evie got her carefree spirit. We told him that we intended to hike through the Alps for a week and he just asked if we had warm sleeping bags. I'm sure he loved his daughter very much, and why he would allow her to trek off into the mountains in a foreign country with a boyfriend he didn't know is beyond me. But off we went.

We took a train to a little village at the foot of the Italian Alps. After we bought our train tickets, we had just our backpacks and about forty bucks between us. The plan was to stay the first night in a cheap hotel in the village and then set off to find our way up into the mountains the next day. We had enough food with us for five days on the trail, and we figured we'd just hitch a ride back when we came off the mountain. After all, it was only a couple of hours from the alpine village to the town of Figline Valdarno, where the farmhouse was, and we wouldn't have enough money for any more tickets. We found a quaint little pensione and paid around twenty dollars for a room. We cooked up some ramen noodles for dinner using my camping stove and drifted off to sleep.

We woke up the next morning to head uphill. We didn't know where the trail up the mountain started or even if there was a trail. There is a certain advantage that American hikers have over the Europeans; it's called the U.S. Geological Survey, which turns out detailed topographical maps of every inch of our national parks and wilderness areas. Apparently the Europeans could never agree on which format to use so the maps of the Alps we had were quite primitive. I had found a tourist map, which showed that we could access the mountains from this village, but the little red dotted line representing a hiking trail just originated from the larger red dot that represented the town—which is why we kept walking uphill hoping that we might find the edge of town and spot a trailhead.

I did my best, using sign language and a little Spanish, to get directions from the villagers, but most of them just stared at us in disbelief. I found out later that people like us, kids with long hair and backpacks, were called *vagabonde,* or vagabonds, which is why most of the people we met did their best to avoid us. We finally got to the end of town, where the forest touched the last houses on the hill, and we saw something straight out of Disneyland. A man with a hand-hewn walking stick was hiking down out of the forest, obviously on a trail of some kind. He was wearing lederhosen, which I had only ever seen worn by the ticket takers at the Matterhorn roller-coaster ride. But in this case, it was not a costume but actually the way the man had chosen to dress for his hike in the forest. When he emerged from the trail I went up to him and started in with my hand signals, at which point he asked in English if we were American. We admitted that we were and asked him where the trail went, and he said that if we kept going, it would take us all the way to Monte Cervino, which is also known as the Matterhorn. I had always thought that the ticket guys at Disneyland looked kind of cheesy in their fake lederhosen but I suddenly had a newfound respect for the attempt at verisimilitude. The man tipped his hat and hobbled off as we took our first steps into the Alps.

I figured that the trailhead was at about four thousand feet and that if my calculations were correct, we could climb a few more thousand feet that day. We planned to hike until about 6:00 p.m., then make camp, cook up some spaghetti, and get cozy in our new handmade tent.

After about an hour of hiking, either we took a wrong turn or the guy in the funny outfit had given us a bum steer because we suddenly found ourselves hiking overland with no trail in sight. We doubled back to where the last vestiges of a trail were and could not see that the trail continued. We decided that all we needed to do was keep going up and eventually we would get to the top, which was our destination for the day. So, up we went, all the time keeping one eye on the sky, which was starting to get pretty gray and mean-looking. I must say that Evie was a trooper. Her pack was not light and her boots were not broken in, but she never complained as we scrambled practically straight up the mountain. We were hiking up through a small ravine when I felt the first raindrop.

Once again, we really could have used "Live Doppler Radar." The rain was light and intermittent at first and I told Evie that we'd be okay because I had a special tarp that I could rig up between rocks in the ravine and that we would be dry if we kept all our stuff under it. I said it was a good time to break for lunch anyway. So, Boy Scout that I was, I stretched the tarp out and with some rope and a couple of bungee cords made the perfect shelter. We were indeed dry as a bone.

It still wasn't raining very hard, but it was getting colder, and I suggested that we cook some ramen to warm us up. I broke out the old Svea camping stove, fired it up, and poured some water from my canteen into a pan. The noodles were at the bottom of Evie's pack and I dug through a lot of clothing and utensils, placing all the stuff on the dry tundra. Evie, who hated to wear shoes of any kind, had taken her boots off to check for blisters. The water started to boil and the rain started to pour down. We remained dry under the tarp and I put the ramen into the hot water. It was getting really cold and we were thrilled that we had a steaming pot to curl our numb fingers around. We were actually feeling pretty cozy under our little shelter when all hell broke loose.

It seems that my Boy Scout-camping-in-the-rain experience hadn't seasoned me as much as I had thought, for I had expertly set up our little temporary camp smack dab in the middle of a dry riverbed. Just as the ramen was ready to pour into our bowls, a wall of water at least two feet high crashed through our stuff, carrying everything down the mountain. Our packs tipped over, spilling out clothing and food and sleeping bags. Evie's boots floated down the mountain, so it was up to me to chase after everything. I was able to recover all the stuff, but we were in for a very cold, wet night. We never got a chance to eat the soup, and the next few hours were an absolute nightmare.

Fortunately the rain calmed down enough for the river to subside and we packed our wet stuff back into the packs. I knew that we had to get farther up the mountain before dark for a number of reasons, not the least of which was to find a flat place to set up our new tent. We also needed fresh water, so we had to find a stream or a lake. We slogged on up the mountain wearing our plastic ponchos. We were kind of glad we weren't on a trail where other people might see us.

Up we went as the wet afternoon wore on. Luckily the rain eventually stopped and we found ourselves hiking through a cloud. We didn't talk much; I think we both knew that this trip was headed south fast. Still no stream, no lake, and no flat ground. We had no choice but to keep going. It was too late to try to get down the mountain before dark so we just prayed that we would find a place to camp by nightfall.

Finally, around eight thirty, just as dusk was upon us, we climbed up over a ridge and looked down at a heavenly sight. Below us was a little lake about the size of a football field with lots of flat grassy land on its banks. There was a little stream going into the lake from the mountain above and an outlet stream that cascaded down through a gorge, so I knew it was an actual lake and not just runoff from the afternoon rains. I wondered if I had time to catch a fat trout before it got too dark. Fresh fish would be a great way to take the edge off what had been a nightmare day. We raced down to the lake and I asked Evie to set up the tent while I rigged my fishing pole and scanned the lake for the perfect spot to cast my line.

We had found a great spot. It was secluded and peaceful and beautiful. Before I went fishing, I filled up our canteens with water from the lake and filled up a pot with water. In case the trout weren't biting, we'd have spaghetti as a backup. I fired up the stove once again, set the water to boil, and marched to the lake to slay the woolly mammoth.

I cast out my line. Nothing. I cast out again. More nothing. That seemed funny. The last time I went fishing in a mountain lake, the trout had practically jumped into the frying pan. I cast again and again and again. It was getting dark as I moved around the lake, sure that I just wasn't in the right spot. Still more nothing. Evie called that the spaghetti was ready so I abandoned my hunt. What was left of my proud male ego was in tatters. First, I had built a shelter in a river and now I couldn't get the trout to bite. At least our roost for the night was in good shape and we were in a very protected spot.

Evie seemed to be in good spirits and she had a good appetite. We were so hungry that we both had two helpings of pasta, which we washed down with fresh mountain lake water. It was dark when we finished dinner and we left the dishes till morning. We climbed into the tent and found that our sleeping bags were not as wet as we had thought. It was actually going to be a cozy first night in the home-made tent.

We had put up the rain fly so if it rained again we'd be dry; the packs were under the tarp; and since the Alps didn't have bears, we didn't have to string up the food as I had done in the Sierras. We could look forward to a quiet night and hopefully better weather tomorrow. We cuddled a bit and fell off into the kind of sleep one only gets after climbing a mountain in the rain all day.

A couple of hours after we drifted off, I woke up to a horrible acrid smell. Evie was sound asleep and farting every few seconds. The tent was like a gas chamber. Maybe she had gorged on too much pasta or the sauce hadn't agreed with her because the girl was farting up a storm. The temperature outside had plummeted so opening up the tent flap wasn't an option. I thought of waking her but figured that really wouldn't accomplish anything. She was going to pass this foul gas awake or asleep, and I thought she would just be horribly embarrassed. I decided to grin and bear it. I tossed around and finally fell back to sleep.

Hours passed and then suddenly someone started ringing a really loud bell. I jolted awake. It was light outside and excruciatingly noisy. It seemed like a hundred bells were being rung just outside our tent. Evie sat up, bleary-eyed, as I opened the tent flap to find several hundred cattle, each with a big fat cowbell, surrounding the tent and rummaging through our gear. Evie looked at the cows, then at me, and then stuck her head out of the tent and vomited all over her boots. It occurred to me that camping in the Alps is a bit different from camping in the High Sierra.

It turned out that we had pitched our camp in a cow pasture, and if it had not been dusk when we got there, we might have noticed the piles of rain-drenched cow shit surrounding the lake. Evie was deathly ill. We had been basically pouring E. coli into our bodies during dinner the night before. It was a miracle that I was not puking my guts out too.

The cows scattered when we emerged from our foul-smelling, handmade, brand-new tent that was now muddy and splashed with partially digested spaghetti. Evie got a few yards away from me and the tent before she stripped off her jeans, crouched down, and drained her body of all fecal matter. Then she stood up and vomited again. I ran over to her with a towel and helped clean her up. She was too sick to be embarrassed and too weak to do anything but cry as a gentle rain began to blanket our little home away from home. I knew I had to get Evie off that mountain and back to her father as soon as humanly possible.

As Evie sat on a rock dry-heaving, surrounded by cows and clanging cowbells. I rushed to pack up all our gear, which was again soaked and muddy. I did my best to scrape the puke off Evie's boots and find her a dry pair of socks. I took the boots to her with a towel and helped get the socks and boots onto her wet feet. She was dark green and running a fever. I decided she was too sick to carry a pack so I stuffed as much as possible into my own and then strapped her pack to mine with bungee cords and rope. We put on our plastic ponchos and I hoisted the double pack up onto my recently broken back. I wasn't ready for the new load, however, and I fell backward into a little ditch, coating my jeans with soggy cow shit and mud. I pulled the pack back up onto my shoulders and this time remained upright, though there was always a strong gravitational tug backward. An old man with grizzled fingers and a white beard walked over to us and started yelling something in a language that sounded like he had a chicken bone stuck in his throat. Many years later I visited Switzerland with my son's mother, who happens to be Swiss, and I heard that sound again. Swiss German is an odd language.

The man was obviously not happy that we were in his cow pasture. I made hand signals to indicate that Evie was sick and I gestured down the mountain. He seemed to understand and he pointed to the other end of the lake and made his own downhill gesture. I looked in that direction and thought I saw a trailhead. We walked over and sure enough we found the trail. We wouldn't have to hike overland down the mountain. We had no water and Evie couldn't keep anything down anyway so we knew we had to get down fast. The weight of the two packs helped propel me down the mountain, and to this day I don't know how she found the strength to do it.

After five hours, we picked up the trail we had lost and were down in the town by two o'clock. There was a *carabinieri* (police) station not far from the trail and I marched Evie inside and asked for water. I was able to communicate that she was sick and that I didn't have enough money for the train back to Figline. I half expected them to lend me the difference, but I could tell by the looks on their faces that we were being harshly judged. After all, I had hair down to my shoulders that was matted with mud and cow shit, and we were Americans with backpacks—just a couple of drugged-out hippies stealing our way across Europe, begging for money. To add insult to injury, Evie looked like she could have been strung out on heroin and I smelled like a camel. They asked me if I wanted to use the phone, but our farmhouse had no phone and this was, of course, decades before cell phones.

I was pretty much out of ideas when it struck me that there must be an American Consulate somewhere in Northern Italy. I gestured some more but was at a loss as to how to say "American Consulate" with my hands, so I just started blabbing in high school French hoping that someone would understand, and someone did. One of the policemen spoke some French and he understood that I wanted to find the consulate. He pointed to Torino on a map of Italy that was on the wall. It looked like it was about an hour away by train. He said the train to Torino would be coming in a few minutes if I wanted to go there.

I told Evie that our only hope of getting her out of there and to a warm, dry place for the night was if I went to the consulate and asked for help. After all, I was an American and we Yankees stuck together, right? I had only enough dough for a one-way ticket for one person so my plan had to work or I'd be stuck in Torino on the street and God knows what would happen to poor Evie. I ran down to the train station, which was a few blocks away, and caught the train to Torino using up my last 10,000-lira note. I was sitting in a compartment with very well-dressed, well-heeled folks who gave me a wide berth, no doubt because I smelled like a donkey and looked like an unshaven ax murderer. I sank as deeply into my seat as possible and tried to disappear. It was definitely another of those "Beam me up, Scotty" moments.

I asked the conductor, who spoke a little English, if he knew where the American Consulate was; luckily he did. It was about a mile from the train station, which we pulled into just past four o'clock. The conductor told me where to go and I ran as fast as I could to that part of town. I asked everyone I encountered where the American building was and finally I rounded a corner and saw Old Glory hanging outside a stately redbrick building surrounded by a tall black fence. I found the front gate and rang the buzzer.

A female voice came over the intercom and asked me what I wanted. I told her my story and she said to come back during business hours the next day. I told her that my girlfriend was really sick and that I needed help right away. It couldn't wait until the next day. She asked me if I had my passport, which I did not, and said that without it there was no way to prove that I was even an American citizen. I reached for my wallet and pulled out my California driver's license.

I spoke into the intercom as calmly as I could, explaining that I was a student from California on a short summer trip to Tuscany. She asked me to stand back and hold my license up to the white box over the gate. Video was a pretty new thing back in 1972 and it had not occurred to me that the girl had been clocking me via video during our conversation. Sure enough, there was a video camera in a white box attached to the top of the fence. I held up the license and she said that a driver's license wasn't proof of citizenship and that I really needed to come back the next day before four o'clock. I was starting to panic and then I remembered that Yale had sent me an ID card for use at the Yale co-op the week before I left for Italy. I had the card in my wallet and it had my picture on it, verifying that I was a student at Yale. I gave it a shot. I held up my Yale ID and told the girl I was in the Ivy League. There was a long silence and then a man's voice came over the intercom. "What college are you in?" demanded the deep baritone. At first I didn't know what he meant, but then I remembered that I had been assigned to Davenport College. I replied in the interrogative, "Uh . . . Davenport?" and the gate immediately opened.

The card that saved my neck in Torino, Italy.

I walked in as the door to the building swung open, and there stood a very tall, good-looking man in his fifties wearing a three-piece suit replete with gold watch fob and bow tie. I shuffled up to him and he almost took a step back when he got a good look and a whiff. I handed him my Yale ID card and said that I was Harry and I was in a real fix. He did not shake my hand, but I then knew what my father meant when he said that Yale would open doors for me.

I followed the consul general inside and we walked into a beautiful wood-paneled room with an exquisite oriental rug on the floor. There was a huge vase of white lilies on a round walnut table in the center of the room. Quite a contrast to the vagabond covered with sweat, mud, cow shit, and vomit standing next to them.

The consul general was stern. Apparently the Yale connection—he had graduated in the fifties—only went so far. He wanted to know what was wrong, why I didn't have any money and what would be required to fix the situation. I told him that I needed $50 to get my sick girlfriend back to safety. He reached into his pocket and pulled out $60 worth of lira. He handed it to me and said I should know better. He didn't specify what I should know better but he didn't have to. I knew he was on to something.

The consul general showed me out and said that I just might make the five o'clock train back to the village. I thanked him. Once again he did not extend his hand, probably thinking that I might have some communicable and quite possibly terminal disease.

I ran back to the station and caught the train. I found Evie, sound asleep, curled up on the floor of the police station. I woke her and told her that we could catch the train to Figline if we went straightaway to the train station. We did and within three hours we were back at the farmhouse in Tuscany, not at all sure what had just happened to us. Evie's father was glad we were back safely even though his daughter was still spending most of her time in the bathroom. He sent a crisp hundred-dollar bill to the consulate with a thank-you note that legitimized my story.

In a couple of days, Evie was feeling like herself again, and during our final week in Italy, we spent our days exploring Florence and our nights doing the nasty as much as possible. Our room was on a bottom floor and away from the rest of the family so if we made noise while in the throes of passion, no one was the wiser.

Our trip to Italy ended in early July and we all flew back to LA to spend the summer with our families. As the summer of 1972 came to a close, Evie got very cold feet about the move to Vermont and called me up one August day to say that she had decided to remain at Berkeley. I couldn't believe what I was hearing and I did my best to convince her not to return to the school that I could not go back to. But she was adamant and said that we would find a way to make our relationship work. I think that between her pitiful driving on that fateful day in Front Royal, Virginia, and the sight of her shitting and puking at the same time on that mountain in Switzerland, I had begun to cool my romantic jets vis à vis Evie anyway. I had no choice but to go on to New Haven so I rationalized our parting as just a natural progression and packed my gear into Beulah for the drive to Connecticut and my new life at Yale.

The only existing photo of me and Evie, 1972.

The Ivy League

It was my fourth time driving across the country. A Mexican thief had stolen the Blaupunkt radio out of my car that spring so I had no tunes to keep me company on the drive. I know the thief was Mexican because the police caught him after they dusted my car for fingerprints. I took Interstate 80, which was the most direct route, and did a whole lot of thinking over the five-day drive. I decided that I really did want to make a career out of acting and that I was still in love with Evie. I pined for her as the white lines of the highway swooshed beneath me. When I got to St. Louis, I almost turned around to head back to Berkeley, but I thought that course of action, though a good thing for my libido, would be a disaster for my life. I kept driving east.

I arrived in New Haven the Friday before classes were to begin. I went first to the administration building to find out where I would be living and with whom. They gave me a fat envelope with lots of dos and don'ts in it and a map of the campus, and they told me that I would be living in the lower court of Davenport College and that my roommate was a junior named Tim O'Brian. I liked his name. I'm one-third Irish so I figured we had at least that in common. It was a hot, humid, and sultry September day and I parked my little Beemer on the street ouside Davenport College directly behind another BMW 2002. It was bright orange and was a souped-up model called a tii. I thought that was an interesting coincidence because you just didn't see too many BMWs around.

I locked up the car, which was stuffed to the gills, with everything from my country jumbo Gibson guitar with the cutout and the mother of pearl inlay to my wadded-up queen-size water bed, which I had decided to bring with me to Yale. I unfolded the campus map and found my way to the lower courtyard and the entrance to the flight of stairs that led to my fourth-floor double room.

I could hear someone playing an acoustic guitar, and playing quite well to boot. I started up the stairs, catching glimpses of other students rearranging furniture in their rooms. Each floor had two rooms and a bathroom, and I got plenty of odd looks from this bunch of extremely clean cut boys. I hadn't shaved in a week, had a scraggly set of muttonchop sideburns and hair well below my shoulders. I'm sure these fellows thought I was somebody's drug dealer come for a fishing expedition on the first day of school.

I reached the fourth floor out of breath and beaded with sweat. The guitar music was coming from inside my room and didn't stop when I knocked, so I knocked again. Still no stop and whoever was playing was really getting into it. I figured it was going to be my room anyway, so I dropped protocol and just opened the door and saw, for the first time, the single most intense human being I have ever, or will ever, meet in my life.

Most of the rooms in Davenport College were triples or quads, for three or four students, but each college had the rare two-bedroom suite complete with fireplace and dark wood-paneled walls. As I opened the door, the first thing that hit me was a nasty wall of unfiltered Camel cigarette and marijuana smoke.

The man playing the guitar was thin, about my size, and quite handsome. He had short, curly brown hair, was wearing a bright red and white striped button-down shirt, jeans, penny loafers, and, somewhat strangely, an eight-inch hunting knife with a black handle in a black sheath was strapped to his belt. The really weird thing about that was that I owned the exact same knife, which I had taken to the Alps with Evie. He was playing a very expensive Martin D-28 guitar, and though he knew I was in the room, he kept playing for another minute or so until the song finished. He clearly wanted me to know that he was a damn good finger picker.

When he stopped, he didn't say hello. He just reached over to the ashtray on the side table to his right, grabbed the still burning joint, filled his lungs to their absolute maximum capacity, and handed the joint to me. I raised my hand to decline as he exhaled a massive amount of marijuana smoke, which would have made any mortal instantly incoherent but which seemed to have no effect on him whatsoever. Then he said in a very sweet voice, "You must be Harry. Hi! I'm Tim. Which bedroom do you want?"

Tim and I, the day we met at Yale.

He could not have been nicer. Nor did he seem the least bit stoned. I told him that he played a mean guitar and he thanked me and asked if I played. I said yes and that I was going to go out to my car to get my guitar and some other stuff. I chose the back bedroom next to the fireplace and he said that was cool and offered to help me bring up my stuff. We walked back down the stairs and he introduced me to all the other guys in the building. He was, at first glance, a great guitar player, a fierce pot and Camel smoker, and a perfect gentleman.

We got to my car and he stopped dead and said, "Is this your car?" I said, "Yes." And he pointed at the orange 2002 in front of mine and said, "That's my car!" I was beginning to like this guy. I had instant respect for anyone who understood what fine driving machines were made by BMW (this was at least a decade before BMW adopted the slogan "The Ultimate Driving Machine"). It was still not a well-known brand in the U.S., but if you owned a BMW, then you knew the good stuff from the bad. Tim helped me get my bags, guitar, and water bed up to the room, which was sparsely furnished with two desks, two wooden chairs, a couple of end tables, and a couch. Each bedroom had a metal-framed single bed with what appeared to be a World War II–issue mattress. I dumped my gear and told Tim I had to find a long hose to fill up my bed. He couldn't believe I was actually going to install a water bed, but he went right along with it, though he did recommend that I not tell anyone.

It so happened that the dimensions of the bedroom were essentially the same as the water bed so I went without a frame and just used the walls as sides of the bed. The only unbordered bit of the bed was at the door. Tim told me about a hardware store not too far away and he and I hopped into his Beemer and raced across town to buy a hose. And when I say "raced," I mean *raced*.

Tim put on a pair of leather driving gloves and lit up another joint as we started off. After that, he never took his foot off the gas. He wanted to show me how much faster his tii was than my pathetic, generic 2002. I'm sure we hit 100 miles per hour at least once on the way over. Somehow we survived the trip to the hardware store, and when we got back, we surreptitiously ran the newly purchased hundred-foot garden hose up the stairway and into my soon-to-be-nothing-but-water-bed room. Tim had run off to do an errand and he returned with a carton of Camels and two six-packs of a canned substance called Olde English "800," which was malt liquor, a beer-like drink, only with several times the amount of alcohol. Within minutes, Tim had consumed the first six-pack and was inviting all the other guys up to have a gander at the hippie from Berkeley installing a water bed in his room.

Tim rolled joint after joint and some of our guests were starting to get pretty loaded. Even Tim was starting to show signs of intoxication. More Olde English miraculously showed up and our little get-together evolved into a genuine ruckus. A guy named Frank started asking Tim if there were any Z bags around and a couple of the others chimed in that a Z bag would be a perfect way to start the year at Yale. I had no clue what a Z bag was and didn't give it much thought. I had some of the turbo beer but smoked no pot and was mainly interested in getting my bed filled up so I had a place to sleep.

I saw Tim give a wad of money to one of the revelers, telling him to get three "bags." The guy, whose name was Steve and who was obviously in awe of Tim, took the dough and disappeared down the stairs. Tim pulled out his guitar and started to play the same tune he was playing when I came in. I recognized the song as "The Fisherman" by Leo Kottke, a hero of mine and one of the best acoustic guitar pickers in the world. Tim was really doing justice to the song and the five or six other guys in the room were clearly also in awe of this man.

Tim played a few more songs as I watched the bed slowly fill with water. After an hour or so Steve wobbled back into the room and said, "Success!" as he held up a little brown paper bag. It was then starting to get dark and some of the guys peeled off to go with Steve, Tim, and Frank to do whatever one did with Z bags.

Once they left, the rest of the guys went off in search of pizza. I stayed behind to finish unpacking and filling my bed. I was still exhausted from the drive and wanted desperately to sleep. I waited up until around eleven to see if Tim would come back, but he didn't, and as I was dead tired, I turned off the lights, climbed into my undulating bed, and immediately drifted into a blissful sleep. What happened next would color every single day of my Yale experience thereafter.

I don't know how long I had been asleep. I didn't own a watch and there were no clocks in the room, but at some point I woke to very strange sounds coming from the other side of my bedroom door. At first it sounded like a wounded animal howling in pain. There was a low grunting sound punctuated by staccato growls that grew louder and louder. As I woke, I tried to orient myself. Where was I? Was I camping somewhere? Was I in Berkeley? Then I really woke up and knew that I was in my new room at Yale. The growling got louder and I reached for my Buck knife, which I had laid on the floor next to my bed. Something was very wrong on the other side of my unlocked door; I unsheathed the knife and my heart raced.

I imagined that at any moment someone or something would burst through my door to try to kill me. The growling persisted and I could hear furniture being moved and things being tossed around the room. Then laughter, then more growling, then silence.

After a minute or two there came a loud thumping noise that sounded like someone throwing something at the wall next to the fireplace. Between each thump there was a loud grunt not unlike those made by Boris Karloff as the Frankenstein monster in the original film. This was repeated twenty or so times, and then silence. Then I heard the sound of breaking glass and the distinctive noise of someone violently vomiting. Then, again, complete silence. After half an hour or so of sustained silence, I drifted back to sleep.

I woke around eight and ventured out to the scene of the crime. I opened my bedroom door and there was Tim's eight-inch Buck knife sticking out of the oiled wood paneling over the fireplace. I could see at least twenty deep gashes in the wood. It seemed that Mr. O'Brian had been practicing his knife-throwing technique on the hundred-year-old mahogany paneling in the middle of the night while stoned on God knows what and growling like a wild boar. Then I saw the blood.

A thin spatter of red ran down the white wall opposite the fire-place. Lying on the ground below was a piece of rubber tubing just like I had seen my old roommate, Gene the junkie, use at Berkeley while tying off a vein to shoot up. Tim's bedroom door was wide open, and there he was, hanging half on, half off the bed, fully clothed. And snoring like a pig. His right hand was caked with dried blood, and I could tell that he had punched out a windowpane and puked into the yard below through the brand-new hole in his room. He must have blown his cookies and then passed out.

In shock, but figuring Tim would be okay, I stumbled to the bath-room, showered and shaved for the first time in a week, threw on my bell-bottoms and poorboy shirt, and went down to the dining room for breakfast, leaving Tim splayed out on his single unsheeted WWII mattress. I assumed he'd be there for at least a day.

In the dining hall I got a lot of stares from my fellow Ivy Leaguers who wondered who this hippie was, getting scrambled eggs and soggy bacon in their exclusive buffet. I was a little nervous and was feeling like I needed Scotty to beam me up again when a voice behind me said, "Hey, Harry. I'm Don. I met you in your room yesterday. Did you get the water bed going?" I turned around and saw my first recog-nizable face of the day. I said, "Yes." And he asked if he could join me for breakfast. Don and I have been good friends ever since.

Don was a senior and had been anointed "Scholar of the House" at Davenport College, which meant that he didn't have to take any formal classes but had only to pursue his passion, which was oil paint-ing. It was a great honor to be Scholar of the House, a title that was reserved only for those deemed "brilliant" or "genius" by the powers that be. Don was, however, part of Tim O'Brian's inner circle, which consisted of four or five other Davenport guys and now, by default, me. There were others who aspired to be part of the inner circle but they would come in and out of Tim's world infrequently because the heat in that room was too intense for all but the most resilient of fel-low musketeers.

Don asked me what I thought of my new roommate and I told him a little about what had transpired in the middle of the night. He smiled a wry, ironic smile and said that he had better fill me in.

First of all, Don explained that the growling and puking were probably due to the Z bags, which were $10 bags of heroin supplied by a mysterious fellow named Zorba, who was the local dealer. (Hence the term "Z bags.") Don told me that Tim had gone to Exeter, a swank boys' boarding school on the East Coast that was a feeder school for Harvard, Princeton, and Yale. Tim had been raised in a privileged but highly dysfunctional family and his father was a famous cartoonist for *The New Yorker* magazine who had divorced his mother some years prior to Tim's acceptance at Yale. Then Don told me why I had been chosen to be his roommate in the fourth-floor two-bedroom suite in the lower courtyard of Davenport College.

The previous year, Tim had lived off campus with another fellow in a small two-bedroom house. He and his erstwhile roommate had become enchanted (that's the kindest way of putting it) with the wares of Mr. Zorba during the winter semester and had neglected their studies. As the story goes—and the "story" had been corroborated by many sources, including the local press—Tim and his roommate had some important papers due in order to finish the winter term, and because of the distraction posed to them by heroin, they were unable to finish, much less start, these assignments. The two of them came up with a brilliant plan to excuse themselves from their obligations. Their house would be randomly firebombed by gang vandals and would burn to the ground, thereby incinerating their work and letting them off the hook.

They put a bunch of books and papers in the ground-floor den, fashioned a Molotov cocktail with some gas and a milk bottle, and then one of them walked outside, lit the bomb, and tossed it through the den window, setting the house ablaze. Tim called the fire department to report the heinous attack and told them that the house was on fire. The firefighters arrived, as did the arson investigators. Since footprints in the snow showed that someone had walked out of the house to the exact spot in front of the window from which the cocktail was launched into the den, and then returned to the front door, it was immediately determined to have been an inside job. Tim and his roommate were arrested, and suspended from Yale for the remainder of the year.

Tim's family made some kind of a deal with the chief of police and the charges were dropped against him, but the other fellow, as the story goes, went away for a while. Tim was allowed to return to school, but only on the condition that he live on campus with a roommate. There was not a soul at Yale who would agree to live with him, so they found me, the unsuspecting hippie transfer student from Berkeley. Thank you, Yale! I have always found it odd that I had two roommates while in college and both had a love affair with heroin. Even Gene the junkie was Winnie the Pooh compared to Tim, who not only liked heroin but preferred to mix it with pot, Olde English "800," cocaine, and occasionally LSD.

Don seemed to relish giving me the more sordid details of Tim's life. I found out that Tim had actually romanced the love of Don's life, whisking her off for a short fling that broke Don's heart. But Tim had a magnetism that caused people to forgive him even for the most egregious betrayals. Long after I had finished my eggs, Don kept recounting stories about this man he loved to hate and hated to love but loved nevertheless. Don was just about to tell me about Tim's latest sexual escapade when we heard a cheery voice behind us. "Hey, boys! What's for breakfast? I'm starving!"

Standing behind us, fresh as a daisy and with a huge grin on his face, was Tim O'Brian, who looked like he had just walked out of a week at a health spa. Who was this guy? What was this guy? Tim sat down with us and proceeded to tell me that he was thrilled I was going to be his roommate. There was no mention of the growling, the knife throwing, or the vomit from the night before. Nor would there ever be. In fact, Tim and I became good friends, and thankfully the only habit I picked up from him was smoking unfiltered Camel cigarettes, which I gave up after my junior year. We remained friends until July of 1974, when an incident outside Mexico City's Anthropological Museum drove a permanent wedge between us, but I'll get to that later.

Yale, Schmale

My first semester at Yale was not pleasant, not only because of the academic distraction caused by my daily association with Tim O'Brian, but also because I was constantly pining for Evie, who had chickened out of her transfer to Bennington and returned to Berkeley to remain three thousand miles away. I was so dogged by the ache in my heart that I packed up my stuff to drive back to Berkeley for the Christmas break, having decided to take everything except the water bed and to just leave New Haven for good.

When I told Tim what I was going to do, he lit up and said, "Hey, I have an old girlfriend in San Francisco. I'll go with you and help drive." I had now driven solo across the country a couple of times so I knew how exhausting it was, but, on the other hand, I doubted how much help Tim would really be. In the end, the pros of having a companion outweighed the cons of Tim's lead foot, and I figured I could get him to slow down a bit. I was pretty reluctant to sit in the passenger seat, given my experience outside Front Royal, Virginia, and I told Tim that I would do most of the driving. As we set off, Tim made a show of organizing a few items he said he needed for the drive. Among them was a bag of marijuana that he put in the glove box, a bottle of Harvey's Shooting Sherry, which he said kept him alert while he drove, a case of Olde English "800" for liquids, and a wooden matchbox that he put on the dashboard along with a straw. I asked what was in the matchbox and he opened it, revealing a bright orange powder. "Pure pharmaceutical Sandoz!" was all he said. I knew what

that was. It was the purest form of LSD made in the Sandoz labora-
tory and available on the street for an exorbitant price. It came in pill
form and Tim had ground up four or five pills into a powder, which
he would snort using the straw whenever he became tired from too
much pot, Shooting Sherry, or Olde English "800." This was going to
be one heck of a cross-country drive!

At some point during the fall, I'd had a new radio with a tape
player installed in the car so at least we had music. Tim was a country
music freak and we listened to endless Hank Williams while I drove
and Tim continued to get as blotto as possible. The good news was
that he was so wasted that he slept for most of the drive, which took
five days. And when he was awake, he was fairly incoherent due to
the combination of pot, LSD, and Olde English "800." He was right
about one thing, though: the Shooting Sherry, taken in the proper
dose, did take the edge off the monotony of the nonstop driving
and also had enough sugar to keep me on my toes. We slept in seedy
motels and arrived in San Francisco on the twenty-second of December. I'll never forget the sound of forty or fifty empty beer cans rolling
around in the backseat every time we went around a corner.

I dropped Tim off at his former girlfriend's house. Her name was
Joan and Tim was obsessed with her. The class of 1974 was the first
class at Yale to ever admit women, and she had the distinction of
being the first female graduate. She had finished her coursework there
in two years and was later the recipient of the MacArthur Founda-
tion's ultraprestigious Genius Award for being inhumanly smart. Joan
went on to work with Jonas Salk on the creation of a vaccination for
the HIV virus. Tim's plan was to stay in San Francisco for a few days
and then fly back to New York, where he would spend the rest of the
holiday with his mother. I would drive south to Los Angeles to see
Evie and to tell my folks about my plans to drop out of Yale.

The news did not go over well with my parents. As expected, they
blew a gasket and could not believe that I would throw away such an
opportunity. I reminded them that they were not paying my tuition

and really had nothing to say on the matter. Regardless of who was paying what, they were beside themselves. I kept telling them I had made up my mind to go back to Berkeley because I was in love and, by God, love always comes first. That argument went over well. My mother, who disliked any girl I brought around, bellowed, "Who is this girl? Where is she from? Does she come from a good family? She's not Jewish, is she?" That, of course, would be the coup de grâce.

My folks were country club people of white, Anglo-Saxon, Protestant descent who could not tolerate even the remotest possibility that I might someday mix our Hamlin blood with what they considered to be the blood of an inferior race or social class. I always wanted to remind them that the name Hamlin meant "swineherd" in German and that we really had no justification for our high-and-mighty attitude. We were descended from pig farmers, for God's sake! That is quite possibly why I find pork disgusting.

I told my mother that my lover's name was Evie Lewis and that her father worked for Occidental Petroleum in their legal department and that I was going to bring her over to the house that night for dinner. They could meet her and judge for themselves. All my mother said was, "Lewis! . . . That's a common name." I wanted to scream back at her that the most famous person in America with her maiden name, Robinson, was a black baseball player, but I didn't. She would have had a coronary.

I had made a date with Evie for that night, but having her meet the parental units was not in my original plan. Rather I had been hoping we might find someplace where we could screw like rabbits since I hadn't seen her in months. But I felt I owed it to someone that I follow through with this meeting, at least to give my folks a chance to see what a sweet and lovely girl she was. I hopped into Beulah and drove from Pasadena to Mandeville Canyon, which was clear across the Los Angeles basin, to see the woman of my dreams. I was not disappointed when I arrived at her father's house. She had not changed a bit. There she was, barefoot and clad only in worn-out overalls and a sleeveless peasant shirt. She smelled so good and we hugged and sucked face for an eternity until I finally broke the news that we were going to be driving out to Pasadena to have dinner with my folks.

To my surprise, she was really excited to meet them and couldn't wait to get started. She said, "Let's go now!" And she jumped into the car. This was all well and good and I was sure glad that she was game to meet the parents, but I guess I had hoped that she might throw on a different outfit. But then I remembered that this was Evie—she never wore shoes, even in the rain, and she only owned overalls and bell-bottoms. She didn't even own a skirt or a dress, and to top it off (or to "add insult to injury," depending on one's point of view), she was hirsute, in the European sense of the word. This meant that she never shaved her armpits or her legs, choosing instead to sport a healthy tuft of black hair under her arms. I had not thought about this angle when I blurted out that I was bringing her over for dinner. Now I was thinking about it, and I could only imagine the disaster this meeting was going to be. I got behind the wheel and drove toward certain catastrophe.

Evie squealed when she saw our Craftsman-style house as I pulled into the driveway. She loved that period and loved the whole Craftsman vibe. I had not warned her about my mother, hoping against hope that everything would magically go smoothly in spite of the wardrobe and underarm hair issues. Evie, always cheerful and full of life, jumped out of the car and raced me to the front door, her bare feet padding alongside me. I opened the door and my mother was standing in the foyer with a glass of gin in one hand and a just-lit Kent cigarette in the other. She had changed into a smart gold skirt and fuchsia blouse for the occasion. She looked Evie up and down and burst into laughter. "Mom, this is Evie," I said. My mother said nothing and the laughter turned into a snarl as she walked toward the girl, as though she was going to hit her. I believe, to this day, had I not pulled Evie out of the way, my mother might have been sent up the river for manslaughter.

I dragged Evie into the kitchen and shut the door only to hear my mother yelling something about the "little tramp" as we darted out the side door and back into Beulah. Evie seemed to take it all in stride, only commenting that my mother wasn't a very nice person, which, of course, was true. I took Evie home, and lucky for us, her father and sister had gone out to dinner so we got to the exchange-of-bodily-fluids thing we had both been hoping for.

As I left her house, she told me that she and her dad and her sister were going out of town until after New Year's Day and that I wouldn't see her again until we got back to Berkeley. She was always doing that. She would hold back vital information that would have an extreme emotional impact on me and then blurt it out at the last minute. Well, I could wait a week and a half. I'd waited this long. I kissed her good-bye and headed back to Pasadena, where I would spend the next eight days being battered and bruised about everything from my horrible taste in women to the absolute stupidity of dropping out of Yale.

Of course, all of that only hardened my resolve until New Year's Eve, when I took a walk down by my old elementary school, which was a few blocks from the house. I ran into a childhood friend and his mother, who were out taking a walk as well. They had heard that I had gone to Yale and were thrilled for me. They asked me how it was going and I told them that Yale was fine but I was dropping out for true love.

My friend's mother, who was a bit looney but very smart, said in a calm voice, "Harry, I'm sure your girlfriend is perfectly nice, but what are the odds that she will be your girlfriend in five years? And if you graduate from Yale, how long will you have that degree?" I had to give that one some thought. Given that the odds were very against my family ever accepting Evie, and given her free spirit, I began to see how much sense this woman was making. Then my childhood friend took me aside and whispered, "Man, if I had the chance to go to Yale I wouldn't let some pussy stand in the way. That would be just crazy!" That clinched it. I decided then and there to drive back to New Haven that night.

Snow Angels

It was New Year's Eve and I had to be registered for the second semester by the fourth of January. That meant I would have to make it from Pasadena to New Haven in three days. I had to leave within the hour. I ran home to inform my parents of my decision, which was both good news and bad news for them. They thought it was crazy for me to start driving across the country at night, especially on New Year's Eve, but I told them I had no choice. I threw my stuff into the car and left a little room in case I picked up a hitchhiker who could help drive.

The first night was uneventful, and even when I tried to, I couldn't sleep, so I just kept driving, stopping only for gas. About halfway across New Mexico, it became apparent that it was January. The temperature dropped like a stone and there was snow on the ground. By the time I was crossing the Texas Panhandle, it was really winter. Route 66 was straight as an arrow for hundreds of miles, and the prairie on either side of me was a blanket of fresh snow three or four feet deep. I had been making good time, driving at least 80 miles per hour most of the way, but out there, in the middle of the night, I decided to step on it a bit more and took it up to 90, flirting with the idea of trying to average 100 miles per hour.

There was no one else on the road and I had my new radio blaring country music, so off I went, occasionally checking the rearview mirror for cops. That's when I had an odd thought. I was on a main interstate and even in the middle of the night there had always been some traffic on the road. Yet I hadn't seen anyone for at least an hour. Where was everyone? Then I began putting two and two together, and it wasn't long before I started questioning my decision to walk away from religion. I would also continue singing the praises of BMW for years to come.

Some fifty miles back, I had decided that I would have my headlights checked at the next service station because they seemed to be pointed downward too much. I hadn't given it much thought. I figured a minor adjustment would fix the problem. The lights were glaring off the highway in a way I had not seen before, and it was somewhat annoying. After driving for some time with this annoying glare, I heard the DJ on the station I was listening to say something about the ongoing problem on 66 and he urged drivers to avoid it altogether. What ongoing problem? Being from Southern California, I had never heard of black ice before, but at that moment it dawned on me that I was driving at close to 100 miles per hour on an invisible sheet of ice, which was why there was no one else on the road. Oh shit!

The good news was that the highway was absolutely straight so I had no reason to turn the wheel, which would have sent me into an immediate spin. I took my foot off the gas and the car began gradually slowing down. Then I saw the one thing I least needed to see: a pair of taillights about a mile ahead. I couldn't put on the brakes because that would also set me spinning. I could tell that the car in front of me was driving at about five miles an hour, which would have been protocol for anyone stupid enough to drive on black ice in the first place. I was now going about 80 and needed to slow down or else I would have to turn my wheels to avoid slamming into the car ahead. What to do? I decided that the least jarring thing to do was to downshift. I was now going about 70. I grabbed the shift knob, stepped on the clutch, and put her into second gear. Whoops! Wrong choice! The car instantly went into a spin, turning like a top and careening down Route 66 totally out of control.

The spinning went on for what seemed like an eternity until I felt the car fly off the road and into a ditch on the side of the highway. Beulah was completely covered with snow but she was upright with the lights still on. And I was still alive. Unfortunately, Beulah's engine had died. She was on a slight incline sideways and down on the right, and I couldn't tell which direction we were pointing. I was, of course, somewhat dazed and confused as I came to the conclusion that, more than likely, the first thing they teach you in "how to drive on black ice school" would be, never downshift! But having never been to that school, now I was in a ditch in a stalled car, covered with snow, at 3 a.m., miles and miles from civilization, with an outside temperature well below freezing.

I tried opening the door but the snow was too heavy. I tried the windshield wipers but they just struggled against the snow. I knew that opening the window would only lead to a cascade of cold snow all over me so I just sat there, contemplating my options, which quickly dwindled to one. The temperature in the car was falling rapidly and it was all I could do to keep my teeth from chattering. I had no idea if the car would start. I knew that if it did start, but I was stuck, I would be tempted to keep the car on to have enough heat not to freeze to death, but I also knew if I did that, by morning I would probably be dead from carbon monoxide poisoning. I had read somewhere that freezing to death wasn't so bad; you got really cold and then went to sleep as you became a human Popsicle. I knew I would be dead in a couple of hours if my one option failed. I had to start the car, put it in first gear, and drive, through the snow, back up onto that road. For that to happen, the car would have to start, I would have to be pointed in the right direction, and there couldn't be anything blocking me.

I remembered that the highway was built a few feet above the prairie, hence the ditch on the side of the road; but because of all the snow, I had no idea if there were boulders or debris in the ditch. I just had to go for it. I reached down and turned the key and, of course, it turned over but didn't start. Maybe it was flooded. I knew that if a carburetor was flooded, the thing to do was put the pedal to the metal and try again. I did that and still nothing. I turned off the lights to save the battery and kept trying. Meanwhile, my breath was steaming and the windshield was fogged with frozen condensation.

The pedal-to-the-metal thing hadn't worked so I decided to wait a few minutes to let the carburetor clear. I had a little Harvey's Bristol Cream in the car that I had filched from my dad's liquor cabinet, so I had myself what could have been my last cocktail as I wondered why I had listened to my friend Steve and his looney tunes mom. I could have been sleeping soundly next to Evie having just had outrageous sex. Instead, I was dying in a ditch in the Texas Panhandle. I finished the bottle of Harvey's and reached down to turn the key one last time.

I drove Beulah for twenty-four years, and when I gave her to my assistant, in 1994, I told him that she was not a car but an angel who had saved my life on more than one occasion. For when I turned the key that last time, she started up and drove right up through the snow and back onto the black ice on Route 66. The ultimate driving machine!

I got to Yale at around 5:00 p.m. on the third of January. I had not slept for seventy-two hours, and though I seemed normal physically, I was beginning to hallucinate. I also hadn't eaten in twenty-four hours. I parked Beulah behind Davenport and dragged myself up to our room. Not much had changed. Tim, Don, and Frank were sitting around smoking a joint and taking swigs from a bottle of Ezra Brooks, a Jack Daniels imitation that cost about half the price of the real thing and tasted like paint remover. Their jaws dropped when they saw me in the doorway. Not a soul knew that I had decided to come back and Tim had already moved into my water bed room. Everyone was glad to see me, though, and they took me out for pizza and beer.

I slept for almost twenty-four hours and was able to register for the winter semester. The seventy-two hours without sleep did some permanent damage, though, and I don't recommend that anyone ever try it. I still had to break the news to Evie that I was three thousand miles away and would be for the foreseeable future. When I told her she seemed okay with it, and I knew then that Mrs. Russell had been right on the money. I did see Evie a few more times, but the writing was on the wall, and soon she fell in love with a saxophone player, married him, had at least one kid with him, and then buried him after he succumbed to leukemia. I have not spoken to her since then, though I did visit when they were living on a houseboat in Sausalito in 1975.

But I remained obsessed with Evie for another couple of years after returning to Yale and only really found that quality of love again when I met Lisa, to whom I have been married for thirteen years.

Mount Washington

The winter semester was all about doing plays. I did an adaptation of John Dos Passos's *U.S.A.* and the American premiere of a play called *Mad Dog Blues* by a new and somewhat avant-garde young playwright named Sam Shepard.

I had forgotten how brutal New England winters could be and I spent every gray day trying to convince myself that I had not screwed up by returning to the Ivy League. But the time passed and winter broke into spring and then I remembered how glorious New England could be. Tim and I were getting along great. He had met a girl named Sarah from an old established and moneyed family. Sarah had a positive influence on him when it came to the drugs and alcohol so there was much less erratic behavior and no growling at all.

One Wednesday in early April, I overheard a conversation at dinner about a great mountain for backpacking in New Hampshire. At about that time of year I would always get a hankering for a hike, and that year the weather was perfect. We were having a heat wave with a string of days in the 80s. I jumped into the conversation next to me to ask about this place. They said it was called Mount Washington and that it was about three hours north. This was sounding pretty good. If I could get someone to go with me, we could rent packs and a tent and go camping for the weekend. Because the weather was so great, I got on it immediately.

I went back to the room and Tim was there with Sarah, Frank, and one of Tim's old flames, Jackie. I told them about the camping idea, and possibly because of the number of joints they had smoked, they all said they wanted in. We scrambled to get all the gear together. There were little three-sided lean-tos a few hours up from the base of the mountain so we wouldn't need tents, just some plastic to cover one side in case it rained, which it wouldn't because the weather was so perfect. And there was a stream for water—and no cows!

We packed everything into both BMWs and set off for New Hampshire early on a Saturday morning. It was a beautiful spring day and we were all thrilled to get into nature after being cooped up all winter. It took a bit longer than planned to get to the base, but we knew that if we got started hiking right away we'd make it up to the lean-tos well before dark. It was blazing hot in the parking lot and we thought about leaving behind some of our warm jackets, but I reminded everyone that it might be cold at the top of the mountain. Our packs were ridiculously heavy, mainly because we all wanted to have our night in the wilderness without sacrificing any creature comforts.

We took up two bottles of red wine, a bottle of Shooting Sherry, and a full bottle of Ezra Brooks whiskey. I carried five plastic plates and we each had a wineglass and silverware we had stolen from the dining hall. I had rented a Svea stove along with my pack and sleeping bag and bought a kerosene lantern for light after dark. I also had a frying pan, spatula, and a small ax for pounding in the roofing nails if we needed to put up plastic. Frank carried one of those fold-up army-issue shovels for pooping purposes. We were fully loaded. I wouldn't dream of packing all that stuff today.

The dinner menu consisted of flank steaks, sautéed spinach, and sautéed mushrooms in a cream sherry sauce. We carried only fresh food, nothing dried. For breakfast we planned eggs with toast and bacon, and for lunch and the hike down we had several Italian salamis. We hoisted up our packs and set off for a great night in the New

Hampshire wilderness. It didn't seem odd to us that when we set off there were only two cars in the base camp parking lot. They were both BMWs, one orange and one beige, or as I liked to call it, Sahara.

Up we went through the beautiful spring foliage. We huffed and puffed and after an hour Tim stopped and reached into his pocket. He pulled out a little envelope and said, "I don't think I'm gonna make it without some help. Here, we oughta all take this." At which point he produced five or six little bits of colored paper, each with a tiny picture of Felix the Cat printed on one side. It was the latest and greatest blotter acid. He said, "This stuff has speed in it and it'll make us fly up this mountain!" Frank, Sarah, and Tim all put Felix on their tongues but Jackie and I took a pass. I knew from experience that it wouldn't have much effect on Tim, but I had no clue what to expect from Sarah or Frank. And if my time in the redwoods of La Honda was any indication, it was going to be a memorable night for them.

We continued on and came to what must have been the halfway point. Just as Frank remarked that he thought he could feel the drug "coming on," we stopped in front of a big sign that said WARNING! MT. WASHINGTON CAN HAVE SEVERE WEATHER CHANGES THAT OCCUR WITHOUT WARNING. HIKERS HAVE DIED ON THE MOUNTAIN. PLEASE USE ONLY THE SHELTERS PROVIDED FOR OVERNIGHT CAMPING. We all looked at one another, and Sarah and Tim and Frank burst out laughing. The acid was working!

Jackie and I were not laughing. We eyed the sky, which was no longer blue but a steely gray. Nor were there any new leaves on the deciduous foliage. The sun went behind the newly formed clouds and the temperature seemed to drop twenty degrees.

But on we marched, and Tim and his merry band were indeed hiking faster than Jackie and I. Soon, however, we began to see remnants of snow, which got thicker and thicker with each step we took, and within an hour we were walking through snow a foot deep and getting deeper. The sky was now dark gray and the slight breeze had turned into a full-blown wind. It was almost six o'clock and starting to get dark. We had no idea how far away the shelters were. We kept trudging through the snow, which was now three feet deep. I mentioned, in passing, to Jackie that we were walking through snow but that ours were the only footprints. She didn't say anything but I knew what she was thinking.

The first snowflake drifted onto my nose at around six thirty. About the same time, the wind began to howl through the trees, and darkness was imminent. The snow was still about three feet thick when we rounded a bend in the trail and saw our first lean-to shelter. Hallelujah!

We all breathed a sigh of relief and practically ran to that lean-to. Tim was the first one there and I saw a look on his face that was not good. The shelter, which only had three sides, was filled with snow right up to the roof. We took off our packs and looked at the other shelters, all of which were packed with a winter's worth of ice and snow. Oh shit!

The snow was coming down hard and the wind was really whipping up. I started to dig the snow out of the first shelter with my hatchet and Frank handed his shovel to Jackie. We dug and dug till we had carved out an igloolike structure. I hung the plastic and secured it with roofing nails, which wasn't easy because the wind was making the plastic flap all over the place.

We piled into our new home and scraped the snow off the floor so it would at least be dry inside. It was pitch-dark by the time we settled in, and everyone was hungry. I fired up the lantern while Frank and Sarah lollygagged blissfully in never-never land. Tim seemed to be okay as he rolled a couple of joints. I was going to be the chef so I made a little space for the kitchen and lit the stove. I started cooking and sent Sarah out to get some water from the little stream nearby for after-dinner hot chocolate. We opened a bottle of red wine, broke out the crystal wineglasses, and once we were organized, we all toasted the fact that we had made it to the top alive.

When the steaks were done, I put everything in the frying pan to warm it up and looked around for Sarah. No Sarah. She had gone outside with a flashlight and a pan for water at least twenty minutes earlier. No one noticed that she hadn't come back. I grabbed a flashlight and ducked out into the blizzard.

"Sarah!" I shouted. No response. "Sarah!" I shouted louder, trying to be heard over the howling wind. Still nothing. I walked over to the stream, and there she was, lying in the snow, holding up a handful of snowflakes to the flashlight. She looked up at me and said, "Have you ever really looked at a snowflake? It's incredible!" Sarah was covered with snow in the middle of a blizzard and transfixed by a snowflake. I pulled her up, brushed off the snow, and got her back inside the structure.

It was almost ten o'clock by the time we got around to eating. The Ezra Brooks and the sherry were set up on a flat log I had found outside so it looked like a little bar. Between the lantern and the stove, which I kept on to boil the water that Sarah had forgotten to get, it was actually getting warm inside our wigwam. I served everyone a plate of steak and sautéed veggies, poured everyone a glass of wine, and we set about our gourmet mountain feast. Just as we dug in, we heard a loud wail just outside the igloo. A few seconds later, the plastic was ripped aside and two bearded men covered with snow tumbled into the shelter. "Oh my God! Oh my God!" shouted one man in a hoarse voice. The other man looked up and, through a completely frozen beard, squealed, "Thank God you are here! We were on the top of the bowl when the storm hit! We lost most of our gear. We saw the light and made it down the mountain. Thank God you are here!"

As they caught their breath, they looked around at the stunned and stoned group they had envisioned as their rescuers. They saw that we were eating steak with silverware and that we each had a crystal glass with red wine, and no doubt they smelled the pot that Tim had been smoking nonstop; I'm sure they had a twilight zone moment. I saw them clock the "bar" and the bottles of wine, and then Frank looked into their eyes and asked, "Wow! Are you guys tripping too?"

The two men, who moments before had been thanking the Lord for finding us, looked at each other, looked one more time at us, and then bolted back out into the blizzard. We never saw or heard from them again. They chose possible death over a bunch of stoned-out Yalies in an igloo.

A Night in the Hamptons

When we got back to New Haven, it was 90 degrees and humid. It may have been spring at Yale but it was definitely winter on the top of Mount Washington. We finished up the semester, I still pined for Evie, and after the last day of classes on June 1, Tim invited me and Sarah and a couple of other friends out to East Hampton to visit his mother. On a beautiful June day, six of us caravanned out to Long Island in two cars, but Tim's mom's house didn't have room for all of us so we decided to have a picnic on the beach and sleep there.

We had a great time. We made a little beach fire, roasted hot dogs, drank wine, and played guitar. It would have been one of those great summer nights that you remember forever solely because it was just plain fun, except that at dawn we were unceremoniously dumped out of our sleeping bags by three of East Hampton's finest. The experience was becoming memorable for a host of other reasons.

We landed in a naked pile on the sand with the officers bellowing that we were being arrested for trespassing. Apparently there is some law about not sleeping on the beach in East Hampton. We were allowed to get dressed, then we were cuffed and led to three waiting police cars. This bust had been carefully planned by these cops, who probably never had more to do than respond to lost cats and dogs. I don't think there's a lot of violent crime in East Hampton. The cops gathered up our stuff for "evidence," and as we were being marched away, I heard one of the officers squeal that he had found drugs. Well, a roach to be exact; probably one of Tim's leftovers.

Now the cops were frothing at the mouth. Not only did they have indigent beach sleepers but *pot-smoking* indigent beach sleepers! We were taken to the station, and when they asked who the roach belonged to and we all replied that we didn't know, they decided to book all of us with possession of dangerous drugs. They fingerprinted us and threw us in the one jail cell in East Hampton. They were nice enough to give us a blanket so that when one of the girls had to pee, the others would hold up the blanket for a modicum of privacy.

Tim made his one call to his mother, who was mortified to have to go to the East Hampton jail to bail out her son and his friends. We had been in jail for about five hours when she finally arrived and we were sure glad to see her. After my experience in Redwood City, I had sworn that I would never see the inside of a jail again but there I was, hating every second.

We all watched as Mrs. O'Brian filled out the paperwork and presented the officers with the bail money. Then one of the cops came over to the cell with the keys, and as he unlocked the cell, he yelled at me to step to the back against the wall. He let the others out and locked me back in. Tim asked the officer why I couldn't come out and the officer replied in a terse voice, "None of your business! Be glad you are out." Tim said, "But there must be some reason." And another cop shouted, "He said it was none of your business! Now get out of here!" And with that they left.

The mood in the station had become very serious and my heart sank when I saw my friends walk out the door. What had happened? My guess was that they had found out about my previous arrest and that I was on probation in California. Technically I was not even supposed to be out of the state of California, but my probation officer had been so overwhelmed that he had told me that I didn't need to check in with him after the first year. I figured that my ass was grass and that I would be extradited to California, where I would have to serve out the rest of my one-year sentence. I was fucked.

One by one, the East Hampton police officers walked by the cell and just frowned at me like I had killed their dog. Then the head cop—I guess you call that guy the captain—came over holding a mimeographed sheet of paper. He looked at me with a scowl and said, "You want to tell me about New Orleans?"

"New Orleans?" I said. "It's a city in the South. I think it's in Louisiana." That was not the answer the captain was after and he went ballistic!

"Don't get smart-ass with me, you sniveling pissant!" he screamed. That was the second time I had been called a pissant in jail. What the fuck was a pissant? I have later learned that the term is used by drill sergeants in one or more branches of our armed forces during boot camp. It is used to make the person on the receiving end shake in their boots. I was not wearing boots, but I was shaking.

The captain calmed himself down and in a much softer voice asked again, "I want you to tell me about New Orleans."

I said, "I don't know what to say. I told you pretty much all I know about it. They have good music and there's a French Quarter, but I've never been there so I really don't know what to say."

"You've never been there?" he said in a sarcastic, interrogative tone.

"No. I have never even been close," I answered.

Then he looked me in the eye and said, "You lie to me, boy, and you will rue the day you ever set foot in East Hampton. Now I want the truth."

I said, "Excuse me, but I think you have the wrong person in mind. What happened in New Orleans that you think I had something to do with?"

Now the whole department, all five officers, were standing around the cell peering in at the caged criminal. One of the cops offered, "You killed a cop in New Orleans in February. That's what you did!"

I didn't know whether to be relieved or terrified. They didn't know about my California parole violation, but now they thought I was a cop killer. My heart was beating a mile a minute. These guys looked like they were going to take me outside and string me up on one of the famous East Hampton elms.

Brushing my teeth in East Hampton Jail, summer 1973.

One of the officers was on the phone at a desk and was looking at me while he was talking. He had the mimeographed rap sheet in his hand. He hung up the phone, pushed his way through the ogling uniforms, and just said in a matter-of-fact tone, "Let him out." The others gasped, "What? Let him out?" The phone cop said, "Yup. Our guy's a nigger! Same name, different color. Let him out." Back in those days the N word was still used to describe the darker race and you could still get pancakes from a place called Little Black Sambo's. We've come a long way, baby, and thank God for it!

They let me out and gave me my things but never once said they were sorry about the mix-up. They let me call Tim's mother and Tim came and picked me up. All the way back to the house, the one thing that dogged me was that there was a black guy somewhere named Harry Hamlin, and he had supposedly killed a cop. I hoped we weren't related. I haven't been back to East Hampton since.

Bill Ball

Tim and I decided to drive back to Berkeley for the summer. I couldn't get Evie out of my mind and I thought there might be a chance for me to pry her away from her saxophone player. After all, what did he have that I didn't besides a big horn? This time the drive out was uneventful. No acid for Tim and only a little Shooting Sherry. We found a house with a couple of rooms for rent that had at least a thousand six-foot-tall marijuana plants in the backyard. This, of course, delighted Tim but was no thrill for me. Not only did I not smoke the stuff but I was still on summary probation from my little experience at the airport in 1970. If the cops busted everyone in the house, I would go up the river for at least a year. Fortunately, on the fourth day of our stay there, someone robbed the backyard and stole every last plant. Tim was destroyed, I was overjoyed.

We didn't have any activities planned for our visit to Berkeley, and since I couldn't even locate Evie, I decided to visit the Zellerbach Playhouse, where I had done the play *Danton's Death* by Georg Büchner. I walked down into the bowels of the theatre and Nate, the stage door man, told me that ACT, the American Conservatory Theater, was going to film their production of *Cyrano de Bergerac* there the following week for PBS. I hatched a plan.

I went up to the street to a pay phone and got the number of ACT from Directory Assistance. I called the theatre and asked who ran the place. The receptionist told me his name was Bill Ball and I said, "Okay, could you put me through to him, please?" She said, "Honey child, no one gets put through to Mr. Ball. I will put you through to his assistant's assistant, though." And she did.

A very gay fellow took my call and I explained to him that I was a Yale theatre arts student and that I had spent two years at Berkeley in the drama department and that I was back for the summer. I knew my way around and I could probably be of assistance to whoever was filming the play. He put me on hold and came back to say that I should come meet with him to discuss how I might be able to help. We set up the meeting and I hung up the phone.

The next day, I arrived at the ACT office and was greeted by a kind and cheery African-American receptionist who, when I told her who I was, introduced herself as Beulah. I almost said, "That's the name of my car!" but thought better of it.

She then said, "Honey child, you've got a lot of nerve callin' up Mr. Ball like that out of the blue. You got yourself some moxie!"

I didn't know the term "moxie," but I figured it was a good thing. She led me into the back office and introduced me to Tony, a raven-haired young man wearing a long scarf—an obvious fashion statement because it was June. Tony looked at me the way a vampire eyes fresh blood and said, "He must meet Gino! Don't you think?" He grabbed my arm and led me down another hall and into Gino's office.

Gino was also gay. He was an older gentleman, around fifty, and well dressed in sport coat and button-down shirt. I introduced myself and told Gino a little of my story: Pasadena, Berkeley, Yale, Berkeley again, etc., and he just put one hand up to his face like Jack Benny and said, "Well, look at you!"

Tony replied, "I think he should meet Mr. Ball. Don't you?"

Gino stood up and took my arm and led me into a glass office containing a huge desk at one end occupied by a small, balding, pink sort of man wearing all white. Gino said, "Bill, this is the young man who called about being your assistant. His name is Harry Hamill."

And Gino left the room. Bill stood up and shook my hand. His hands were pink and soft as though they had never held anything rougher than a pencil. This man was obviously brain, not brawn. I corrected Gino and said that my name was Harry Hamlin, not Hamill. Unfortunately the Hamill mistake persists, as I am called Mr. Hamill on an almost daily basis—that along with Mark. Of course, that's because Mark Hamill was the lead in *Star Wars*.

Mr. Ball said, "Please call me Bill," and asked me to take a seat in an ornate gold-leafed chair opposite the desk. He stared at me for a few moments in silence. It wasn't quite the same vampire look I had seen on young Tony's face—it was more restrained—but there was a thirst there nonetheless. It felt as though I had inadvertently walked into the lion's den.

Bill then said in a matter-of-fact voice, "Can you cook? Can you drive a car?"

I saw my chance to set the record straight (no pun intended) and replied, "I have my own car, and as for cooking, my girlfriend says I make a mean western omelet." I could see the fangs start to recede as Bill realized we didn't bat for the same team. To his credit, he remained interested, and after asking a slew of other questions about my life and ambitions, he hired me to be his personal assistant during the three-week shoot at Berkeley.

Bill was a chain-smoker and coffee drinker, and my duties were mainly to light his cigarettes and always make sure he had a fresh cup of coffee within arm's reach. I wasn't supposed to leave his side unless he sent me on an errand. For this, he would pay me $200. I took the job and spent the next three weeks as Bill Ball's shadow. I'm certain that everyone else thought I was his "boy toy" and that I was being rear-ended every day after work. I didn't have a girlfriend to parade around to dispel the rumors, and for years people thought I had had it off with Bill. But the production of *Cyrano* was sublime and I immediately saw why this man was considered a genius, which he was.

In the course of my "work," Bill and I became sort of friends. On my last day as his assistant, we were saying our good-byes in his office and I finally got up the nerve to tell him that I had decided to pursue a career as an actor. I had thought that if I told him before then, he would think I was trying to weasel into his company or his training program, which was not the case. When I told him he just looked at me and said, "Oh, that's interesting." And that was the end of that. He told me I'd been a great assistant, handed me a couple of crisp hundred-dollar bills, wished me luck at Yale, and showed me the door. Case closed, or so I thought.

Rebecca

Our senior year at Yale was pretty much all work and no play. Tim, Frank, and I took a house off campus, which, ironically, was right next door to the chief of the New Haven police department. The same man who had busted Tim for arson two years before. Occasionally they would make eye contact if they were coming or going at the same time. I'm not sure the chief ever made the connection but it made Tim a nervous wreck, and he always checked to see if the man was in his front yard before leaving the house. The rental was a dowdy, unfurnished, four-bedroom. When we moved in, we made countless trips to junk shops for beds and couches. Essentially the place was a dump. But it was our dump and we loved it there.

Senior year was also when I met Rebecca. She was a really cute blond junior who had also been a childhood friend and adolescent paramour of Tim's. She and I first became friends, and then one thing led to another, and we started exchanging bodily fluids on a regular basis. Rebecca looked like she was fourteen even though she was twenty-one. She was quite short and thin and small-boned, and she was a sweet, cute girl without a mean hair on her little head, which was apparently filled with trillions of brain cells because she was also the smartest girl I have ever been with.

I was infatuated with her and we had great sex, which we discovered could be even better after viewing a little porn. Porn was a new thing back in the early seventies. *Deep Throat* had come out when I was at Berkeley and had caused quite a sensation. The university sponsored screenings of it for "cultural purposes" at the International House across the street from the DKE house. Evie and I had attended one of those screenings. Wow! That was my and Evie's first experience with sex on film, and we went back across the street and did the nasty till neither of us could walk.

Happily Yale had a similar screening program. Every Saturday night after midnight the latest, greatest porn was shown in the main dining hall. That is, no doubt, where Justice Clarence Thomas, who was at Yale Law School while I was an undergraduate, might have been exposed to the now infamous Long Dong Silver. It was Long Dong that almost derailed his nomination to the Supreme Court.

Rebecca and I went to one of those dining hall screenings, which was filled to the rafters. They were showing a film called *The Devil in Miss Jones*. There was endless hooting, hollering, and applause during the movie. And, as with Evie, when the movie ended, Rebecca and I went back to my place and did the nasty till dawn. We discovered that there was a theatre in town that served up a new X-rated flick every Wednesday night and we decided to check it out.

The law in New Haven was that there had to be a cop standing in the back of a porn theatre checking IDs and making sure that nothing untoward was going on in the audience, which was surprisingly mostly couples. When we walked in, the officer saw what looked to him like a twentysomething guy with a fourteen-year-old blond goddess. He insisted that we leave immediately until Rebecca pulled out her driver's license and Yale ID, which proved that she was twenty-one. I had to show my ID, too, and after giving us a funny look, the cop smiled and said, "Enjoy the movie." Which we did very much, and that became our ritual for several months.

We couldn't wait for Wednesday! Every couple of weeks we would show up and a cop would tell us to leave because Rebecca looked so young. But she'd whip out her ID and in we'd go.

We usually walked home from the theatre holding hands and critiquing the film. Anyone seeing these two fresh-faced kids walking across the Yale campus in the moonlight would probably have thought we were debating the merits of Proust or Sartre, but no, it was more than likely that we were discussing what we were going to do to one another when we got home. I would say that was the year of my sexual awakening. You can learn a lot from watching those movies and we did. I never dreamed that I would be introduced to them with such a sweet and innocent girl.

But I also learned a lot about Proust and Sartre that year and worked really hard writing my senior thesis, which was, and remains, completely incomprehensible. I got an A. Probably for incomprehensibility.

The year passed quickly, and Rebecca and I stayed glued to the hip—or thereabouts. I had become fascinated with a place called the Yucatán. The name sounded so exotic and primitive. I proposed to Tim, Frank, and Don that we organize a road trip down there. I showed them some brochures and told them about the miles and miles of unspoiled beaches and the ruins of the ancient Mayan civilization. At first they seemed more than a little skeptical, but eventually I convinced them.

We graduated in late May and Tim managed to find a used blue VW camper for $900. We had it checked out and dubbed it Beulah II. We had decided Beulah was a good name for transcontinental vehicles. I went into New York and bought some scuba gear for $200 and had my dad ship his portable air compressor out by Greyhound bus. We packed up the van and off we went—four recent Yale graduates driving into the complete unknown.

Don, me, and Frank with our VW Bus, "Beulah II,"
in the background, summer 1974.

Mex Trip

We drove pretty much straight through to the Mexican border, stopping only once in Brownsville, Texas, to do laundry at the coin-op. While we were waiting for the clothes to dry, Frank decided to take a spin in the big industrial dryer. He climbed in and Don pushed the On button. He had a hell of a ride for a few seconds, then started screaming his head off. I think he thought it would be something like Disneyland, and had forgotten that dryers get really hot inside.

That was Frank. He was a loveable, affable guy who took life as it came, didn't complain, and never seemed to worry. He'd go along with just about anything and he had a twisted, ironic sense of humor. Don was much more serious and introspective. He was a philosopher/painter who would have thrived in Paris in the late nineteenth century drinking absinthe and ruminating over the absurdity of existence. Tim was a junkie but a loveable junkie who, we discovered after we crossed the U.S.-Mexico border, had spirited away some thirty tabs of high-grade LSD for fun and games on the journey. Tim was an intellectual with a heart of gold. He carried a copy of James Joyce's *Ulysses* with him at all times during the trip and was always quoting odd Joycean lines as he read. He was an alcoholic and a drug addict, but he was also a cum laude graduate of Yale University. Every day Tim would update us on the exploits of Leopold Bloom as he made his way around Dublin.

Frank, me, and Don just before crossing the border—
Frank had banged an eye in the dryer!

Of the group, I was the responsible one. I didn't take acid and have never much liked pot. I was the main driver and navigator. As such, I picked the route we would take to get to the Yucatán Peninsula. That route took us to our first overnight stop deep in Mexico at a town called Palenque where, rumor had it, there was a magnificent Mayan pyramid with a bas-relief of an actual spaceship inside. There was also a very special breed of cow that inhabited the pastures outside of town. As legend had it, the cow shit from these particular cows spawned a certain mushroom with a purple band that, when harvested properly and ingested by a willing cosmic voyager, sent that person deep into the rabbit hole for at least six hours.

Tim and Frank had done extensive research on these mushrooms and told us that they had to be picked from the cow pies at dawn, and that the picker had to wear a special hat. As each mushroom was picked, thanks were to be made to Quetzalcoatl, the winged god of the Mayans. Then the mushroom was to be put into the hat and placed back on the picker's head. The mushroom was then to be washed thoroughly and eaten within twenty-four hours. The recommended dose was four to six mushrooms.

Driving in Mexico in 1974 was not pretty, but we made it to Palenque, where we found a room with three single beds in a cheap pensione not far from the cow pastures.

The plan was to get up before dawn and go hunting for shrooms, and if we actually found any, we would stash them for use in the late afternoon after we had explored the temple with the spaceship. Tim had a Pulsar digital watch, which was the very first digital watch ever sold. It cost more than a thousand dollars and had been a graduation gift from his rich uncle. He was extremely proud of it and would constantly show off its special functions, like an alarm that beeped. No one had ever seen such a thing and we were all suitably impressed by this technological wonder. Now, of course, they can be had for under a dollar. That watch came in handy for our predawn expedition and it woke us up in time to get out into the pasture.

There we were, four Yale graduates clad in jeans and hats, marching into pastures with cows mooing, "What the hell are you doing in our yard?" We spread out in search of the perfect magical pile of shit. We carefully inspected each cow pie but to no avail, until we heard a squeal from Frank in the next pasture. We hopped the rustic wooden fence and saw, to our amazement, that every single plop of cow shit had a six- or seven-inch mushroom growing out of it, each with a thin stem, round top, and, most important, the famous purple band around the center of the stem. Jackpot!! We each picked one, thanked Quetzalcoatl, put it in our hat, put the hat back on, and repeated the process eight times. Done! That was easy.

We traipsed back to our humble room, washed the mushrooms in the sink, and stored them so that we could go explore the ruins. We found the cool sarcophagus cover, but you would have to have a vivid imagination or have eaten lots of magic mushrooms to see aliens and spacecraft in the bas-relief.

Once back at our digs, it was time to sample the organic psychedelics. I was not much of a drug taker but I figured, when in Palenque . . . !

We divided them up into groups of eight and started munching away. They were quite bitter and would have been much better sautéed with a bit of garlic and butter. We persevered, however, and soon they were all down the hatch. We looked at each other, wondering, What next? We decided to take a walk into town. It was a very hot night and we went in search of cold beer.

Tim told us that we shouldn't eat anything but that a few beers wouldn't hurt. We found a little joint that served tacos and beer and made that our home for the evening. We all kept waiting to feel something from the mushrooms, but all I noticed was a slight buzz-on from the cerveza. No one else seemed to feel much either. Tim suggested we go back to the pasture and get a lot more. And then it happened. Almost in unison, we were all belching and farting. My stomach expanded as though someone was blowing it up like a balloon. We went outside, and I projectile vomited all over Don. That started a chain reaction and soon there were four recent Yale graduates puking in the streets of Palenque. I was the sickest and ended up blowing my cookies again all over Don as we slept later that night. It's amazing that Don and I have remained friends for all these years after I barfed on him twice in the same night. We never did get high enough to distinguish between the shrooms and the copious amounts of Corona we had consumed.

The next day, we left for the Yucatán. As we left town, we saw an American hitchhiker and offered to give him a lift. It turned out he really didn't want to go very far—mostly he was trying to sell pot to American tourists. Tim, of course, was overjoyed and shelled out $50 for a one-pound brick of what looked like nothing but buds. Buds

Don, Frank, and I headed for the Yucatán.

were the most-sought-after part of the marijuana plant and Tim had just purchased a pound of them for a paltry $50. We told the fellow about our experience with the mushrooms and he laughed out loud, saying that we had indeed found magic mushrooms, but that they had to be soaked in purified water for a day and washed at least ten times before you could eat them. He said if we washed them in the tap water only once, we had either been poisoned by the water or by the massive amounts of E. coli bacteria that most certainly remained on the mushrooms. He also said that even if we had done that, if the mushrooms had been fresh, we would have had to eat a lot more of them to get really high. So much for the magical mushroom mystery tour! We let our new friend/dealer out and kept going.

Now we were four Yale grads driving toward the Yucatán with enough dope in our vehicle to get us tossed into a rat-infested Mexican jail for life. Being the only person in our little group who had been through all of that before, I was the only one to consider the implications of having that much contraband on board. I reminded the others that we were being stopped at military checkpoints every three or four hundred miles and that, from time to time, the Federales had looked into the car and gone through our stuff. Not to mention the fact that a pound of fresh marijuana buds has an extremely distinctive and overpowering "fragrance." The Federales would certainly "nose" the dope even if they didn't see it. I got more and more paranoid by the mile, until I finally insisted that we dump the dope. No one was happy about my stance on the matter, especially Tim, who had not only paid for it but was most certainly planning on smoking it all. But I wouldn't budge. Finally a compromise was reached.

We inspected the outside of the vehicle and discovered that the two steel beams on either side of the van supporting the chassis were hollow. We broke up the brick and wrapped quarter-pound chunks into rolls that we stuffed into the beams. At the very least, this got the dope out of the car and eliminated the smell. Problem solved, sort of.

Beulah II—you'd never know there was so much pot
stashed in the chassis.

We pulled into the little town of Playa del Carmen on the Yucatán coast late the next day and asked some of the local shopkeepers if it was okay to sleep on the beach. This was definitely not East Hampton, but we wanted to be respectful anyway since we planned to stay on the beach for a month. We found a guy who spoke some English and he said the best place to set up camp would be much farther down the road, not far from a place called Tulum.

Tulum was a small Mayan ruin partially overgrown with vines. There was one other building in Tulum called the Crossroads Café and we ventured in to get our bearings. It turned out that the Crossroads Café was the only store/restaurant/bar for fifty miles in either direction, and they had cold beer and music from 5:00 p.m. to 8:00 p.m., when they turned on their generator to cool down the fridge. They also had a nice menu of tacos and other local delights. They were pretty low on provisions, though, with only a few tins of canned butter from Denmark, some canned milk, and an assortment of canned meats like Spam, and sardines. We were told that the locals brought in bread and fruit each morning. We had no choice but to go on the extreme Tulum diet plan.

We asked about the beach, and the proprietor, who spoke reasonably good English and who said his name was Tony, pointed back up the road and told us to go to Rancho Tankah and ask if we could stay on their beach. We each had a warm beer and then we drove back about three kilometers to a little dirt road with a hand-painted sign that said RANCHO TANKAH. We drove down the little road and came to a run-down hacienda nestled amid a grove of coconut palms. Standing next to the front door was a handsome fiftysomething fellow smoking a cigarette. He didn't budge as we drove up to him. He didn't speak much English but he understood that we wanted to stay there, and he showed us a shed near the beach where we could string up four hammocks. We first tried to build our own palapa on the beach but soon gave up in the extreme heat and decided to accept the shed offer.

The room had a thatched roof and rustic boarded walls supported

Frank and Don on our first day on the beach near where we stayed
at Rancho Tankah. This was our first attempt to build a palapa—
the tent is the one I built with Evie.

by hand-hewn logs that were somehow strong enough to support
our hammocks. The floor was the dirt variety. The place was filled
with old baskets that must have been used to transport coconuts. He
motioned for us to toss the baskets out the rear door and said it would
be thirty-five pesos a night. And with that, we had found a home.

We explored the beach and discovered that there were live conch
snails all over the sand in the shallow water between the beach and
the barrier reef about a hundred yards offshore. There were coconuts
everywhere. There was another little cottage much closer to the beach
and it seemed to be inhabited because there were men's trousers and
shirts pinned to a line to dry on the front porch.

We pulled Beulah II up to our room and unloaded our stuff, each
one of us taking a corner. We hung up our hammocks, and the man,
who introduced himself as Francisco, brought us a kerosene lantern,

Our digs at Rancho Tankah, summer 1974.

a pitcher of water, and four glasses. He said, as we looked suspiciously at the water, *"Agua purificada!"* Up to that point we had been drinking only this bubbly water called *Tehuacán,* beer, and Coke. They did sell gallon jugs of water that was purified by being electrocuted but it was disgusting and tasted dead. We found that we much preferred Corona.

Francisco poured us each a glass of *agua purificada* and we all looked at each other and said, "What the hell?" It was absolutely delicious. He took us out back and showed us the elaborate system that produced this fresh H_2O. First, large cisterns collected rainwater from the roof of the hacienda. Then a small generator kept the water moving through the cisterns, producing the same effect as a stream, which kept the water from stagnating. It was quite an impressive setup and Francisco seemed very proud of it. Francisco then took us to the beach and showed us how to open a conch shell using a screwdriver and a stone. He pried the meat out and put it on an outside table and pounded the meat with his fist. Then he took us inside the hacienda and showed us how to fry it up with butter and a little garlic. Delicious!

Francisco picked up a coconut and, seeing the big Buck knife on

Tim's belt, motioned for him to open the nut. Tim smiled at the challenge, whipped out his knife, and had at the coconut. Fifteen minutes later, with sweat pouring off his face and somewhat humiliated, Tim gave up and Francisco just laughed and laughed. He led us over to a cement block about two feet square with a steel bar, pointed at the end, sticking out. He took a coconut and brought it down on the pointed end of the bar and the skin peeled right off. I tried it and failed miserably, but soon, after a few more lessons, we got the hang of it, and from then on we had as much coconut as we could eat, which we discovered was not very much.

We now had an endless supply of fresh water, coconut, and giant sea snails. We would not starve to death.

Tim, climbing to get a coconut. Note the Pulsar watch!

Not long after we got settled, a car pulled up and an American fellow popped his head into our hut and introduced himself as Arthur Miller from Pennsylvania. I loved Arthur Miller's plays and had always wanted to meet him, so I was very excited to make this man's acquaintance. "Not that Arthur Miller. I'm an archaeologist." He explained that he was in Yucatán deciphering hieroglyphics and trying to decode the ancient Mayan language. He was staying in the little hacienda by the water. We introduced ourselves and he was impressed that we were a bunch of Yale grads. Then he asked about the scuba gear piled up outside the hut. When I told him it was mine, he asked if I would teach him how to dive.

Arthur had discovered an ancient Mayan place of ritual deep in the jungle. This hidden cave had a *cenote* inside it, which is a body of fresh water connected to a network of underground limestone caves that wind their way throughout the Yucatán. The caves have underground rivers and every so often they bubble to the surface in the form of a clear pool, or cenote. He said that his find was of extreme significance, and he needed to go into the cenote to see what the Mayans had thrown into it. Legend had it that the Mayans covered virgins with gold chains and threw them into these cenotes as sacrifices to the gods. Miller was sure that no one had ever found this cave since the mysterious demise of the Mayan civilization some seven or eight hundred years ago and he was determined to be the first man inside. I told him that I had no experience with cave diving but that I would be happy to teach him how to scuba.

The next day, we charged up the tanks with the compressor, and late in the afternoon, he drove me to a nearby cenote purported to have a manatee living in it. I never saw the fabled creature but I did give Miller the rudiments of scuba diving. The following day, he offered to show us his secret discovery but warned us that the cave had fallen under the "curse of the Arashob." The Arashob were small, crafty leprechaun-like creatures. He had determined this based on an elaborate bas-relief carved into the wall of the cave. We told him we were cool with the curse and hacked our way through the jungle with him until we came to the cave.

When we got there, we saw that it was not like a normal cave that goes deep into a mountain. It was more like an overhang with bas-reliefs of people carved into the leading wall. Just below the wall was a small, shallow-looking pool of water no more than nine feet in diameter. The water was jet black and dirty. "How will you ever see anything in there?" I asked. Then Arthur took a small pebble and tossed it into the pond. The water was crystal clear; it only looked black because the rock around it was black. We could see the pebble perfectly as it descended deeper and deeper until it disappeared at least fifty feet below. My heart was beating fast and I told Miller that I didn't feel up to going down into such a pool. The golden rule of scuba is: "Never dive alone. Always dive with a buddy." He wanted to go it alone, but I refused to let him use my equipment unless he found someone else to go with him. Little did I know how connected this guy was.

We cut our way back through the jungle and he asked us to drive him a few miles up the road to the place that had the only telephone for fifty miles around. It was a ship-to-shore arrangement that Miller had used a couple of times. The place we were going was called Akumal and it was a small, private scuba resort for invited guests only. It was behind gates and completely walled-in. It was so private that we had to wait in the car while Miller went in to use the phone. He emerged a few minutes later with a huge smile on his face and shouted, "Success!" We asked him what was going on but he just said, "You'll find out." And he smiled all the way back to Rancho Tankah.

It rained for the next three days. Late June is the rainy season in Yucatán, but it was more like monsoon season. We still were able to snorkel and scuba on the reef, and I had brought a spear gun and speared some fish, which we fried on our little Coleman stove. We sometimes poached the fish in coconut milk for a bit of a change of pace. We found ourselves spending more and more time at the Cross-roads Café between five and eight. We thought about leaving early because of all the rain, but then a caravan of trucks and jeeps arrived at Rancho Tankah. It seems that Arthur Miller was a bit of a celebrity in his own right and he had called *National Geographic* from Akumal to tell them of his discovery and they had sent the premier cave-diving team in the world to explore his cave and film a documentary of the experience.

Suddenly we had a team of Russian cave divers and their film crew for neighbors. They arrived just as the skies cleared and the scalding Mayan sun reappeared. They wasted no time and wanted to be taken immediately to the cave. Arthur Miller jumped into our van and we led the caravan of trucks to a place on the dirt road where they could hoist their equipment to the site. Dr. Miller and a few other locals had to cut a path through the jungle with machetes. The entire experience was filmed by a crew that followed Dr. Miller's every move. When they reached the cave, the crew set up lights and laid cable from the portable generator they had wrestled through the jungle.

The star cave diver was a tall, thin Russian who spoke very little English and didn't seem to have any hair on his body. I imagined, though, from the color of his skin, that he had once been blond. He was in his early fifties and seemed to be very excited. He tossed a stone into the cenote and watched it sink into oblivion, and then raced to put on his gear. The first man to go down was an advance diver who dragged a cable down with him, possibly for lighting. He also had a powerful underwater flashlight. He had on a full wet suit and gloves, assuming that at depth it would be really cold.

We watched as he descended in the crystal-clear water. The men above fed the cable out as he went down, twenty feet, forty feet, and we could still see him, sixty feet, one hundred feet, and he disappeared entirely. He pulled another twenty feet, then tugged hard on the cable signaling that he was coming back up. All the other divers and crew huddled around the little pond nestled beneath the curse of the Arashob.

I wondered if they had been told of the curse, which, as Dr. Miller had explained, was supposedly that anyone entering the cave would suffer grave injury or death. In fact, he had told us that his partner, with whom he had discovered the cave, had been in a terrible car accident a few weeks before we arrived as he drove to Mérida and was in the hospital there with two broken legs. It had been a very hot day when they first discovered the cave and his partner had dipped into the pool to cool off. Dr. Miller had not. I worried about the fate of these divers.

I peered down into the seemingly black water and could see our advance man slowly making his way to the surface. A diver must surface from a depth of a hundred feet slowly so as not to get the bends, or bubbles of nitrogen in the joints that cannot only be very painful but can also kill you. As he got closer to the surface he seemed to be making faces and was holding something in front of him in his right hand. He broke the surface and tore out his mouthpiece, shouting, "Aheeeeee!!! It's amazing! There are bones and pottery and all kinds of artifacts!"

I had never seen an adult male quite so excited. This must be the jackpot for cave divers. He reached the side of the pool and opened his right fist and said, "It's a human mandible with the teeth still embedded, probably female!" He handed it to the bald Russian and they all crowded around for a better look. The Russian guy said a bunch of stuff in Russian to his men, and then in broken English he said, "This was surely a sacrificial cave. This is truly an amazing discovery!" He hoisted on his tank and he and the advance guy and one other diver went down into the abyss.

The divers stayed at Tankah for several days and brought up lots of artifacts, including a small Aztec calendar stone that proved the theory that the Aztecs and the Mayans traded with each other. The entire experience was filmed by the *National Geographic* crew and was shown on public television some years later. I never saw it but heard all about it.

The day after that first dive into the Cave of the Arashob, our motley crew packed up Beulah and headed west toward Oaxaca. I'm not sure why we wanted to go there, probably because there was a lot of buzz at the time about the pot in Oaxaca. It was undoubtedly something on Tim's agenda. It was sort of on the way home, though we would have to cross over a mountain range to get there. There seemed to be more and more checkpoints with nosey Federales as we headed toward Oaxaca, and I was getting very paranoid about the pot stashed in the chassis. I kept saying we ought to dump it but Tim and Frank always overruled me. We made it to Oaxaca without being busted but we didn't find the place as enchanting as we had imagined so we kept driving. Don had a book on the Anthropological Museum in Mexico City and kept saying that it was an absolute must-see so we decided that we'd hotfoot it to Mexico City for a little culture.

Just outside Oaxaca, we fueled up at the nearest PEMEX station. PEMEX, for the uninitiated, is the state-owned monopoly that supplies all the fuel for all of the automobiles, trucks, trains, and planes in Mexico. While we were filling up, a handsome blond fellow wearing shorts, flip-flops, and a multicolored peasant-boy shirt wandered over to the van and announced that his name was Libre, or "free" in English. He was American and as hippified as they came in those days, with long blond hair to his waist and a bright purple macramé shoulder bag. He said he needed a lift up the highway about fifty miles and could he ride along. What the hell. There was room for one more if he sat on the gear. So off we went north, toward Mexico City and anthropology, with Libre telling stories of the Federales busting American tourists right and left for pot.

Libre told us that if we were caught, we would need to bribe the first police because every layer of law enforcement would cost more and more, and that if we actually got into a jail, the chances of getting out, even with bribes in the hundreds of thousands, were very slim. He said, "Listen. If you guys have any pot, get rid of it. If you do get busted, you can bribe the first guys with a couple of hundred dollars, but after that, forget it." He said, "The bribe is called *mordida* . . . that's slang for 'bribe' but it works in a pinch." I chimed in from behind the wheel and said that we had about a half pound of pot and we should get rid of it.

Libre's stories of other Americans now rotting in Mexican jails had apparently had an effect on Tim and he offered to give all of our pot to our hitchhiking friend. We pulled off the highway near where he was going to get off anyway and pulled out all the remaining dope from the chassis and handed it to the platinum blond hippie who was not only free but now in possession of some killer weed. But not *all* the pot went to Libre. Unbeknownst to us, Tim had kept an ounce or two for himself.

We asked him how he was going to deal with the police and he said he had the program down, but he did say that he wanted to give us something in return. He set about drawing a map to a place called Estación de Catorce, or "Station Fourteen" in English. According to Libre, if we followed the map and asked around for a guy name José Jiménez, José would hook us up with something amazing and that we absolutely had to take his word that this would be the best thing we would do in Mexico.

I was a bit suspect because when I was a kid there was a program on TV that featured a Mexican guy whose name was José Jiménez and that was an iconic Mexican name for me. The show had been a comedy and this José Jiménez was kind of a bozo. As Libre stuffed the pot into his backpack and handed us the map to Estación de Catorce, he said, "Now promise me you'll use the map!" In spite of my skepticism, we said we would, and Libre walked out of the van and out of our lives forever.

Our next stop was Mexico City and the famed Anthropological Museum. We were running out of money so Tim and I had called home to get some cash wired down to the Western Union office in the city. I felt a bit like a loser for having to go to the "rents" for dough, but we really had no choice unless we wanted to hustle in the Zona Rosa for boys in Mexico City. Now that I think about it, Frank might have been game just so he could say that he'd once been a hooker in the Zona Rosa. Frank was a very adventurous fellow.

The next morning, we set off to see what Don called the Louvre of anthropology.

He was not far off. This museum was then, and I'm sure still is, one of the most amazing cultural experiences one can imagine.

We left our Jimmy Buffett heads at the door and slipped back into our Ivy League mentality to absorb as much culture as possible. All of us, that is, with the exception of Tim, who peeled off at one point to get some "fresh air" in the park outside and take in a chapter or two more of *Ulysses*.

Frank, Don, and I learned about the first arrivals in the Americas, who had crossed the Bering Strait when it was still a solid landmass. About an hour after Tim had gone outside, he reappeared, out of breath and white as a sheet. I was alone at that point, as Don and Frank had gone ahead into another section of the museum. When Tim saw me, he cried, "Thank God I found you!"

He was so out of breath that he couldn't get out another word. I said, "What happened to you? You look like you've seen a ghost!"

He just sat down on the ground and said, "I'm fucked! We're fucked! I got busted in the park! Two plainclothes cops caught me smoking a joint. They took my passport and the bag of pot and they sent me to get you because you speak Spanish."

I didn't really "speak" Spanish. I could say stuff like "Where's the bathroom?" and "Which direction?" and "I want a beer," but I certainly couldn't carry on a conversation with Mexico City's finest, who would, more than likely, arrest me, too, if I went anywhere near them. I had visions of rat-infested Mexican prisons with smelly, unshaven banditos trying to get us to bend over to pick up the soap. We tried to find Don and Frank but they were deep inside the labyrinth of anthropology by then, so I screwed up my courage and my stupidity and decided to help my erstwhile roommate by going out to talk to the Mexican police. As we walked out, I let Tim have it.

"What the fuck were you doing smoking pot in a public park in one of the biggest cities in the world?" He had no answer for that one. He just made a very contrite face and hung his head. He pointed to the two men who were about a hundred yards away and watching us like hawks. I told Tim that our only chance was to bribe the guys right away. We each had the $200 our parents had just wired us. I said, "Let

me do the talking. We'll offer them fifty and see if they take it. Whatever we do, we can't get into a police car!"

We walked up to the police officers, both of whom were sporting
thin mustaches. They were wearing black leather lace-up shoes, gray
slacks, and button-down shirts with no ties and dark sport jackets.
They looked like they were in their early thirties. When we got close
to them, one of them grabbed my wrists and held my fingers up. He
was inspecting them to see if I had any pot residue on my hands. Then
he smelled them and smelled my breath. I glanced down at Tim's
hands and, sure enough, his right thumb and index finger were yellow. My hands, thank God, were clean.

The cops showed me their IDs and their guns, which were in hol-
sters under their jackets. These guys were the real deal and they meant
business. They had very stern looks on their faces as they went on and
on about what was going to happen in a language that was 99 per-
cent incomprehensible to me. I listened as though I understood every
word, and when they finished, expecting me to jabber back at them
in the same Martian, I simply said, in a calm voice, *"Es posible por
'mordida'?"* Which basically meant "Would you be scumbag enough
to take a bribe?"

To use *mordida* as the word for bribe gets the point across but the
implication is that the bribe taker is an idiot. Anyway, it got the point
across and the two men looked at each other, then scanned the park,
presumably to see if any of their compatriots were nearby. Then one
of them said, in English, "What you got?" I said, "Fifty dollars." He
laughed and started to pull out handcuffs. I said, "A hundred dollars?"
He looked at me funny and said again in English, "Empty your pockets." We were screwed.

Out of my pockets came the $200 and a Swiss army knife. Tim
had only $200. They took the $400 and then the one who didn't
speak any English motioned for Tim to remove his Pulsar watch. The
two men looked at the watch as though it was the coolest thing they

had ever seen, which, of course, it was. They put the dough in their pocket along with the watch, handed Tim his passport back and my knife back to me, and reached out to shake our hands. They both smiled and said, "Amigos!" at the same time.

As the two cops turned to walk away, Tim said, "Hey, what about my pot? Can I at least have that back?"

The English-speaking cop turned slightly, held up the Baggie, and said with a wry smile, "Hell no! This is really good stuff." And they kept walking.

Tim turned back to me as the two cops walked off and, for some primal reason, I just decked him with a right hook. He went down like a stone and I turned around and walked back to find Don and Frank so I could share with them the good news that we were now back to being broke and quite possibly had no choice but to become young male hookers in the Zona Rosa.

From that day on, Tim O'Brian and I ceased to be friends, which was just fine with me. We remained cordial throughout the rest of the trip, but after that we saw each other only every few years and only to pass superficial pleasantries. I am truly sorry to say that Tim died when he was far too young from the abuse he wreaked on his body. I can only imagine the pain he was trying to cover and what childhood nightmare must have caused that pain.

Frank and Don were somewhat more forgiving than I, but they were also miffed at Tim's blatant stupidity. We decided that we couldn't tap the parents for more dough so we were going to have to sell stuff. I suggested Tim sell his $3,000 guitar and, of course, that wasn't going to happen. We found a scuba shop in town that evening and were able to sell the tanks and regulators for $250. I sold a spear gun for $25. I didn't want to sell the compressor because it belonged to my dad. We had $275 plus about another $50 that we had left so we figured that if we drove straight through to Connecticut, we could just make it. We still had one more night in Mexico City and one more day of the museum and Don wasn't willing to give that up. It was also agreed that after Mexico City we had to go to Libre's Estación de Catorce because we had promised him we would.

Tim and me, before Mexico City. Notice the Pulsar watch!
Tim could have been the poster boy for Pulsar.

The next morning, we drove back to the museum, and Frank, Don, and I spilled out of the van but Tim wouldn't leave it. He said he didn't want to run into the cops again. We said, "Come on! We paid them off. They're happy. Anyway, they're not going to be inside the museum." Tim was unmoved and said he would wait in the van. We said, almost in unison, "All right." And we slid the van door closed.

Five hours later, we came back to the van and slid the same door open only to be knocked backward by a foul, acrid odor. There, lying facedown in a puddle of urine was a passed-out Tim O'Brian clutching an empty bottle of tequila in his right hand. We had bought that bottle the night before and had not cracked it, which meant that Tim had consumed the entire bottle before he passed out and wet himself. He had been too frightened to leave the van and pee. Things were not going well for Tim and apparently didn't go well for him for many years to come. When he sobered up, he was good old Tim again and as likeable as ever to everyone but me. I took the driver's seat and off we went to find out what treasure Libre had assured us we would find at the hands of José Jiménez.

We drove through the night, and though we followed Libre's instructions to a T, we were convinced that we must have taken a wrong turn along the way. We drove for hours on an isolated, rutty, one-lane dirt road. When one of us would say, "Let's turn back," inevitably someone else would say, "No! This is the right direction. Keep going!"

I kept going. Eventually we saw an outcropping of adobe buildings come into view on the horizon. We were elevated on one side of a dusty valley and we could see that train tracks intersected the little town. Then a little rusty sign on a wooden post announced that we had arrived at Estación Catorce. Jackpot!

I drove into the town, which seemed deserted. It was more of a tiny pueblo than a town and was essentially one dirt road with adobe and cinder block buildings on either side. There was a little store for dry goods and another for groceries. But we saw no signs of human activity. It was around one in the afternoon and excruciatingly hot so we figured everyone was down for a siesta.

It looked like a town out of an old John Ford cowboy movie. Then we saw what looked like a saloon. It even had the double swinging doors. I pulled the van over to the side of the road and we hopped out into the swelter hoping to find José Jiménez and an ice-cold beer. We pushed through the double doors into a dark, hot room with a wooden bar on one side and a twenty-foot-long tin urinal on the other side. The room smelled of piss and stale beer, and once again there was no one in sight, just cases of warm Superior beer piled up behind the bar.

We looked around and saw no cooler or refrigerator and then noticed that there were no light fixtures. That meant no ice-cold beer, and since no one was around, probably no José Jiménez either. Suddenly the doors behind us opened and a barefoot, snot-nosed seven-year-old boy walked over behind the bar and asked, *"¿Quieren cerveza?"* Which meant "Do you want beer?" Beer, warm beer, was probably all they had, and that didn't seem too refreshing to any of us so we answered, *"No, gracias. ¿Dónde está José Jiménez?"*

Apparently those were magic words because the boy's eyes lit up and he ran out of the bar and disappeared up the street. I went over to the super-urinal and relieved myself. There were buckets of water on a ledge above the trough and we dumped the water onto our piss and it drained out of a hole at one end. I could only imagine what the place was like on a rockin' Saturday night. It was obviously a "men only" establishment because there were no accommodations for the full female bladder. We each relieved ourselves and commented on the ingenuity of the Mexican plumber who had come up with the super-urinal.

After a few minutes the little barefoot boy burst back into the bar carrying two large green turniplike vegetables in each hand. He held them up proudly and said, *"¿Quieren peyote?"*

Peyote, that's what Libre was offering us in return for our pot! None of us was that familiar with peyote but I could see Tim's eyes light up. Frank was most knowledgeable on the subject and explained that peyote was a cactus that contained a powerful hallucinogen called mescaline and that it had been used by the indigenous people of central Mexico during certain religious rituals. Basically he said that if we ate the cactus, we would have the "trip" of our lives.

Just then, an old blue, topless jeep pulled up in front of the saloon and out hopped a spry, sixtysomething fellow with a cowboy hat and a big brass buckle on his handcrafted leather belt. He tipped his hat and announced that he was José Jiménez and that for thirty-five pesos he would show us where the peyote fields were.

We agreed on the price, which was a couple of dollars, and we followed José for about an hour on an even ruttier dirt road out into the absolute middle of nowhere. We were awfully trusting. This fellow could have had a shotgun and robbed us all in the desert and blown our heads off. On the other hand, he might have just been the jolly purveyor of peyote to gringos that he seemed to be. Thankfully for us he turned out to be the latter, and when he stopped his jeep and motioned for us to get out, he just walked over to the side of the dirt track, took off his straw cowboy hat with his right hand, swept the hat across the horizon, and said with a loud laugh, "PEYOTE!!"

We looked out at the prairie in front of us and saw only miles and miles of flat desert covered with tumbleweed. He could see that we didn't know what the fuck he meant and he laughed a "you guys are really green" laugh and whipped out a six-inch pocketknife. He reached down and pushed aside one of the big weeds and there, growing in a circle under the weed, were four doughnut-size green cactuses. He pried one out of the ground and held it up. It was about the same size as the ones the kid had back at the bar, but this one we could smell and it was not pleasant. It was an acrid, metallic smell that seemed to say, "Come near me and I'll hurt you!"

José dusted off the "button" as they were called, and cut little bits of white hairlike spines out of the top. He said, "Very bad," as he swept them off the button to the ground. Then he cut off the root until the thing was about the size of a Dunkin' donut. He made a motion as if to take a big bite of the thing and just laughed again. He handed the button to Frank, put his hat back on, and climbed into his jeep. He drove back the way we had come and we never laid eyes on José Jiménez again.

We all looked at each other and then out at the miles and miles of tumbleweed and felt as though we had just found King Solomon's mines.

We started digging under the weeds and, sure enough, each one had at least three big buttons under it. Ah! The folly of youth! We were like kids in a candy store. We dug up at least a hundred buttons and I used my eight-inch hunting knife to cut the root away from the button and remove the white stuff from the top. The smell was really beginning to get to me but I pressed on, "cleaning" the buttons for the hallucinogenic feast that lay ahead.

There were four of us and about a hundred buttons. We were crossing the border the next day, and of course we couldn't cross with contraband. That meant we would each need to eat twenty-five plump, juicy peyote buttons. We had no idea of the correct dosage but we figured that we would eat a few, wait an hour or so, eat a couple more, and just play it by ear. We looked around and figured that the spot we were in wasn't ideal for having the spiritual journey of a lifetime, so we scanned the horizon for a more hospitable place to trip our brains out.

We saw, way off in the distance, a small set of green foothills and figured that would be an ideal spot if we could just get to it. So off we went toward what looked like a lush paradise compared to the dusty desert floor of the peyote fields. It was just our good fortune that our little jeep trail was taking us right there.

As we got closer and closer to our tropical paradise in the desert, it became apparent that the green lush hillsides were not covered with trees, ferns, and lush vines but cactus . . . lots and lots of spiny, hateful, prickly cactus. It was green, though, and from a distance looked inviting. We stopped at the foot of the smallest hill, which was a few hundred feet high, and figured we could wind our way through the cactus to the top so we would at least have a view for our trip. The sun was getting lower on the horizon and we decided we had found our Shangri-La, thorny though it was.

When we found a relatively level spot, we set up our peyote-eating factory. We had a little cutting board, and Tim whipped out his Buck knife and started slicing the buttons into bite-size pieces. Yum-yum!!

We gathered around, as we knew Tim would be the first to down the hallucinogen. He grabbed a handful of plump, juicy green slices and said, "Well!! Down the hatch!" He opened his mouth wide and flung the bits in. No sooner had the first piece crossed the threshold of his lips than the three of us were sprayed with whatever he had eaten for lunch. Tim was what you could call a hard-core drug taker and I had only known him to vomit after taking drugs if he had taken far too many or eaten mushrooms covered with cow shit. But none of the peyote juice had even grazed his lips and he was retching like he had the plague.

Then Frank mentioned that the peyote cactus was difficult to eat and that it was usually dried out first or eaten with an orange or some other fruit. Tim said through dry heaves, "Thanks for telling me now!" We spent the next two hours trying to get even a morsel of the magic cactus into our bodies but to no avail. We all tried and we all puked. We did, however, climb to the top of the hill to watch the sunset and drink tequila on our last night in Mexico.

We slept near the van that night well away from the smell of our own vomit, and the next morning, before we left for the border, we played a game of "How far can you fling the wretched peyote button" until all the buttons were gone. Don had the best arm and he won hands down.

A friend and I, somewhere near Palenque, Mexico.

The Graduate

W hen we got back to New Haven, we said our good-byes and went our separate ways. Tim sold the van and I took my share of the dough, which was just enough to get me home. The drive out to Pasadena from New England was uneventful, and once back at the family spread, I spent many days flipping through old *Playboy* magazines and floating on a plastic raft in our pool à la Dustin Hoffman in *The Graduate*—a film that was essentially about my family and others just like mine, since it had been written by the brother of my mother's gynecologist, who was, no doubt, privy to many of the Pasadena peccadillos of the day. I was a Yale graduate with no particular place to go. I had survived a raucous and, in hindsight, extremely dangerous trip through Mexico and really hadn't given much thought to my next move. There was no excited neighbor whispering that I needed to go into plastics, and my parents didn't seem to have much of a plan for me either. I knew that I liked acting but didn't have a clue how to pursue an acting career.

My eldest half brother, Clay, had a friend who was somehow in the top echelon of the Public Broadcasting System and who, upon hearing of my unemployed Ivy League status, offered me a job as a production assistant at WNET in New York. The pay was to be $250 per month, hardly a living wage in New York, but my parents thought it would be a good way for me to "get my foot in the door" in the entertainment industry to which they knew I was drawn. They offered to subsidize me if I took the job.

My parents hated the idea of my becoming an actor. *Hated* is not nearly a strong-enough word. "You'll be on the dole your whole life!" they'd say. "You'll be a bum!" There was no end to the many ways that they characterized the life I would have if I attempted an acting career. I didn't know how to become an actor anyway so I acquiesced and decided to make the move to New York.

I called my half brother Jerry, who lived on the Upper East Side, and asked if I could crash at his place till I found my own apartment. The answer was, of course, yes. With timing as ironic as any could be, the moment I hung up the phone with Jerry, it rang again. When I answered, I heard a somewhat familiar voice ask if Harry was home. I said, "Speaking."

The voice replied, "Hi, Harry! It's Bill Ball and I would like to offer you a scholarship to come study acting in our advanced training program." He was that brief and to the point.

I said, "Wow! Why?"

He said, "You know, I remember you telling me that you wanted to become an actor and we just had a cancellation in our first-year program and I thought of you. Are you still interested in acting? The program starts next week."

The next three words out of my mouth changed my life forever. I said, "I'll be there!" I didn't give it a millisecond's further thought.

An Actor's Life for Me

I was supposed to leave for the Big Apple the following week. Going to San Francisco to ACT would mean that I would have to quit my job with WNET before I started, which would piss off my half brother Clay no end. And I would have to tell my parents that I was going to acting school instead of taking a "real" job. At least I had been offered a full scholarship and I wouldn't have to ask them for dough; that would not have gone over well. I waited a couple of days before I broke the news to my folks. I marched into the study where they were drinking their first martinis of the night and announced that I would not be joining the Public Broadcasting System; instead, I would be studying acting in San Francisco for the next three years.

My mother stood up, martini in hand, and pursed her red lipstick-stained lips, and growled, "Over my dead body, you will!" My father also started to protest, but I cut him off, saying, "Sorry but I've made up my mind. You won't have to pay a cent. I have a full scholarship and a $45 a week stipend so you can bark all you want but this is what I'm going to do."

My mother screamed that I was ruining my life, as I walked out of the room and started packing up Beulah for the drive north. With all the brouhaha in the house I figured I had better leave sooner rather than later so I decided to drive north the next morning. I was already pretty well packed for my trip to New York so all I had to do was throw in a few last items and my guitar. Then I went to bed.

My father came into my room and tried to dissuade me from

going. My mother wouldn't even speak to me. Even my brother, David, came in and tried to tell me what a mistake I was making, saying that I would be asking him for money as he was going to become a really rich accountant and financial wizard and that he wasn't going to lend me a cent. I told them all to leave me alone. I knew that I was setting some bridges on fire, but I was pretty sure they wouldn't burn completely. I fell asleep.

I woke up on a drizzly Saturday morning. I was up long before any of the other alcoholics in the house and I showered and fired up some eggs, wrote a good-bye note and jumped into Beulah for the six-hour drive to San Francisco. I slipped the key in the ignition and cranked her for the zillionth time. Nothing! I tried again. Nothing! I got out and popped the hood and there, staring me in the face, was betrayal!

Someone had pulled the distributor out of the engine. That's like ripping out the heart of the automobile. Beulah was dead as a doornail!

My brother, potbellied, unshaven, and in blue boxer shorts, came to the front door and announced, "You're not going anywhere!"

I asked nicely, "Where's the distributor?"

"What distributor?" he answered.

This was a true Cain and Abel moment and a certain dead end so I repacked a few essentials into a single suitcase, grabbed my guitar, and set off on foot toward the bus stop. I had no money in my checking account, and for the first and last time in my life, I deliberately bounced a check—$25 to Pacific Southwest Airlines for a one-way ticket to San Francisco. I didn't speak to my mother for two years.

The Kindness of Strangers

I arrived in San Francisco and traveled via airport shuttle to Union Square, which was just a couple of blocks away from the American Conservatory Theater, or ACT, as everyone called it.

I hoisted my suitcase and guitar up the street to 450 Geary, where the school and the administrative offices for the theatre were located. ACT had won the Tony award for best regional theatre the year before, and was at that time considered the premier repertory theatre in the country. I was in heaven except for a few minor details: I didn't know any of the other students; I had exactly $10.75 to my name; and I had no place to sleep that night, or any other night thereafter. I did know Bill Ball and his assistant, Gino, and Beulah, the reception-ist, and I figured one of them would point me in the right direction.

I took the elevator to the fifth-floor reception and there was Beu-lah with her shining black face and beautiful white smile. She was a sight for sore eyes and somehow she knew it as soon as I walked in the door. There were lots of other kids milling about but she took me to Gino's office straightaway and said to Gino, "Look what the cat dragged in!"

Gino seemed genuinely pleased to see me and said that he'd heard I might be coming to the training program. He said, "There's some-one I want you to meet and she's coming this way right now." He motioned outside his office to a cute, shortish girl about twenty-five years old with short brunette hair and a round pretty face. She marched into his office as though she owned it and Gino said, "Skit, this is Harry. Harry, meet Skit."

We shook hands as I thought to myself what a strange name she had. I had never met a Skit before and I said, "That's a cool name."

And she said rather shyly, "Well, it's actually Katharine, but everyone calls me Skit."

Gino said, "Skit will be in the first year with you. I just know you'll be friends." And he was right. Skit and I hit it off from day one. There was an informal orientation that afternoon and Skit and I went around the building together as we were introduced to the teachers and the various studios. There were studios for acting and studios for dance and fencing and singing and movement. Our heads were spinning by the end of the tour and Skit said, "Let's get a bite!" And we headed back out on to Geary Street. Right next to the school there was a deli and a cheap soup place and I said, "Soup or sandwich?" She just made a face and said, "Neither, darling!" And grabbed my arm and led me down the street to a swank eatery near The St. Francis hotel.

As we walked in, I pulled back and said, "Whoa, this is a bit above my pay grade."

She laughed and said, "Oh, come on! My treat." I felt it would be rude to resist anymore and, besides, I loved that kind of joint.

During lunch we filled each other in on our lives and dreams and nightmares. She told me her last name was Stapleton and that she was from Denver and that she was good "friends" with one of the main contributors to the theatre, one Cyril Magnin, who owned a bunch of clothing stores named I. Magnin. Now the picture was becoming clearer. I knew of the Magnin stores. They were the Saks Fifth Avenue of California and Cyril Magnin was one of the richest men in the state. Who was this girl? If I had ever flown into Denver, I would have known that Stapleton Airport was named after her grandfather; that's who she was! We had a great time at lunch, which was over a hundred dollars, more than my entire food budget for a month. I had explained my situation to her and she offered up the couch in her apartment until I found a real place to live. Since I knew no one else, and considering that I was actually destitute, I took her up on her offer.

I was not the least bit attracted to Skit in an animal sense and knew that this was going to be a cheap lodging situation only. I was going to spend my first night in San Francisco among Colorado royalty! I lugged my stuff up to the top of Nob Hill where she had a beautiful one-bedroom apartment with a killer view of the bay. She had a three-panel foldout screen that she put in front of the couch for a modicum of privacy. Skit used the bathroom first, then said, "G'night!" And left me to my own devices. It was a hot September night and all she had was an extra blanket for covers so I ended up sleeping in the nude to keep cool. I slept like a baby.

I awoke the next morning to a soft rat-a-tat on the front door. It was so soft that I thought it might be coming from next door. Then again, very softly, came a rat-rat-a-rat-rat-tat-tat. This was someone who knew Skit well and was waking her with a familiar knock. But Skit was out like a light. I fell back asleep, but then again I woke to a rat-a-tat-tat. Bleary-eyed I got up and was halfway to the door when I realized I was buck naked. I reached around for something to cover my manhood and the closest thing was an eight-inch by eight-inch throw pillow, which I jammed in front of my privates as I opened the door.

There, standing straight as an arrow, was a man in his late sixties, impeccably dressed with morning coat and ascot and white morning shoes with a tiny lapdog attached to a dainty leather leash. The dog immediately started licking my naked ankles and the man asked if Katharine was in. The dog kept licking and jabbering but I had to keep one hand on the door and one hand on the little pillow. I said that Skit was asleep and that I was just a houseguest and did he want me to wake her? He said in a very calm voice, "No, thank you. Just mention that Cyril and Tippecanoe dropped by for a chat." And with that he and his annoying little dog were off and I knew that I was going to have a tough row to hoe at ACT.

A couple of days later, Bill Ball called me into his office to welcome me and see how I was doing. I thanked him for the scholarship and the stipend and said I was having a great time with the classes, which were, in fact, brutal. When I became a student at ACT I discovered what a force Bill Ball was in the theatre world; I was very intimidated by him. When I had been working for him as his assistant, our relationship was friendly. Now it was strictly professional. As I left his office I thanked him again, and just as I got to the door he said, "Harry, I hear you met Cyril Magnin."

I turned and said, "Yes, I did and I just . . ." But Bill cut me off as though he already knew the story. Then he simply said, "You know he's our biggest supporter and without him there would be no ACT?" It was obvious that my face time with Mr. Ball was over and he didn't require a response to his question. He just waved me out the door and was sure that I got the point.

Like I said, the classes and class schedule were brutal. It was non-stop, seven days a week of memorizing, studying theatre history, dance, movement, speech, diction, fencing, and ballet, yoga, singing, and, of course, acting. We were required to see all the plays in repertory and we would have long sessions discussing the direction and the acting and even the playwriting. I was on fire, and my ambition to become a great actor grew with every class. I knew I had found my calling. But I had to find my own place to live and I had to find a way to get my car back. Skit was getting annoyed with her couch guest, and I'm sure Mr. Magnin, whatever his motivation, was none too happy to have me in the picture every time he took Tippecanoe for a walk on Nob Hill.

Eventually Skit gave me $50 and helped me buy a reconditioned distributor for Beulah as well as a one-way ticket to LA on PSA. I stole down to Pasadena and replaced the distributor head, left a note to my father that I had come and gone, and wished them well. I was back in San Francisco in under twenty-four hours.

Sometime during the fifth week of classes, a fellow first-year student named Greg approached me with a proposition. He had located a three-bedroom basement apartment on California Street up by the Catholic cathedral. The rent was $200 a month and he had another guy, Wayne, who wanted in. Would I be interested? I said without a moment's hesitation, "Sure!" That would be $70 a month from me and I figured I could afford that since I got a $45 stipend once a week. That would leave me with a cool $110 a month to live on. Fat! Actually I would have moved onto the street to get out of Skit Stapleton's apartment—not because I had anything against her but I didn't want to be responsible for the end of the American Conservatory Theater.

Gino had asked me several times in the hallways of the school how things were going with my apartment hunting and I'm sure there was another message attached to those inquiries. The day after I moved in with Greg I knocked on Bill's door just to tell him the news. "Wonderful!" he bellowed.

As the weeks wore on, it became apparent that there were two distinct camps or "schools of thought" about the ACT approach to theatre and acting. One approach, and the one that seemed most respected by the faculty and students, was sponsored by Allen Fletcher, who was co-artistic director of the main theatre and head of the acting program. The other, which was respected by the theatre administration and the actors in the company, was sponsored by Bill Ball, the founding artistic director and codirector with Mr. Fletcher. There was a kind of unspoken rivalry between the two men and it became clear that Mr. Fletcher had less respect for Mr. Ball than did Mr. Ball for Mr. Fletcher. As it happened, it was Mr. Fletcher's responsibility to vet all the applicants to the school and he served as the chairman of admissions.

I was the only student in the first year who had not actually applied to the school and so I had not been vetted by Mr. Fletcher. Bill had simply pulled rank on Mr. Fletcher and invited me without even so much as an audition. I came to learn that this arrangement did not sit well with Mr. Fletcher, and he never really accepted me as a worthy student even though the critiques of my work were as good as or surpassed those of the other students. It became my mission to impress Allen Fletcher, and by the time I left ACT, I think I had.

Rebecca Redux

The first year was going by in a flash. Throughout the fall, I had abandoned sex and pined for Rebecca. Finally I couldn't take it anymore, so I fired up my TWA Getaway Card for a quick Thanksgiving trip to New England, roast turkey, and raw Rebecca. It was pretty fantastic except that the weather was brutal and Rebecca and I took a few wrapped-up walks during which we discussed the inevitable end of our relationship.

The night before I left for San Francisco, Rebecca said, "Before you go, I have something to show you. It involves you and it's in the attic. Follow me." Now I was intrigued. What could Rebecca have in her mother's attic that involved me?

We pulled the stairs to the attic down from the ceiling and made our way up the creaky ladderlike steps. In one corner of the large dark room there was a wooden trunk, the kind you will find in New England antiques shops for around $400. Rebecca walked over to the antique trunk, knelt down, and slowly opened the lid. In the dim attic light, I could see some clothing, picture frames, a few knick-knacks, and some papers. Rebecca dug around inside until she came up with the wood stock to what must have been a small-gauge rifle. She set it down gently on the floor and then grabbed one of the pictures. She turned it over and there was a photograph of a young man in his teens. Rebecca then said, "Take a closer look."

I took the framed photo and went over to the window to look at it in the light. I was looking at a photo of a young, good-looking boy in his early twenties. I noticed a slight resemblance to me. Then she told me that it was a photograph of her brother, who had been heartbroken when his first love, an older female actress, had left him to go to California to become a star. He had become withdrawn and despondent and, in a final act of despair, had shot himself in the head with a .22-caliber rifle that belonged to his father. The stock of the gun on the floor was the stock of that rifle.

I took Rebecca into my arms and held her for what seemed to be an eternity. Then I asked her why she had never told me about her brother before. She replied that I had reminded her of him every time she heard my voice. She said it was spooky how much we sounded alike. I was having a little trouble processing all of this new information and was somewhat shocked by the whole thing. I couldn't help but wonder, Had she just liked me because I reminded her of her brother? It seemed slightly incestuous.

I helped Rebecca put the stuff, including the stock of the gun—weird—back into the trunk and we went down to her bedroom, where we held each other until dawn. I returned to San Francisco a single man.

Eventually I fell for a sweet and very witty girl named Gina whose dad was the Fly in the original motion picture of the same name. We had a tumultuous relationship, which was a lot of fun but also nasty at times, and I don't mean it in the good sense of the word. Gina and I ended up being on-again, off-again lovers throughout my years at ACT. There wasn't a lot of time for romance in that first year but we managed to squeeze in some exhausted sex from time to time. There is certainly nothing glamorous about the day-to-day life of an acting student, and the life of a working stage actor is even less glam—as I was about to discover.

Wisdom Lost

In late winter of our first year, we were assigned roles in various Shakespearean plays for what were called the "First Year Shakespeare Projects." I was assigned the role of Biron in *Love's Labor's Lost*. It was a huge role with a word count rivaled only by Hamlet. *Love's Labor's Lost* is a kind of romantic comedy and is not frequently performed because the language is very difficult. Playing Biron was an extraordinary privilege for me and I saw it as the challenge of a lifetime.

I was sure I was up to it if only I could memorize the thousands of lines. I spent hours with a tape recorder going over and over the scenes, and all seemed to be going well until I began to feel a pressure in my jaw somewhere behind my last set of molars. Every day, I did my vocal warm-ups and went dutifully to rehearsal, and every day the pain in my jaw got worse and worse. I looked into the back of my mouth with a flashlight but couldn't see anything. It seemed fine back there, but eventually the pain became unbearable and I asked Beulah, the receptionist, if she knew of a dentist I could see.

It was a Friday and she hooked me up with a dentist who could take X-rays that afternoon. It turned out that I had two heavily impacted wisdom teeth in my lower jaw—one on each side—that had to be removed immediately. The only problem was that my performance as Biron was scheduled for the following Friday, and the only time I had to have the teeth pulled was the very next day, Saturday. Beulah set about finding a dental surgeon who would work on Saturday and, bless her heart, she found a naval dentist who worked at the Presidio who agreed to extract my teeth, not only on a Saturday but also on extremely short notice.

The dentist said he would do the procedure for $250 and Beulah arranged to get the money through the theatre. She put me on the phone with the doctor, who asked me to bring the X-rays and asked what kind of anesthesia I wanted. I had asked around about wisdom teeth extraction and everyone said, without hesitation, "You wanna be out for that!" I took that to mean full anesthesia: sleep! I told the dentist that I didn't want Novocain; I wanted to be "out." He said, "No problem. I'll see you tomorrow at my office at eleven hundred hours." He was a military guy, all right.

The next morning, I arrived at his office but the door was locked. I looked around and a car drove up and parked next to mine. Out stepped a well-groomed man in his forties with graying hair and a pencil-thin black mustache. I believe a mustache like that is called a Boston Blackie. In any case, I will never forget that man or his Boston Blackie. The "doctor" stepped briskly toward me and announced that we would have to get right to it, as he had another engagement that he couldn't miss. He made it clear that he was doing me a huge favor by coming in on a Saturday. He opened the door to his office and switched on the lights. It was cold and depressing and he motioned me into the room with the chair. He told me to take a seat and he attached a big bib to my neck. He looked at the X-rays and then poked around in my mouth for a couple of minutes and said, "Ah-ha." Then he took a breathing apparatus and placed it over my nose and disappeared into the next room.

He came back a few minutes later with a silver hammer and a silver chisellike spike about eight inches long. He asked, "How are you doing?" I said, "Fine." I wondered where his assistant was and when the anesthesiologist was going to make an appearance. Then he said, "Open your mouth as wide as you can." Which I did, and he put the spike in my mouth and rested it on my lower right jawbone and then hit it as hard as he could with his silver hammer.

I'm pretty sure the tears shot horizontally from both eyes as I screamed. The man had just broken my jaw with a hammer and I had been administered no pain medication whatsoever. I bolted out of the chair and grabbed my now bloody face as the "dentist" stood back with a look of horror on his face. I cried out through the ruins of my mouth, "What the fuck are you doing?" He said, hammer and bloody chisel in hand, "I thought you told me no Novocain so I gave you gas instead. You shouldn't have felt a thing!"

I couldn't believe what I was hearing. The man didn't understand when I told him that I wanted to be "out." I wanted to be asleep and have no memory whatsoever of the procedure. Now I would remember this moment in detail for the rest of my life. He told me to calm down and he would give me a shot of Valium and then anesthetize my mouth with Novocain, but that we had to continue.

The thing was that I had never had Nitrous Oxide in a dentist's office before and had not been told to breathe through my nose so I was not the least bit sedated when he broke my jaw.

I sat back down in the chair, the bib covered with blood, and allowed this butcher to finish his dirty business. He had given me a massive dose of tranquilizer and so many shots of Novocain that I couldn't feel my head for twenty-four hours. I don't know how I made it home that day.

He ended up breaking both jawbones with the same little silver hammer. He then cauterized the wounds with some hot poker–like instrument. He gave me a bottle of Aspergum and told me to gargle with salt water four times a day for two weeks. When I left his office, my face was twice the size it had been when I entered, and I knew that if I could endure that, I could have endured torture at the hands of the Third Reich.

The next morning, I woke up in excruciating pain. I looked in the mirror and saw only Quasimodo staring back at me. My mouth was still swollen and there was dried blood caked all over my face, which was the size of a basketball. I had a dress rehearsal that day at noon for *Love's Labor's Lost*. I tried to move my jaw and wailed with pain as I opened my mouth wide enough to brush my teeth. This was not going to be a good day. But there was no way that the cast could do the run-through without my character, who was the absolute center of the play. I had to be there.

That is one of the ten commandments of the theatre: "The show must go on!" I put three or four Aspergum into the hatch and fluffed and puffed as much as I could. Somehow I made it to the studio just in time. People where aghast when they saw my face and some didn't recognize me at all. The whole way to the theatre, I had been working my jaw slowly back and forth to loosen it up before having to recite the second-highest number of words spoken by any character in the Shakespeare lexicon. The rehearsal began and, to my amazement, I was able to mumble and gurgle and grunt the words so that my fellow thespians could follow along.

I did notice, however, that my leading lady kept her distance during the love scenes; in fact, everyone was playing their part just a few feet farther away from me. Finally my roommate, Greg, whispered that the odor coming from the hole in my face was intolerable and smelled like rotting meat. I said, "It *is* rotting meat! So sorry." I asked for a break and ran to the drugstore and bought a dozen spray bottles of Binaca.

I will never forget the flavor of Aspergum mixed with Binaca, and I relive that taste in my mouth whenever *Love's Labor's Lost* is mentioned. By the following Friday, I had healed enough to give a decent performance of Biron in front of a packed audience, though people kept a wide berth for weeks due to the stench of the slowly healing, barbarically extracted wisdom teeth.

That's Just the Way It Is

By early spring, all the first-year students had begun appearing in the main-stage productions as what we called "spear carriers"—and that's mainly what we did. It gave us some experience on the big stage in front of a couple of thousand people and that was invaluable. It was during those nonspeaking moments on stage that we came in contact with the professional actors who were members of the company. We looked up to them as if they were gods, or at least I did. I would watch with wonder and awe as they took the stage and made the plays come to life with perfect clarity, movement, and diction.

I was backstage during an early rehearsal for one such production when I rounded a hallway corner and bumped into one of the actresses, of whom I was not only in awe, but to whom I was also secretly attracted. Of course, she was older and she was a member of the company—and we had all been instructed to keep our professional distance from the pros.

Her name was Elizabeth and I had been watching her from day one. She was luminescent on stage, but a bit matronly offstage, which didn't matter to me—I thought she was amazing.

Around the corner I went and—flump!—we had a head-on collision. I was mortified and said, "Oh, I'm so sorry! I didn't see you there." I looked into her eyes and she into mine, and then a look of absolute terror crossed her face. I was still not completely healed from the botched wisdom tooth extraction and I was sure she must have caught a whiff of my putrid breath. The horror! She put her hand to her mouth and screamed a little scream as she ran past me and down the hall. I guessed that any chance I had with Elizabeth, the actress of my dreams, had been destroyed by my fetid halitosis.

The next day, there was a note in my mailbox at the school. It just said, "I must see you today. I will be at Salmagundi at 5:00 p.m. . . . Elizabeth C." I knew the note was from the actress I'd bumped into the night before, but why did she have to see me? With more than a little excitement, I slung my books over my shoulder and traipsed into the soup joint, Salmagundi, at five. I looked around and there she was, sitting alone in a far corner of the restaurant, cradling a cup of coffee in her hands, much like Jessica Lange has done in every movie she has ever made. This coffee cradling, of course, predated Jessica's neurosis by several years. I cautiously walked up to her and said, "Hi, I'm sorry about last night. I'm such a klutz!" She reached out her hand and said, "I'm Liz. And I didn't need to see you because of what happened at the theatre."

She looked right through me, as if she was opening me up to see what made me alive. It was very creepy and at first she didn't apologize, she just kept staring, her eyes wide and penetrating as though she was asking my soul some secret question. A tear rolled down her cheek as she lifted a small photograph out of her purse. She held it, facedown, and asked, "Who are you and where did you come from?"

I explained that I was Harry Hamlin from Pasadena and that I had recently graduated from Yale. She stopped me and said, "I know all that. But there has to be something else." Now I was really puzzled. What else could she want to know about me? Then she said, "I'm going to show you something and tell you something I have never told anyone."

With that, she recounted the story of her first true love and how, when she was young and foolish and far too ambitious, she had thrown away that love in pursuit of fame and fortune. She told me of the sweetest boy she had ever known and the only man she had ever truly loved, who was so heartbroken when she left him that he fell into a horrible depression and finally took his own life with a bullet to his head. Then she slowly turned over the framed photo and there, in the palm of her hand, was a picture of Rebecca's brother. Just like the photo from Rebecca's attic, it could have been a picture of me, the resemblance was so striking.

She went on to say that not an hour had gone by since she had learned of his death that she had not thought of him, and when she had seen me the night before and heard my voice, she really had thought she was seeing a ghost. Then she laughed a little laugh and said she was sorry to drag me into all of this but that she just sensed a connection. Nothing in the world could have prepared her for what I told her next.

At first she just stared at me in utter disbelief, but when I described the family farm and told her that I had actually held a photograph of the very same man before, as well as the stock of the gun that killed him, she got up and ran from the restaurant. To this day, I wonder about things like that; they seem completely random, yet somehow too perfect. Of course I would end up meeting Liz, Rebecca's dead brother's ex-girlfriend. That's the way the world works. That's just the way it is.

Liz and I became lovers for a brief instant, but for me there was just something too darned strange about that arrangement and I broke it off. I have not seen her in thirty years, yet I still consider us friends joined at the hip.

Ambition Unchecked

As the first year of the actor's training program came to a close, I realized that I had indeed found my passion. I had discovered my purpose in life and it was simple: to become the greatest actor in the history of the world. I had not heard the term "narcissism" yet and so I remained unaware of how grandiose my ambitions really were. All I knew was that I would work 24/7 to achieve my goal. Late spring was audition season for summer stock and we all worked like dogs perfecting our audition pieces. Then came "Hell Week," when all the summer stock companies came to ACT to find their actors. We were going to audition for five companies, but one was a cut above the rest, the Oregon Shakespeare Festival in Ashland. It was the most prestigious Shakespeare theatre in the country, and, of course, the one place I felt I belonged.

I auditioned for all five groups and was rejected by only one, the Oregon Shakespeare Festival. I was devastated for a moment, but then I realized that most of my friends from ACT were going to the Pacific Coast Center for the Performing Arts (PCPA), where Allen Fletcher would be directing a production of *Peer Gynt* by Ibsen. Having done the play once before in the nude, I wanted a crack at it again, this time fully clothed and directed by a genius. So off I went to PCPA.

Allen Fletcher was the country's premier expert on Ibsen and had done his own translation of the epic poem, which he adapted into a play. Daniel Davis, who went on to play Fran Drescher's butler in the television series *The Nanny*, was to play Peer. Allen was such a purist that he made us call the play *Pear Gunt,* which is the Norwegian pronunciation, rather than the familiar and Anglicized *Peer Gynt.* In addition to *Peer Gynt,* PCPA was performing a number of other shows that summer; I was cast as Jud in *Oklahoma,* Demetrius in *A Midsummer Night's Dream,* and several smaller roles in *Peer Gynt.* I understood Demetrius, the young lover of Hermia in the Shakespeare, I understood the three roles I was to play in *Peer Gynt,* but I was puzzled that anyone would cast this baby-faced, innocent kid as Jud Fry, the meanest, snarliest dude in Oklahoma.

I worked like a maniac on all three projects, and when opening night came around for *A Midsummer Night's Dream,* the "love" scenes were somewhat dampened by the fact that Gina, the girl playing my love interest who was also my on-again, off-again lover in real life, had to throw up in a bucket offstage before each of her entrances. Overall the play was a success, in large part because of Tony Plana's performance as Puck. Tony Plana went on to perform in many films as well as play Ugly Betty's father in the TV series of the same name. But when the reviews for *Midsummer* came out, I was not mentioned, and I came to the conclusion that I must have worn a cloak of invisibility that night.

Peer Gynt was the next to open, and once again, though the play received raves in the press, I was not mentioned. Obviously my cloak of invisibility knew no boundaries.

The role that most frightened me was that of Jud because I was so unlike him in type. I also had to sing a song called "Lonely Room," which was pretty much all in a deep baritone, and ever since childhood I had been told by my brother that I was tone deaf. Oddly enough, when the play opened, the cloak of invisibility came off and I got rave reviews! I was shocked, and from then on, I knew that I could never be an accurate judge of my own performance.

The summer of 1975 gave me the "lift" necessary to get me through the most grueling year of the three-year training program. The original forty-person class for the first year at ACT was culled to twenty for the second year. Half of our class was essentially told to pursue another profession. Fortunately I was not. But the cuts didn't stop at year two. We were also aware that the third-year class would consist of ten or fewer students. This meant that we had to be fiercely competitive and consistently be the absolute best we could be if we were to have a future in the theatre. And it was just that, a future in the theatre (not film or television—theatre), that we all craved. Film was like the dirty stepchild of the theatre and television was like the filthy bastard. We all swore off Hollywood and vowed that we would remain true to our values and only pursue a life in the theatre. Obviously I didn't do a very good job of keeping my promise.

The second year was more "spear carrying" on stage at the Geary Theater, one of San Francisco's oldest and largest theatres and also the home of ACT. We were not allowed to speak unless we were members of the union, the Actors' Equity Association. There is a certain conundrum that goes along with trying to break into the acting business. It's a major "chicken or egg" paradox: One cannot become a member of the union without being hired by an "Equity theatre" and one cannot be hired by an "Equity theatre" without being a member of the union. The same applies to the Screen Actors Guild (SAG), which is the union for film actors. No card, no job; no job, no card. So it comes down to the luck of the draw and the lucky ones get hired without a card and the theatre or film company petitions Actor's Equity or SAG to let them in. Sometimes it works, sometimes it doesn't. Have I mentioned how hard it is to become an actor?

We all were looking for that golden opportunity to get our union card. Without it, we knew, we would have no career beyond "summer stock," which is almost always nonunion.

Of the twenty remaining students, ten of us were absolutely focused on our ambition to become the best actor in history, but I believe that I was the most consistent in my efforts to fine-tune my technique and to be noticed by anyone in a position to give me that golden opportunity. I watched every play at the Geary over and over until I knew every actor's lines and felt I could have said them better. I stayed in the training studios until midnight practicing vocal techniques and speeches from different plays in different genres. Meanwhile, my classmates were usually downstairs at a local pub called the Curtain Call getting sloshed, a custom of which I also partook on occasion. But I was like a Stinger missile, quite possibly because I felt that gnawing sensation of inadequacy that had dogged me since childhood. My brother had always told me I was ugly, stupid, and uncoordinated. My mother and father were certainly not supportive of my decision to pursue an acting career, and they told me on numerous occasions that I was doomed to failure and that they wouldn't support me when I came calling for help. I had a lot to prove and I was determined to win.

Still pursuing my backup plan of rock stardom
in San Francisco at ACT.

The Big Easy

In the winter of 1976, the great American playwright Tennessee Williams came to ACT to put up a new play entitled *This Is (An Entertainment)*. It was his latest work and was almost entirely incomprehensible. Most of Tennessee's later plays seemed to be written in outer space and *This Is* was no exception. We all thought that he was a genius, which of course he was, but it seemed as though he had taken some strange back road on his literary journey and was experimenting with new forms of speech and thought. Or it might have just been drugs. I chose to believe that this great writer had discovered a crack in the armor of Western rational thinking and was attempting to deconstruct some of the linguistic conventions that were the adhesive keeping our civilized interactions from exploding into irrational and purely emotional outbursts. He invited chaos through nonsensical scene and linguistic structure.

I've often wondered if the guy was just toasted all the time and if we give him way too much credit. But he was, after all, responsible for *A Streetcar Named Desire*, *The Glass Menagerie*, *Summer and Smoke*, *Sweet Bird of Youth*, *Orpheus Descending*, *Cat on a Hot Tin Roof*, etc., etc., etc.!! The man was an American treasure and I had the pleasure of meeting him for the first time in the lobby of the Geary Theater during a dress rehearsal for his most dreadful accomplishment, *This Is (An Entertainment)*.

It was a late weekday afternoon and rumor had it that Tennessee Williams was coming to town to observe the final week of rehearsals for his new play. Of course, I was thrilled. I had massacred one of his greatest works with my dreadful broken-backed portrayal of Stanley Kowalski in *Streetcar* back at Berkeley, but I knew that I was destined to play the role again, and I believed I would find redemption in the second attempt. I had kept working on the play from time to time, and now its author was going to be somewhere within arm's reach.

I walked over to the theatre with the intention of finding the great master, and when I opened the lobby door I ran smack-dab into a short man in a rumpled suit. We collided and a folder of papers the man had been carrying fell to the floor. We both reached down to gather up the folder when I realized that I had just whacked into Tennessee Williams.

He stood up, and just when I thought he was about to say, "Watch where you're going, you idiot!" he said, "I am so, so sorry. I always seem to be bumping into things." Then, looking me in the eye, he said with that famous drawl, "I'm so glad I bumped into you and not the door!" There was plenty of innuendo in that statement but I ignored it and introduced myself, blabbering that I had played Stanley in college and that I had a few questions about the play and if he ever had a minute, I would love to . . . He interrupted me, putting his right index finger up to his lips.

It wasn't so much "Shut up!" as it was "Okay, I hear you. Ask away!"

I said, "Well, really, I only have one question. Did Marlon Brando capture what you intended in the character of Stanley?" I had always, of course, loved Brando's performance in the film, but having studied the text, I was haunted by what seemed to me a note in his performance that was not in step with the rest of the play and I couldn't put my finger on it. His performance was luminescent and thoroughly engaging, but I was nagged by the question, Was it the character Tennessee wrote? Only the author could answer that and now I had asked him.

Tennessee just smiled a broad, knowing smile, and, grabbing my left shoulder with his right hand, he said, "Son, go back and read the play again tonight. Come find me tomorrow and tell me what you think." He patted me on the shoulder and walked out the door. It was as ambiguous an answer as possible, but it was not a no and it was definitely not a yes. I reread the play word for word that night and found my answer.

Brando played Stanley with a slight New York accent. A lower-class man of Polish descent, born and raised in New Orleans, Stanley would have had a thick Southern Louisiana twang. The next day, I raced to the theatre and found Tennessee sitting in the orchestra watching the absolutely dreadful rehearsal. I waited until a break and sat down next to him. He looked at me like I was invading his space for a second, then seemed to remember our collision of the day before.

I said, "I read the play again and Stanley was supposed to be from New Orleans and Brando . . ." Tennessee stopped me once again with a finger to the lips. Then he said, "You did read the play. Good for you!" And with that, the rehearsal began again and our conversation was over.

I came away from that moment thinking that there was another way to interpret Stanley and that an actor could play that role and make it his own. Over the years, I had several more conversations with Tennessee Williams, but I never again asked him about Stanley or *A Streetcar Named Desire*.

In the early eighties, a very talented director named John Erman was tapped to direct a television production of *Streetcar*. At the time, I was a hot young film actor bred on the stage and perfect to play Stanley opposite Jessica Lange as Blanche DuBois. My agent called me on a Monday afternoon and told me that I was on a "short list" of actors who would read for the part for the director and the producer later that week. Here was my chance at redemption and possibly even an award if I could bring my own interpretation to the screen.

I was living alone at the time in a 900-square-foot shack in Laurel Canyon, and when I hung up the phone, I grabbed a camera, a tape recorder, my toothbrush, and one change of clothes, and drove straight to the airport. I found the next flight to New Orleans and, with no itinerary, went straight to the Big Easy to find Stanley Kowalski and bring Tennessee's real vision of Stanley to life.

I arrived at night and slung my tape recorder and my camera over my shoulder and walked out into the wonderful chaos of the French Quarter. I had recently played a gay writer who seduced a married man in a film for Twentieth Century Fox. It was one of the the first films in which the actors were portraying "normal" homosexuals and had caused quite a stir. Most everyone who saw the movie came away thinking I was gay and I thought that was kind of cool—in a twisted sort of way.

When I walked out onto Bourbon Street, I started asking around for bars that would have locals rather than tourists, but most everyone I asked must have seen my gay movie because they all pointed me to the same bar, which, when I walked in, was a room full of men who fell into complete silence. I guess I had become somewhat of a hero in the gay community in New Orleans. The bar treated me like I was royalty, but I was on a mission, and after some cordial conversation and a couple of beers, I extricated myself and kept hunting for the elusive Stanley Kowalski.

I worked my way across town and around three o'clock in the morning I found myself sitting next to the man I had been trying to find. I was at a bar on Decatur Street talking with a Polish truck driver named Sam who hailed from the Ninth Ward. Sam told me that in the thirties, forties, and fifties, the New Orleans Polish community was centered in the Ninth Ward. I asked him if he would mind my putting our conversation on tape and he obliged. He went through a litany of words and how they would be pronounced by a true New Orleans Pole. There was a definite drawl and words like bird were pronounced "boid."

This guy was definitely not Brando but was exactly the man Tennessee described in his notes on the play, which had originally been titled *The Poker Night*. In the stage directions, Mr. Williams describes the Kowalskis' house in great detail, and the next day, after getting an hour of Sam on tape, I went in search of the very house that had inspired the play. I found my way to Elysian Fields Avenue and, sure enough, there was an old grass "right of way" where a streetcar line had once traveled. The tracks were long gone and trees had been planted in their place but it was definitely a "right of way."

I walked up and down both sides of the street with a copy of the stage directions in one hand. The notes described a white frame house on a corner with a staircase leading up to a second floor with "quaintly ornamented gables." The interior description was of a large room with a curtain in the middle that separated it into two sections. I looked at each corner house to no avail until I noticed one home that was for sale and under construction. I walked over to it and there it was: a white clapboard house with an outdoor stairway that led to a second-floor apartment. The gables below the roof were carved and quite ornate. I noticed that the front door was open for the workers to come in and out. I walked in as though I belonged there and no one paid me any attention. I could see that there was a floor-to-ceiling-length accordion-type divider that, when pulled out, would have separated the room. Bingo! Not only had I found the real Stanley, but I also was standing in the very room that had inspired the play. I knew the part was mine!

I flew back to LA that afternoon armed with my tape of Sam the Pole from the Ninth Ward and the distinct odor of the French Quarter. I spent the next day working on the reading I had prepared for the director and went into his office feeling like a million bucks. I was so excited to tell the director about my conversation with Tennessee and I couldn't wait to read the part the way I was sure the playwright had intended. I showed the director the pictures of the actual house and then read the confrontation scene after Stanley comes back from the hospital and finds Blanche drunk and dressed to go on her moonlight cruise. I incorporated the essence of Sam the Polish truck driver from the Ninth Ward and channeled Stanley direct from the soul of the then dearly departed playwright. In my own fantasy I was brilliant, and I could see Tennessee giving me that sly wink of approval he had given me when I first asked him if Brando had nailed it. I finished the speech and the director just said thank you and indicated that our face time was over.

Wait just a minute! I had flown to New Orleans, found the "real" Stanley after discussing it with Williams himself, visited the real house, and that was it? "Thank you for coming in."

Yes, that was it! Treat Williams was hired to play Stanley in that production, and though I admire Treat's work, I felt that his performance was pretty much a clone of Brando's. Just as well. I'm sure that anything other than a Brando-type interpretation would have been considered sacrilege by the throngs of Brando fans and I would have been tarred and feathered by the press and everyone else. Had Tennessee still been around, he might have come to my defense, but even that would have been unlikely. I probably dodged a huge bullet.

But a few years before my trip to the Big Easy and my fruitless audition, ACT put up *This Is (An Entertainment),* which opened to horrible reviews. It was a colossal failure, even by regional theatre standards. I still felt that I had been in the presence of genius when I had spoken to Mr. Williams and I cherish those brief conversations about Marlon Brando and *A Streetcar Named Desire* to this day.

Hung Like a Horse

Early that spring, I received a note during my afternoon acting class. This was a very odd occurrence. For one thing, acting class was considered sacred and we were never to be disturbed or distracted during class. It was highly unusual for a session to be interrupted and one never left a class early unless it was for a medical emergency. But the note was from Bill Ball, instructing me to meet him immediately in a different rehearsal studio. I was being summoned by the boss; I had no choice but to leave class.

I couldn't imagine what was going on and my head was filled with all manner of scenarios. Maybe Cyril Magnin wanted me banished from the training program. Maybe Bill was going to try to jump my bones! I was perplexed. I arrived on the fifth floor and knocked gently on the rehearsal studio door. "Come in!" Bill's voice boomed from behind the door. I stepped into a large empty room and Bill said, "Take a seat." There was a single empty folding chair opposite Bill. I sat down and wondered what on earth this could be about.

Bill looked at me for what seemed like an eternity. Then he said in a low voice, "I have been asked to direct a play but I can't tell you what it is just yet." I didn't know if I should respond to that statement, but after a moment he went on, "I've been following your progress and I think there is a part in this play that you should audition for." There was more silence as he watched my reaction, which was, I'm sure, pretty easy to read.

I was in shock that I was being considered for a role in a play that Bill Ball was going to direct. He said, "I wish I could tell you more but everything is still up in the air and quite hush-hush. You know how it is." Actually I didn't have a clue how it was, but I nodded as though I did. Then he said something that truly blew my mind. "I won't know if you are right for the part unless I see you with no clothes on, so if you wouldn't mind, would you please take off your pants and your shirt."

I asked, "Just my pants and my shirt?"

He replied with no discernible expression, "And your underwear." There was more silence.

I felt as though I had finally come to that big fork in the road—the one every actor hears about and pretends they may never have to face. The gay artistic director wants me to get naked with him alone in a room and he won't tell me why. There was an empty table between us, but that didn't seem like much of an obstacle for him if he wanted to have his way. A line had been drawn in the sand and I had to make a decision.

I stood and thanked him for considering me but I didn't feel that it would ever be necessary for an actor to take off his clothes to get a part. Oddly he smiled and said he understood and said that he respected my position but that he wouldn't be able to recommend that I audition for the part. He said he was sorry and wished me luck as I left the room. I walked down the stairs toward what remained of my acting class and I just kept asking myself, "What the fuck was that?"

I told no one of my encounter with Mr. Ball in the fifth-floor rehearsal room and only after several weeks did I learn that the play he had been asked to direct was Peter Shaffer's *Equus*. ACT had been tapped for the West Coast premiere of the play, which had just taken London and New York by storm, racking up more awards than any drama in recent Broadway history. In New York, the play starred Richard Burton as a desperate and confused psychiatrist trying to figure out why a young teenage boy had blinded a number of horses with a hoof pick. The boy was played by Peter Firth, and he and Burton had won many awards for their performances.

The thing about the play that attracted the most attention around the water cooler, however, was the fact that the boy, Alan Strang, and his girlfriend spent the last twenty minutes of the play totally nude on stage. When I heard all of this, I pondered whether my reaction to Mr. Ball would have been different if I had known about the play before he asked me to take off my clothes. I still didn't really understand why he needed to see the penis of the actor who might play the boy. What was he looking for? A big one? A small one? Circumsized? Uncircumsized? Perhaps he wanted to make sure that the actor's penis was not deformed.

Bill Ball directed the West Coast premier of *Equus,* which opened in the spring of 1976. Another young actor was hired from outside the company to play the boy. He obviously had the right penis and had no problem showing it to Mr. Ball. The show was a huge hit and made big money for ACT.

As it happened, Mr. Ball and the professional company had made plans the year before to visit Moscow and perform a play by Eugene O'Neill for the Moscow Art Theatre, which had, somehow or other, become our sister company even though our respective countries still had enough atom bombs pointed at each other to destroy this planet and several more in the solar system.

Equus was making too darn much money for the company and needed to be extended in order to pay for the Moscow trip. That's when Mr. Ball called me back into the fifth-floor rehearsal studio for a second peek at my postadolescent pudendum.

The young actor playing "the boy" was going with the troop to Moscow. Now Mr. Ball needed to find a suitable replacement for the San Francisco run. Once again, I entered the bare room. As I sat down facing him, he asked me how I liked the play. I flashed back on the first questions he ever asked me: "Can you cook? Can you drive a car?" I told him I was amazed by the play and the part of the boy, which was all true. I knew his next question was going to be "So, are you ready to show me the goods?" It was. Though the wording was a bit more civilized. I said yes and dropped my trousers.

His eyes went down to the frightened and certainly shriveled penis that really wanted nothing to do with this full frontal nudity stuff. His gaze rested there for only a second or two, and he immediately said I could audition for the part the following week. I had passed penis inspection. His assistant later told me that Bill had been looking for an actor that was not "hung like a horse," which would have been distracting for the audience. Not to mention the fact that to be hung like a horse would also not have been in keeping with the story, which was about horses that were hung like horses and a young man that was hung like a young man.

I wasn't quite sure how I felt about having passed the "test" but I was excited about the possibility of getting my first professional job as an actor, even though I would have to run around on stage in my birthday suit in front of a couple of thousand people eight times a week.

Bacon and Eggs

A week later, I auditioned in front of ten or twelve people in the theatre. I played a couple of the scenes, alone on stage, holding the script while being read the other actor's lines from the audience. I was not asked to whip out my penis.

The next day, Bill called me into his office to tell me I got the part. As I stood in front of his desk, listening to the words that were sure to change my life forever, I had my second recognizable bipolar moment. I was, on the one hand, overwhelmed with joy by the fact that I was being given my first professional gig, while at the same time I was totally overwhelmed with dread at the prospect of full frontal nudity. My God! What had I agreed to do!?

I had six weeks to prepare. My first rehearsal was that afternoon in the same room where I had proven to the gay director that I wasn't hung like a horse. I was given a copy of the script and measured for my costume, which was a pair of white jeans and a cream-colored, long-sleeved thermal.

The actor playing the lead horse in the play, Nugget, which the boy rides from time to time, was very concerned about my weight. His name was Michael. He was tall and handsome and had been a year ahead of me in the training program. The horses in the play were very stylized and the actors playing the horses had to wear huge hooflike boots as well as horselike head gear that gave them an extra two feet of height. That, of course, made them somewhat unstable, which meant that the actor/horses had to be very strong and very coordinated. Michael was perfect for the part of Nugget. Though tall and strong, he was still quite thin and weighed only 160 pounds. I weighed in at 165 on the first day of rehearsal and he told me I had to lose at least ten pounds by opening night. He was right. I was going to have to jump up onto his back like Will Rogers while he stood still in twelve-inch boots on a slanted stage.

I had never had to lose any weight before and had no clue how to do it. Michael was very helpful, though, and gave me a workout and running regimen as well as a recently published book titled *Dr. Atkins' Diet Revolution* by Dr. Robert Atkins. That was my first exposure to the "Atkins diet," which has come in handy over the years for getting ready for love scenes on film. During my thirties and forties, I used the diet so much that my cholesterol levels soared to above 280. Thankfully, for me and any future audience, my love scene days are over and my cholesterol is back to normal.

The six weeks leading up to my first nude night on stage were grueling. I would wake up a dawn and run up and down the hills of San Francisco and then eat nothing but eggs and bacon all day long. I was still living on my $45 per week stipend and that, augmented by U.S. Government-issued food stamps, which all the students collected, was just enough to cover my $100 rent and the cost of bacon and eggs from the local co-op. The Atkins diet is a high-protein diet, and steak, roast beef, and ground sirloin were the recommended meats of choice—all of which were way beyond my pay grade. So it was bacon and eggs for breakfast, bacon and eggs for lunch, and bacon and eggs for dinner.

Halfway through the rehearsal process, I was presented with my first professional contract to sign. I was to be paid the grand sum of $126 per week while performing, but I would have to give up my student stipend and pay taxes on the dough. I still came out ahead, and was happy as a pig in you-know-what to finally be making the "big money."

The "full frontal nudity" thing kept haunting me throughout the rehearsals and I kept waiting for Mr. Ball or the stage manager to ask me to get naked for the final act. Curiously they never did, so, during the final week before we "opened," I asked the understudy if she would practice the scene with me in the buff. It so happened that the understudy was none other than Gina, my on-again, off-again girl-friend, who, at this point in time, happened to be off again.

The girl that I would be doing the actual play with was a professional actress who would only rehearse with me during the final week and then only fully clothed. Gina and I booked a small studio on the Wednesday before our Tuesday opening and went through the clothed scenes and made a plan to actually get naked for the nude scene. We were alone in the room and felt reasonably comfortable about the whole thing since we had spent a year exchanging fluids on a regular basis anyway. We got to the final act and brazenly disrobed at the appropriate moment, imagining that there were a couple of thousand people out in front of us. Everything went great until the moment when I was to attempt to mount her in the missionary position.

In the play, the boy wants to do the nasty with the girl but can't, and the horses witness his failure, hence, the blinding of the beasts. Unfortunately Gina and I still had some heat between us, and as I came down toward her naked vagina, I lost all control and became hard as a rock. That, of course, defeated the whole purpose of the rehearsals and informed me that I would, more than likely, never be a good method actor. Unlike the characters in Peter Shaffer's award-winning play, we consummated right then and there on the floor of the studio. Just like that, we were on again, at least for a few minutes. The rehearsal was a bust.

I kept asking the stage manager when we were going to rehearse the last act in the nude, and finally he told me that Bill had decided to let the opening night be the first time we actually got naked. I was relieved and terrified at the same time. I was very comfortable doing the scene clothed but I, of course, had no idea what it would be like to do it naked in front of all those people. And, to add insult to injury, there would be a gallery of students who actually sat on the stage with us throughout the whole play and who would be less than three feet from my naked penis as the pants came down.

I had started talking to my penis throughout each day. "Now listen, when the time comes, I don't want you to be afraid. You hear!?? I want you to be big and strong and allow lots of blood to flow and I want you to make me and our kind proud!" I knew I was farting in the wind but I kept at it anyway.

By the day of the dress rehearsal, I was down to 155 pounds—I had turned into a skinny, walking, talking egg that smelled like bacon. I had no energy and in addition to being terrified about what was to come in a matter of hours, I was starving. Around noon, Bill Ball found me at the theatre going over my lines with the stage manager. He took one look at me and said, "Oh my!" He turned to the stage manager and whipped out a hundred-dollar bill. "Get this man a rare filet steak and mashed potatoes from the bistro across the street. And I want him to have a filet steak and potatoes every day three hours before the performance."

I'm not sure I had ever had filet steak in my life, but over the six-week production, I developed a taste for it that follows me everywhere—even to this day.

I devoured the meat and potatoes with relish but still felt a gnawing sense of dread. The thought of being naked in front of all those
people tore at my insides, and before I knew it, I was glued to the toilet, having relinquished the expensive meat and potatoes through the
back door. I just couldn't stop doubting myself.

What would become of me after that first night? Would I have
any friends left? Would I still have respect after baring it all? I was
still haunted, from time to time, by those huge red polished fingers
that had held my tiny four-year-old penis over the urinal at nursery
school. Would I be laughed out of the theatre? What had I agreed
to do!?

Tenderloin

Curtain time for ACT was 8:00 p.m., which meant that the actors had to be at the theatre by seven thirty at the latest. At six on opening night I was beside myself and couldn't sit still, so I decided to take a lone walk through the city.

I walked down toward Market Street and found myself in the middle of the Tenderloin district, which was mostly porno houses, seedy bars, and bums. Why I chose to walk in that direction I'll never know, but the contrast between life's underbelly and what I was about to do on stage must have seemed appropriate to me.

I thought about my parents and their lack of support for what I was doing with my life and I wondered if they would be proud to know that I was now a paid union member of my chosen profession. The Republican in them would have liked the "paid" part but hated the "union" part. I hadn't told them of my good fortune yet because I would have had to mention the part about the family jewels, which they would most certainly have wanted me to keep covered up.

I remembered how random it was that I was an actor at all as I flashed on my first days at Berkeley and my dashed dreams of architectural glory. I felt like "dead man walking" and relived much of my life up to that point, knowing that by the final curtain a few hours later my fate would be sealed. I would either be a triumphant success or doomed to the giant trash heap of would-be actors whose dreams were dashed by a single terrible performance on a single night. I was determined not to be one of those actors.

I walked up Leavenworth Street, which was notoriously seedy, toward Geary and couldn't help but put two and two together, and I thought about my time behind bars and how I had told my jailbird mentor and savior, Brother Robinson, that someday I was going to be an actor and he had said in his high squeaky voice, "If you gonna be a actor, you better be a star 'cause then they can't touch ya!" There I was, walking up Leavenworth Street, toward my chance at stardom. The irony was almost too much to bear. I wondered where Brother Robinson was and if he would even remember me if I became a star. Maybe somewhere along the line he's seen me on film and hollered out, "Hey, that guy was my roommate . . . in Redwood City!"

I got to the theatre at seven fifteen and went to my dressing room, which was awash with flowers and cards from friends and well-wishers. There was a single ecru card from Mr. Ball that had six words written in his own hand: "You have greatness within you! Continue!" I closed the door to my room and cried as I read and reread his card. I would like to have shown that to my father—and I planned to but never did.

The stage manager barked out, "Half hour!" over the PA system and I got down to business. My costume was laid out. One pair of white jeans, no belt, one long-sleeved cream thermal, and a pair of off-white slip-on Keds sneakers. No underwear. I slipped off my bell-bottom jeans and T-shirt and was in costume within seconds. I sat down at the makeup table and perused my makeup, which had been meticulously laid out by my dresser, Elaine, who also happened to be Michael's girlfriend. She was my "dresser" but I would really only need her to dress me after the final curtain and before the curtain call, which I was to take in my white jeans. There would not be enough time to get a shirt on after I ran off stage naked in the dark at the end. Her main job would be to get me "decent" before my bow. How hard could that be?

There I was, fifteen minutes before my professional career was to begin, and I had no idea what to do about makeup. The week before, I

had asked the stage manager about the makeup thing and he told me that everyone used it. He said I should buy a Ben Nye professional kit for $50, which I did, using the last of my money before my first big paycheck would hit my account the next week. I stared at the pots of powder and paste. I was twenty-six, without a line on my face, and by the end of the play the audience would be able to count my pubic hairs if they so chose, so makeup seemed somewhat superfluous, even a bit ridiculous. I never did use any of it, but it had been so nicely arranged by Elaine that I left it there untouched for the entire run of the play.

"Places, please!" The stage manager was in a good mood. "Have a great show, everyone!" I took it as a good omen. Stage managers have seen it all and if they are in a good mood at "Places" it means they like the show. I must have been doing something right.

As I rose from my dressing room chair, I felt like I was about to walk the plank, but as I approached the stage I got excited. I could hear the full house murmuring as we took our positions backstage, and then the hush of more than a thousand voices as the house lights went to half. Then, magically, silence! My heart was pounding out of my chest as I walked out in the pitch dark to take my place in the opening tableaux. I stood, center stage, bolt upright, with Michael as Nugget, the stallion, hovering above me, nuzzling my neck. Then one single spotlight exploded over us like a bolt of lightning and the play began.

There had been such great press about the play and the first run had been such a success that the audience was clearly on our side, which always makes a big difference. They laughed and held their breath in all the right places. I was very pleased with how it was going up until the final scene of act 1 when the boy has an orgasm while riding Nugget. I always thought the scene was a bit over the top, but Bill convinced me that there was no way I could be "too big" as I reached my climax.

As the curtain came down at the end of the first act there was thunderous applause, presumably because I had executed such a fine bareback orgasm. During the intermission, everyone seemed very up and said that I was doing a great job, but they all had the same look in their eye, as if they were thinking, "Now for the real test!" or "Let's see what you're really made of!"

I went back to my dressing room and stared at myself in the mirror. Could I do it? Did I have the "right stuff"? And what did that mean? Would I freeze at the moment of truth and keep my pants on? Someone told me that had happened when an understudy went on once in London. I banished the thought and forced myself to believe that the words and the play would carry me to my fully frontal nude artistic destiny.

"Places, please, for act two," came the stage manager's voice. I took one last glance in the mirror and said calmly to the image staring back at me, "You can do this, boy . . . you can do this." Then I got up, walked out of the dressing room, and into the rest of my life, silently singing "Climb Every Mountain" as I went.

The second act of *Equus* is mainly about the boy and a girl named Jill he meets at the stable. She is much worldlier and finds the boy, Alan, to be quite fascinating and sexy in his own innocent way. Ironically, for me personally anyway, she takes him to a porno movie to see if she can get a rise out of him, so to speak. While there, his father comes into the theatre for his own "rise" and a very awkward moment ensues. Jill takes the boy back to the stables, where she asks him to take off his clothes.

Things continued to go well as the second act marched on. Then, after what seemed like only minutes on stage, the big scene arrived. I heard the actress playing Jill say, "Take your sweater off."

I delivered my line: "What?"

And she said, "I will if you will."

Now that I think about it, that character of Jill is a cheeky little bitch! I pulled my sweater over my head. I was absolutely dead-on in the middle of the scene artistically—right there in the moment, in the groove, the muse showering me with her grace as I went to unbutton my pants.

Acting is a true bipolar experience because we can be right "there" in the scene, totally absorbed by the artistic moment, and at the same time, we are also aware of the other "there," which in this case was a couple of thousand people, none of whom was breathing and each of whom was waiting to see just what lay beneath those white jeans. This was literally a "pin drop" moment. I slowly pulled the zipper down and began to peel the jeans over my thighs.

Then a sense of perfect harmony coursed through my soul. I had experienced that sensation only once before, as I woke in the passenger seat of that Datsun 1600 and realized that I was certainly going to die in a head-on collision. It was the peace that comes with total acceptance of whatever the moment has to offer. It was Full Frontal Nudity in the presence of that which is divine in all of us and in everything else.

When the final scene ended and the house went to black, the audience broke into thunderous applause. I ran offstage and Elaine, my dresser, was waiting with my jeans, but my body was so sweaty that she couldn't get them on. I pulled and she tugged and the audience cheered as the stage manager waved me frantically toward the stage to take my bow. I guess Elaine's job was harder than I thought because we never did get the pants all the way up, but they at least covered the main event. As I walked onto the stage, the entire audience stood and cheered as I took one bow and then another.

I looked to the side and the stage manager motioned for me to keep taking bows as the crowd cheered. I ran off the stage and Peter Donat, who played the doctor, came out to the same thunder. He beckoned for me to come back and the audience went wild—and kept going wild throughout a two-season run. As I walked off the stage that first night, Bill Ball stood in the wings. He said nothing. He just shook my hand, and, with a wry smile, gave me one wink. And that was that.

This Week in San Francisco and the Bay Area

Key

June 4-12, 1976

Harry Hamlin is featured as a demented stable boy and Michael Keys-Hall portrays the horse Nugget in A.C.T.'s spellbinding thriller, "Equus". Directed by William Ball, the Peter Shaffer drama is playing through June 19 at the Geary Theater.

Epilogue

This new version of the play was such a huge success that I was asked to return the next season to reprise the role, which landed me on the cover of almost every gay magazine in the country, as well as caught the eye of some casting directors from Hollywood.

I did go back to ACT for one more season, but sometime in the fall, I saw an actress filling out some forms in the green room and I casually asked her what she was up to. She said she was applying for a Fulbright scholarship that, if she won it, would pay for her to study at the Royal Academy of Dramatic Art in London. I asked where she got the forms and she said she had an extra and that I could have it. I took the form, thanked her, and, on a whim, filled it out, requesting a scholarship to the Moscow Art Theatre. I sent the application in and forgot about it.

That season, I did several plays for the professional company, of which I was then a member. I also continued taking classes toward the master of fine arts degree that it would take me another ten years to get.

In February, I got a very thin letter from the Fulbright people and assumed that it contained a terse rejection. I ripped it open and dejectedly read that my application had been approved and that arrangements were being made for me to study at the famed Moscow Art Theatre in the Soviet Union!

My first thought was that I had to learn Russian, fast! Though Bill Ball asked me to return to ACT for another two seasons as the young male ingenue of the professional company, I opted for the Fulbright and our Soviet enemies. I started taking Russian classes and learning about Russian history as the spring season came to an end and the company packed up for its annual trip to Hawaii.

It had become a tradition that Bill would reward the company with a one-play tour to Honolulu every year that lasted for a week. I also think Mr. Ball loved the mai tais at the Royal Hawaiian Hotel, where all the company actors were put up.

I packed my Russian language books along with my swimming gear in preparation for our South Pacific journey. We arrived in Honolulu and it was everything I had imagined. The air smelled of plumeria flowers and the wind was somehow both warm and refreshing. We were doing a production of *Ah, Wilderness!* by Eugene O'Neill, in which I had hardly anything to do, so the week was mostly a vacation for me.

One balmy night after our final performance, my friend Michael, the same Michael upon whose back I had jumped for two seasons of *Equus,* asked me if I'd like to take a walk on the beach with his friend Dan. It sounded like a great idea as it was a perfect starry night. We made our way to the beach and soon we were laughing and joking about how cool it was to be in Hawaii and how sad it was going to be to have to leave the next night. Mike nonchalantly whipped out a joint and lit up as we walked. I was not a pot smoker and was still very gun-shy about doing anything illegal in public. I had just always had very bad luck when it came to marijuana so I declined to smoke and peeled off toward the water for a little alone time while my buddies got shitfaced.

Within a minute, a very cool-looking dude with dreadlocks in a Hawaiian shirt sauntered up to Michael and asked if he could have a toke from the joint. Mike handed him the reefer and out came the badge and three other plainclothes officers from behind the coconut trees.

Here we go again!

The dreadlock guy yelled down to me on the beach, "You know these guys, man?" I yelled back that I did know them and he proceeded, of course, to arrest me too. We were taken into the cop shop, fingerprinted and photographed, and ended up spending the night on the jailhouse floor. We were arraigned the next morning and I told my two friends to plead "not guilty."

The one thing I learned in jail, other than how to tie a cigarette in a knot, stamp on it, throw it against the wall, and still smoke it, was that you never, ever plead guilty to anything, even if you are caught red-handed as these fellows had been. Over and over, as we waited our turn in front of the judge, I reiterated, "Do not plead guilty. We can beat this." They both agreed and swore that they would say, "Not guilty," when asked.

Finally our names were called. Michael was first to go before the judge. "How do you plead?" the judge asked.

"Guilty, you honor," Michael replied.

I winced and looked at him with horror. What had he done? Now we were all fucked! Then Dan was called before the judge. "How do you plead?" asked the judge.

"Guilty, your honor," Dan replied.

Then it was my turn. "How do you plead?"

"Not guilty, your honor!" I said in a loud voice.

"Very well then," said the judge. "For the two of you who pled guilty, that will be a fifteen-dollar fine each. See the bailiff outside the courtroom to pay your fine. For the gentleman who pled not guilty, I'm setting your court date for a week from this Thursday at eleven a.m."

I immediately raised my hand and asked to speak to the judge. He agreed to hear me and I asked if I could change my plea to guilty. He looked at me with a stern face and asked, "Are you guilty?"

I said, "No, but it will cost me at least a thousand dollars to stay in Hawaii for an extra week and I'll have to hire an attorney and it's only fifteen dollars if I'm guilty, so I'd like to change my plea to guilty."

He said, "I will not allow an innocent man to plead guilty in my court for expedience's sake. Court date stands, defendant released on his own recognizance!" With that he pounded his gavel and stood up holding the Baggie with the partially smoked joint as evidence in his right hand. He looked right at me and said, "This looks like pretty good stuff," and walked out of the courtroom.

Michael agreed to stay on in Hawaii as my witness. I found a cheap lawyer through the company manager, and Mike and I went camping in the Kalalau Valley on the island of Kauai for a week at no appreciable cost to us. We returned to Honolulu the following Wednesday for my court date and within minutes the judge threw the case out due to lack of evidence. The joint was missing and the dreadlock dude failed to appear for the state. I was acquitted. I have kept a healthy distance from illegal drugs since that day.

Me, camping out in Kalalau Valley on the island of Kauai, awaiting trial for possession of pot in Honolulu, June 1977.

I had gone back to Los Angeles to pack my bags for Moscow when I received word from the Fulbright folks that my Russian visa had been pulled because Jimmy Carter and Leonid Brezhnev had gotten into a pissing match and it looked like nuclear war was back on the table. They told me I could still take the money and go to London for a year but that I couldn't go to school because I had already had too much of that. They just wanted me to go to London and soak up whatever was British and theatrical and write a paper on that and come home.

I had already left ACT and they had hired some new guy to be the young star so I had no place to go but London. I had learned how to say, "Hello, I don't know how to speak or understand your language but would you like to have sex with me anyway?" in Russian but that was the extent of it. Good thing my English was pretty good.

I was getting ready to go to London when a casting director who had seen *Equus* called me to talk about the movie business. I told her I wasn't interested in acting on film but she insisted that I make the trip to Warner Bros. studio to meet her. While I was at her office, she asked me to read a scene for a producer who was putting together a miniseries for NBC. I said that I wasn't interested, but once again she insisted, and I went into this guy's office and read a scene with a handsome young blond actor named Corbin. The whole thing was over in a flash and I was back in the casting director's office when her phone rang and she squealed and said the producer was offering me the lead in his miniseries. I just laughed and told her that I was off to London to study Shakespeare and to thank the producer kindly for his offer, at which point I got up and left her office and the studio.

After that first no, I kept getting offers from the film world for the next couple of weeks. I never made it to London because I finally got an offer that I just couldn't refuse—but that's another story.

Addendum

My family and I are packing to go to our cabin on the lake in Canada. I have spent the past year in "criminal rehab" and have filled out countless forms and tried to get letters from the courts in San Francisco, East Hampton, and Hawaii. No record of my crimes exists in any of those jurisdictions. I have been fingerprinted for the FBI and the state of California. The FBI does have a record of my criminal activity but it seems I have no criminal record in the state of California. Last week, I received the attached letter from the government of Canada declaring that I have been "deemed rehabilitated" by that country. Thank the Lord!

Government of Canada
Consulate General of Canada

Gouvernement du Canada
Consulat général du Canada

June 30, 2009

File: D090600063

Harry Robinson Hamlin

Dear Sir:

This is in reply to your application for criminal rehabilitation under Canada's *Immigration and Refugee Protection Act*. I am pleased to inform you that your application has been approved.

Concerning your conviction for possession of narcotics and marijuana that occurred in California in 1970 equating to CDSA 4(1) punishable by a prison term not exceeding three years, you would be described as inadmissible under Section 36(2)(b) of the Immigration and Refugee Protection Act.

Given that you have only one conviction that is not considered serious criminality and because of the passage of more than ten years since the completion of sentence, you are deemed rehabilitated. You are now considered a member of a prescribed class that is deemed to have been rehabilitated pursuant to A36(3)(c) that reads as follow: *"the matters referred to in paragraphs (1)(b) and c) and (2)(b) and (c) do not constitute inadmissibility in respect of a permanent resident or foreign national who, after the prescribed period, satisfies the Minister that they have been rehabilitated or who is a member of a prescribed class that is deemed to have been rehabilitated;"*.

As this is the only document that will be issued establishing your rehabilitation under the *Immigration and Refugee Protection Act*, I urge you to guard it safely and to carry a photocopy with you whenever you travel to Canada.

Please note that approval of this application for rehabilitation does not exempt you from any other requirements of the *Immigration and Refugee Protection Act* or Regulations.

Yours sincerely,

Erin Brouse
Consul

Acknowledgments

I would like to thank a few folks who have been an enormous help along the way as I wrote this book. Andy Conrad for insisting that I put pen to paper. Beth Wareham for her leap of faith. Whitney Frick for continuing to believe and work and work and work. Rex Bonomelli for listening to my silly design ideas and then, thank God, using his own. Katie Rizzo for "crashing" the book. Kate Lloyd for all the hard work she is going to do and Susan Moldow for staying at the helm and not tossing me out with the bathwater. Eugene Spirito for just being alive. Special thanks to Michael Brussard for believing that I had a voice and blowing my horn for me. And, of course, I always thank my kids for their patience and my wife, Lisa, for her unwavering support and for the great sex.

—HH